FREE Study Skills Videos/DVD Offer

Dear Customer,

Thank you for your purchase from Mometrix! We consider it an honor and a privilege that you have purchased our product and we want to ensure your satisfaction.

As part of our ongoing effort to meet the needs of test takers, we have developed a set of Study Skills Videos that we would like to give you for <u>FREE</u>. These videos cover our *best practices* for getting ready for your exam, from how to use our study materials to how to best prepare for the day of the test.

All that we ask is that you email us with feedback that would describe your experience so far with our product. Good, bad, or indifferent, we want to know what you think!

To get your FREE Study Skills Videos, you can use the **QR code** below, or send us an **email** at studyvideos@mometrix.com with *FREE VIDEOS* in the subject line and the following information in the body of the email:

- The name of the product you purchased.
- Your product rating on a scale of 1-5, with 5 being the highest rating.
- Your feedback. It can be long, short, or anything in between. We just want to know your impressions and experience so far with our product. (Good feedback might include how our study material met your needs and ways we might be able to make it even better. You could highlight features that you found helpful or features that you think we should add.)

If you have any questions or concerns, please don't hesitate to contact me directly.

Thanks again!

Sincerely,

Jay Willis
Vice President
jay.willis@mometrix.com
1-800-673-8175

SCAN HERE

Mometrix
TEST PREPARATION

SHRM CP Exam Prep

SHRM CP Certification Secrets Study Guide

2 Complete Practice Tests

Detailed Answer Explanations

2ndEdition

Written and edited by the Mometrix Human Resources Certification Test Team

Printed in the United States of America

This paper meets the requirements of ANSI/NISO Z39.48-1992 (Permanence of Paper).

Paperback
ISBN 13: 978-1-5167-1536-7
ISBN 10: 1-5167-1536-5

Ebook
ISBN 13: 978-1-5167-1920-4
ISBN 10: 1-5167-1920-4

Hardback
ISBN 13: 978-1-5167-1897-9
ISBN 10: 1-5167-1897-6

Dear Future Exam Success Story

First of all, **THANK YOU** for purchasing Mometrix study materials!

Second, congratulations! You are one of the few determined test-takers who are committed to doing whatever it takes to excel on your exam. **You have come to the right place.** We developed these study materials with one goal in mind: to deliver you the information you need in a format that's concise and easy to use.

In addition to optimizing your guide for the content of the test, we've outlined our recommended steps for breaking down the preparation process into small, attainable goals so you can make sure you stay on track.

We've also analyzed the entire test-taking process, identifying the most common pitfalls and showing how you can overcome them and be ready for any curveball the test throws you.

Standardized testing is one of the biggest obstacles on your road to success, which only increases the importance of doing well in the high-pressure, high-stakes environment of test day. Your results on this test could have a significant impact on your future, and this guide provides the information and practical advice to help you achieve your full potential on test day.

Your success is our success

We would love to hear from you! If you would like to share the story of your exam success or if you have any questions or comments in regard to our products, please contact us at **800-673-8175** or **support@mometrix.com**.

Thanks again for your business and we wish you continued success!

Sincerely,
The Mometrix Test Preparation Team

TABLE OF CONTENTS

Introduction

Thank you for purchasing this resource! You have made the choice to prepare yourself for a test that could have a huge impact on your future, and this guide is designed to help you be fully ready for test day. Obviously, it's important to have a solid understanding of the test material, but you also need to be prepared for the unique environment and stressors of the test, so that you can perform to the best of your abilities.

For this purpose, the first section that appears in this guide is the **Secret Keys**. We've devoted countless hours to meticulously researching what works and what doesn't, and we've boiled down our findings to the five most impactful steps you can take to improve your performance on the test. We start at the beginning with study planning and move through the preparation process, all the way to the testing strategies that will help you get the most out of what you know when you're finally sitting in front of the test.

We recommend that you start preparing for your test as far in advance as possible. However, if you've bought this guide as a last-minute study resource and only have a few days before your test, we recommend that you skip over the first two Secret Keys since they address a long-term study plan.

If you struggle with **test anxiety**, we strongly encourage you to check out our recommendations for how you can overcome it. Test anxiety is a formidable foe, but it can be beaten, and we want to make sure you have the tools you need to defeat it.

Secret Key #1 – Plan Big, Study Small

There's a lot riding on your performance. If you want to ace this test, you're going to need to keep your skills sharp and the material fresh in your mind. You need a plan that lets you review everything you need to know while still fitting in your schedule. We'll break this strategy down into three categories.

Information Organization

Start with the information you already have: the official test outline. From this, you can make a complete list of all the concepts you need to cover before the test. Organize these concepts into groups that can be studied together, and create a list of any related vocabulary you need to learn so you can brush up on any difficult terms. You'll want to keep this vocabulary list handy once you actually start studying since you may need to add to it along the way.

Time Management

Once you have your set of study concepts, decide how to spread them out over the time you have left before the test. Break your study plan into small, clear goals so you have a manageable task for each day and know exactly what you're doing. Then just focus on one small step at a time. When you manage your time this way, you don't need to spend hours at a time studying. Studying a small block of content for a short period each day helps you retain information better and avoid stressing over how much you have left to do. You can relax knowing that you have a plan to cover everything in time. In order for this strategy to be effective though, you have to start studying early and stick to your schedule. Avoid the exhaustion and futility that comes from last-minute cramming!

Study Environment

The environment you study in has a big impact on your learning. Studying in a coffee shop, while probably more enjoyable, is not likely to be as fruitful as studying in a quiet room. It's important to keep distractions to a minimum. You're only planning to study for a short block of time, so make the most of it. Don't pause to check your phone or get up to find a snack. It's also important to **avoid multitasking**. Research has consistently shown that multitasking will make your studying dramatically less effective. Your study area should also be comfortable and well-lit so you don't have the distraction of straining your eyes or sitting on an uncomfortable chair.

The time of day you study is also important. You want to be rested and alert. Don't wait until just before bedtime. Study when you'll be most likely to comprehend and remember. Even better, if you know what time of day your test will be, set that time aside for study. That way your brain will be used to working on that subject at that specific time and you'll have a better chance of recalling information.

Finally, it can be helpful to team up with others who are studying for the same test. Your actual studying should be done in as isolated an environment as possible, but the work of organizing the information and setting up the study plan can be divided up. In between study sessions, you can discuss with your teammates the concepts that you're all studying and quiz each other on the details. Just be sure that your teammates are as serious about the test as you are. If you find that your study time is being replaced with social time, you might need to find a new team.

Secret Key #2 – Make Your Studying Count

You're devoting a lot of time and effort to preparing for this test, so you want to be absolutely certain it will pay off. This means doing more than just reading the content and hoping you can remember it on test day. It's important to make every minute of study count. There are two main areas you can focus on to make your studying count.

Retention

It doesn't matter how much time you study if you can't remember the material. You need to make sure you are retaining the concepts. To check your retention of the information you're learning, try recalling it at later times with minimal prompting. Try carrying around flashcards and glance at one or two from time to time or ask a friend who's also studying for the test to quiz you.

To enhance your retention, look for ways to put the information into practice so that you can apply it rather than simply recalling it. If you're using the information in practical ways, it will be much easier to remember. Similarly, it helps to solidify a concept in your mind if you're not only reading it to yourself but also explaining it to someone else. Ask a friend to let you teach them about a concept you're a little shaky on (or speak aloud to an imaginary audience if necessary). As you try to summarize, define, give examples, and answer your friend's questions, you'll understand the concepts better and they will stay with you longer. Finally, step back for a big picture view and ask yourself how each piece of information fits with the whole subject. When you link the different concepts together and see them working together as a whole, it's easier to remember the individual components.

Finally, practice showing your work on any multi-step problems, even if you're just studying. Writing out each step you take to solve a problem will help solidify the process in your mind, and you'll be more likely to remember it during the test.

Modality

Modality simply refers to the means or method by which you study. Choosing a study modality that fits your own individual learning style is crucial. No two people learn best in exactly the same way, so it's important to know your strengths and use them to your advantage.

For example, if you learn best by visualization, focus on visualizing a concept in your mind and draw an image or a diagram. Try color-coding your notes, illustrating them, or creating symbols that will trigger your mind to recall a learned concept. If you learn best by hearing or discussing information, find a study partner who learns the same way or read aloud to yourself. Think about how to put the information in your own words. Imagine that you are giving a lecture on the topic and record yourself so you can listen to it later.

For any learning style, flashcards can be helpful. Organize the information so you can take advantage of spare moments to review. Underline key words or phrases. Use different colors for different categories. Mnemonic devices (such as creating a short list in which every item starts with the same letter) can also help with retention. Find what works best for you and use it to store the information in your mind most effectively and easily.

Secret Key #3 – Practice the Right Way

Your success on test day depends not only on how many hours you put into preparing, but also on whether you prepared the right way. It's good to check along the way to see if your studying is paying off. One of the most effective ways to do this is by taking practice tests to evaluate your progress. Practice tests are useful because they show exactly where you need to improve. Every time you take a practice test, pay special attention to these three groups of questions:

- The questions you got wrong
- The questions you had to guess on, even if you guessed right
- The questions you found difficult or slow to work through

This will show you exactly what your weak areas are, and where you need to devote more study time. Ask yourself why each of these questions gave you trouble. Was it because you didn't understand the material? Was it because you didn't remember the vocabulary? Do you need more repetitions on this type of question to build speed and confidence? Dig into those questions and figure out how you can strengthen your weak areas as you go back to review the material.

Additionally, many practice tests have a section explaining the answer choices. It can be tempting to read the explanation and think that you now have a good understanding of the concept. However, an explanation likely only covers part of the question's broader context. Even if the explanation makes perfect sense, **go back and investigate** every concept related to the question until you're positive you have a thorough understanding.

As you go along, keep in mind that the practice test is just that: practice. Memorizing these questions and answers will not be very helpful on the actual test because it is unlikely to have any of the same exact questions. If you only know the right answers to the sample questions, you won't be prepared for the real thing. **Study the concepts** until you understand them fully, and then you'll be able to answer any question that shows up on the test.

It's important to wait on the practice tests until you're ready. If you take a test on your first day of study, you may be overwhelmed by the amount of material covered and how much you need to learn. Work up to it gradually.

On test day, you'll need to be prepared for answering questions, managing your time, and using the test-taking strategies you've learned. It's a lot to balance, like a mental marathon that will have a big impact on your future. Like training for a marathon, you'll need to start slowly and work your way up. When test day arrives, you'll be ready.

Start with the strategies you've read in the first two Secret Keys—plan your course and study in the way that works best for you. If you have time, consider using multiple study resources to get different approaches to the same concepts. It can be helpful to see difficult concepts from more than one angle. Then find a good source for practice tests. Many times, the test website will suggest potential study resources or provide sample tests.

Practice Test Strategy

If you're able to find at least three practice tests, we recommend this strategy:

Untimed and Open-Book Practice

Take the first test with no time constraints and with your notes and study guide handy. Take your time and focus on applying the strategies you've learned.

Timed and Open-Book Practice

Take the second practice test open-book as well, but set a timer and practice pacing yourself to finish in time.

Timed and Closed-Book Practice

Take any other practice tests as if it were test day. Set a timer and put away your study materials. Sit at a table or desk in a quiet room, imagine yourself at the testing center, and answer questions as quickly and accurately as possible.

Keep repeating timed and closed-book tests on a regular basis until you run out of practice tests or it's time for the actual test. Your mind will be ready for the schedule and stress of test day, and you'll be able to focus on recalling the material you've learned.

Secret Key #4 – Pace Yourself

Once you're fully prepared for the material on the test, your biggest challenge on test day will be managing your time. Just knowing that the clock is ticking can make you panic even if you have plenty of time left. Work on pacing yourself so you can build confidence against the time constraints of the exam. Pacing is a difficult skill to master, especially in a high-pressure environment, so **practice is vital**.

Set time expectations for your pace based on how much time is available. For example, if a section has 60 questions and the time limit is 30 minutes, you know you have to average 30 seconds or less per question in order to answer them all. Although 30 seconds is the hard limit, set 25 seconds per question as your goal, so you reserve extra time to spend on harder questions. When you budget extra time for the harder questions, you no longer have any reason to stress when those questions take longer to answer.

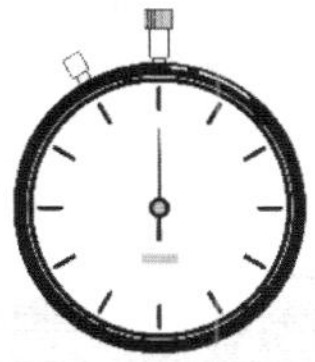

Don't let this time expectation distract you from working through the test at a calm, steady pace, but keep it in mind so you don't spend too much time on any one question. Recognize that taking extra time on one question you don't understand may keep you from answering two that you do understand later in the test. If your time limit for a question is up and you're still not sure of the answer, mark it and move on, and come back to it later if the time and the test format allow. If the testing format doesn't allow you to return to earlier questions, just make an educated guess; then put it out of your mind and move on.

On the easier questions, be careful not to rush. It may seem wise to hurry through them so you have more time for the challenging ones, but it's not worth missing one if you know the concept and just didn't take the time to read the question fully. Work efficiently but make sure you understand the question and have looked at all of the answer choices, since more than one may seem right at first.

Even if you're paying attention to the time, you may find yourself a little behind at some point. You should speed up to get back on track, but do so wisely. Don't panic; just take a few seconds less on each question until you're caught up. Don't guess without thinking, but do look through the answer choices and eliminate any you know are wrong. If you can get down to two choices, it is often worthwhile to guess from those. Once you've chosen an answer, move on and don't dwell on any that you skipped or had to hurry through. If a question was taking too long, chances are it was one of the harder ones, so you weren't as likely to get it right anyway.

On the other hand, if you find yourself getting ahead of schedule, it may be beneficial to slow down a little. The more quickly you work, the more likely you are to make a careless mistake that will affect your score. You've budgeted time for each question, so don't be afraid to spend that time. Practice an efficient but careful pace to get the most out of the time you have.

Secret Key #5 – Have a Plan for Guessing

When you're taking the test, you may find yourself stuck on a question. Some of the answer choices seem better than others, but you don't see the one answer choice that is obviously correct. What do you do?

The scenario described above is very common, yet most test takers have not effectively prepared for it. Developing and practicing a plan for guessing may be one of the single most effective uses of your time as you get ready for the exam.

In developing your plan for guessing, there are three questions to address:

- When should you start the guessing process?
- How should you narrow down the choices?
- Which answer should you choose?

When to Start the Guessing Process

Unless your plan for guessing is to select C every time (which, despite its merits, is not what we recommend), you need to leave yourself enough time to apply your answer elimination strategies. Since you have a limited amount of time for each question, that means that if you're going to give yourself the best shot at guessing correctly, you have to decide quickly whether or not you will guess.

Of course, the best-case scenario is that you don't have to guess at all, so first, see if you can answer the question based on your knowledge of the subject and basic reasoning skills. Focus on the key words in the question and try to jog your memory of related topics. Give yourself a chance to bring the knowledge to mind, but once you realize that you don't have (or you can't access) the knowledge you need to answer the question, it's time to start the guessing process.

It's almost always better to start the guessing process too early than too late. It only takes a few seconds to remember something and answer the question from knowledge. Carefully eliminating wrong answer choices takes longer. Plus, going through the process of eliminating answer choices can actually help jog your memory.

Summary: Start the guessing process as soon as you decide that you can't answer the question based on your knowledge.

How to Narrow Down the Choices

The next chapter in this book (**Test-Taking Strategies**) includes a wide range of strategies for how to approach questions and how to look for answer choices to eliminate. You will definitely want to read those carefully, practice them, and figure out which ones work best for you. Here though, we're going to address a mindset rather than a particular strategy.

Your odds of guessing an answer correctly depend on how many options you are choosing from.

Number of options left	5	4	3	2	1
Odds of guessing correctly	20%	25%	33%	50%	100%

You can see from this chart just how valuable it is to be able to eliminate incorrect answers and make an educated guess, but there are two things that many test takers do that cause them to miss out on the benefits of guessing:

- Accidentally eliminating the correct answer
- Selecting an answer based on an impression

We'll look at the first one here, and the second one in the next section.

To avoid accidentally eliminating the correct answer, we recommend a thought exercise called **the $5 challenge**. In this challenge, you only eliminate an answer choice from contention if you are willing to bet $5 on it being wrong. Why $5? Five dollars is a small but not insignificant amount of money. It's an amount you could afford to lose but wouldn't want to throw away. And while losing $5 once might not hurt too much, doing it twenty times will set you back $100. In the same way, each small decision you make—eliminating a choice here, guessing on a question there—won't by itself impact your score very much, but when you put them all together, they can make a big difference. By holding each answer choice elimination decision to a higher standard, you can reduce the risk of accidentally eliminating the correct answer.

The $5 challenge can also be applied in a positive sense: If you are willing to bet $5 that an answer choice *is* correct, go ahead and mark it as correct.

Summary: Only eliminate an answer choice if you are willing to bet $5 that it is wrong.

Which Answer to Choose

You're taking the test. You've run into a hard question and decided you'll have to guess. You've eliminated all the answer choices you're willing to bet $5 on. Now you have to pick an answer. Why do we even need to talk about this? Why can't you just pick whichever one you feel like when the time comes?

The answer to these questions is that if you don't come into the test with a plan, you'll rely on your impression to select an answer choice, and if you do that, you risk falling into a trap. The test writers know that everyone who takes their test will be guessing on some of the questions, so they intentionally write wrong answer choices to seem plausible. You still have to pick an answer though, and if the wrong answer choices are designed to look right, how can you ever be sure that you're not falling for their trap? The best solution we've found to this dilemma is to take the decision out of your hands entirely. Here is the process we recommend:

Once you've eliminated any choices that you are confident (willing to bet $5) are wrong, select the first remaining choice as your answer.

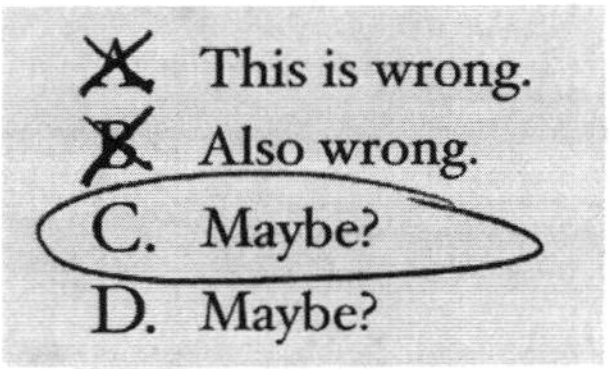

Whether you choose to select the first remaining choice, the second, or the last, the important thing is that you use some preselected standard. Using this approach guarantees that you will not be enticed into selecting an answer choice that looks right, because you are not basing your decision on how the answer choices look.

This is not meant to make you question your knowledge. Instead, it is to help you recognize the difference between your knowledge and your impressions. There's a huge difference between thinking an answer is right because of what you know, and thinking an answer is right because it looks or sounds like it should be right.

Summary: To ensure that your selection is appropriately random, make a predetermined selection from among all answer choices you have not eliminated.

Test-Taking Strategies

This section contains a list of test-taking strategies that you may find helpful as you work through the test. By taking what you know and applying logical thought, you can maximize your chances of answering any question correctly!

It is very important to realize that every question is different and every person is different: no single strategy will work on every question, and no single strategy will work for every person. That's why we've included all of them here, so you can try them out and determine which ones work best for different types of questions and which ones work best for you.

Question Strategies

☑ Read Carefully

Read the question and the answer choices carefully. Don't miss the question because you misread the terms. You have plenty of time to read each question thoroughly and make sure you understand what is being asked. Yet a happy medium must be attained, so don't waste too much time. You must read carefully and efficiently.

☑ Contextual Clues

Look for contextual clues. If the question includes a word you are not familiar with, look at the immediate context for some indication of what the word might mean. Contextual clues can often give you all the information you need to decipher the meaning of an unfamiliar word. Even if you can't determine the meaning, you may be able to narrow down the possibilities enough to make a solid guess at the answer to the question.

☑ Prefixes

If you're having trouble with a word in the question or answer choices, try dissecting it. Take advantage of every clue that the word might include. Prefixes can be a huge help. Usually, they allow you to determine a basic meaning. *Pre-* means before, *post-* means after, *pro-* is positive, *de-* is negative. From prefixes, you can get an idea of the general meaning of the word and try to put it into context.

☑ Hedge Words

Watch out for critical hedge words, such as *likely*, *may*, *can*, *sometimes*, *often*, *almost*, *mostly*, *usually*, *generally*, *rarely*, and *sometimes*. Question writers insert these hedge phrases to cover every possibility. Often an answer choice will be wrong simply because it leaves no room for exception. Be on guard for answer choices that have definitive words such as *exactly* and *always*.

☑ Switchback Words

Stay alert for *switchbacks*. These are the words and phrases frequently used to alert you to shifts in thought. The most common switchback words are *but*, *although*, and *however*. Others include *nevertheless*, *on the other hand*, *even though*, *while*, *in spite of*, *despite*, and *regardless of*. Switchback words are important to catch because they can change the direction of the question or an answer choice.

☉ FACE VALUE

When in doubt, use common sense. Accept the situation in the problem at face value. Don't read too much into it. These problems will not require you to make wild assumptions. If you have to go beyond creativity and warp time or space in order to have an answer choice fit the question, then you should move on and consider the other answer choices. These are normal problems rooted in reality. The applicable relationship or explanation may not be readily apparent, but it is there for you to figure out. Use your common sense to interpret anything that isn't clear.

Answer Choice Strategies

☉ ANSWER SELECTION

The most thorough way to pick an answer choice is to identify and eliminate wrong answers until only one is left, then confirm it is the correct answer. Sometimes an answer choice may immediately seem right, but be careful. The test writers will usually put more than one reasonable answer choice on each question, so take a second to read all of them and make sure that the other choices are not equally obvious. As long as you have time left, it is better to read every answer choice than to pick the first one that looks right without checking the others.

☉ ANSWER CHOICE FAMILIES

An answer choice family consists of two (in rare cases, three) answer choices that are very similar in construction and cannot all be true at the same time. If you see two answer choices that are direct opposites or parallels, one of them is usually the correct answer. For instance, if one answer choice says that quantity x increases and another either says that quantity x decreases (opposite) or says that quantity y increases (parallel), then those answer choices would fall into the same family. An answer choice that doesn't match the construction of the answer choice family is more likely to be incorrect. Most questions will not have answer choice families, but when they do appear, you should be prepared to recognize them.

☉ ELIMINATE ANSWERS

Eliminate answer choices as soon as you realize they are wrong, but make sure you consider all possibilities. If you are eliminating answer choices and realize that the last one you are left with is also wrong, don't panic. Start over and consider each choice again. There may be something you missed the first time that you will realize on the second pass.

☉ AVOID FACT TRAPS

Don't be distracted by an answer choice that is factually true but doesn't answer the question. You are looking for the choice that answers the question. Stay focused on what the question is asking for so you don't accidentally pick an answer that is true but incorrect. Always go back to the question and make sure the answer choice you've selected actually answers the question and is not merely a true statement.

☉ EXTREME STATEMENTS

In general, you should avoid answers that put forth extreme actions as standard practice or proclaim controversial ideas as established fact. An answer choice that states the "process should be used in certain situations, if..." is much more likely to be correct than one that states the "process should be discontinued completely." The first is a calm rational statement and doesn't even make a definitive, uncompromising stance, using a hedge word *if* to provide wiggle room, whereas the second choice is far more extreme.

⊘ Benchmark

As you read through the answer choices and you come across one that seems to answer the question well, mentally select that answer choice. This is not your final answer, but it's the one that will help you evaluate the other answer choices. The one that you selected is your benchmark or standard for judging each of the other answer choices. Every other answer choice must be compared to your benchmark. That choice is correct until proven otherwise by another answer choice beating it. If you find a better answer, then that one becomes your new benchmark. Once you've decided that no other choice answers the question as well as your benchmark, you have your final answer.

⊘ Predict the Answer

Before you even start looking at the answer choices, it is often best to try to predict the answer. When you come up with the answer on your own, it is easier to avoid distractions and traps because you will know exactly what to look for. The right answer choice is unlikely to be word-for-word what you came up with, but it should be a close match. Even if you are confident that you have the right answer, you should still take the time to read each option before moving on.

General Strategies

⊘ Tough Questions

If you are stumped on a problem or it appears too hard or too difficult, don't waste time. Move on! Remember though, if you can quickly check for obviously incorrect answer choices, your chances of guessing correctly are greatly improved. Before you completely give up, at least try to knock out a couple of possible answers. Eliminate what you can and then guess at the remaining answer choices before moving on.

⊘ Check Your Work

Since you will probably not know every term listed and the answer to every question, it is important that you get credit for the ones that you do know. Don't miss any questions through careless mistakes. If at all possible, try to take a second to look back over your answer selection and make sure you've selected the correct answer choice and haven't made a costly careless mistake (such as marking an answer choice that you didn't mean to mark). This quick double check should more than pay for itself in caught mistakes for the time it costs.

⊘ Pace Yourself

It's easy to be overwhelmed when you're looking at a page full of questions; your mind is confused and full of random thoughts, and the clock is ticking down faster than you would like. Calm down and maintain the pace that you have set for yourself. Especially as you get down to the last few minutes of the test, don't let the small numbers on the clock make you panic. As long as you are on track by monitoring your pace, you are guaranteed to have time for each question.

⊘ Don't Rush

It is very easy to make errors when you are in a hurry. Maintaining a fast pace in answering questions is pointless if it makes you miss questions that you would have gotten right otherwise. Test writers like to include distracting information and wrong answers that seem right. Taking a little extra time to avoid careless mistakes can make all the difference in your test score. Find a pace that allows you to be confident in the answers that you select.

✓ KEEP MOVING

Panicking will not help you pass the test, so do your best to stay calm and keep moving. Taking deep breaths and going through the answer elimination steps you practiced can help to break through a stress barrier and keep your pace.

Final Notes

The combination of a solid foundation of content knowledge and the confidence that comes from practicing your plan for applying that knowledge is the key to maximizing your performance on test day. As your foundation of content knowledge is built up and strengthened, you'll find that the strategies included in this chapter become more and more effective in helping you quickly sift through the distractions and traps of the test to isolate the correct answer.

Now that you're preparing to move forward into the test content chapters of this book, be sure to keep your goal in mind. As you read, think about how you will be able to apply this information on the test. If you've already seen sample questions for the test and you have an idea of the question format and style, try to come up with questions of your own that you can answer based on what you're reading. This will give you valuable practice applying your knowledge in the same ways you can expect to on test day.

Good luck and good studying!

Four-Week SHRM-CP Study Plan

On the next few pages, we've provided an optional study plan to help you use this study guide to its fullest potential over the course of four weeks. If you have eight weeks available and want to spread it out more, spend two weeks on each section of the plan.

Below is a quick summary of the subjects covered in each week of the plan.

- Week 1: Behavioral Competencies: Leadership, Interpersonal, and Business
- Week 2: HR Expertise: People
- Week 3: HR Expertise: Organization and Workplace
- Week 4: Practice Tests

Please note that not all subjects will take the same amount of time to work through.

Two full-length practice tests are included in this study guide. We recommend saving any additional practice tests until after you've completed the study plan. Take these practice tests without any reference materials a day or two before the real thing as practice runs to get you in the mode of answering questions at a good pace.

Week 1: Behavioral Competencies: Leadership, Interpersonal, and Business

Instructional Content

First, read carefully through the Behavioral Competencies: Leadership, Interpersonal, and Business chapters in this book, checking off your progress as you go:

- ❑ Leadership and Navigation
- ❑ Ethical Practice
- ❑ Relationship Management
- ❑ Communication
- ❑ Global and Cultural Effectiveness
- ❑ Business Acumen
- ❑ Consultation
- ❑ Critical Evaluation

As you read, do the following:

- Highlight any sections, terms, or concepts you think are important
- Draw an asterisk (*) next to any areas you are struggling with
- Watch the review videos to gain more understanding of a particular topic
- Take notes in your notebook or in the margins of this book

After you've read through everything, go back and review any sections that you highlighted or that you drew an asterisk next to, referencing your notes along the way.

Week 2: HR Expertise: People

Instructional Content

First, read carefully through the HR Expertise: People chapter in this book, checking off your progress as you go:

- ❑ Human Resources Strategic Planning
- ❑ Talent Acquisition
- ❑ Employee Engagement and Retention
- ❑ Learning and Development
- ❑ Total Rewards

As you read, do the following:

- Highlight any sections, terms, or concepts you think are important
- Draw an asterisk (*) next to any areas you are struggling with
- Watch the review videos to gain more understanding of a particular topic
- Take notes in your notebook or in the margins of this book

After you've read through everything, go back and review any sections that you highlighted or that you drew an asterisk next to, referencing your notes along the way.

Week 3: HR Expertise: Organization and Workplace

INSTRUCTIONAL CONTENT

First, read carefully through the HR Expertise: Organization and Workplace chapters in this book, checking off your progress as you go:

- ❑ Structure of the Human Resources Function
- ❑ Organizational Effectiveness and Development
- ❑ Workforce Management
- ❑ Employee and Labor Relations
- ❑ Technology Management
- ❑ Human Resources in the Global Context
- ❑ Diversity and Inclusion
- ❑ Risk Management
- ❑ Corporate Social Responsibility
- ❑ U.S. Employment Law and Regulations

As you read, do the following:

- Highlight any sections, terms, or concepts you think are important
- Draw an asterisk (*) next to any areas you are struggling with
- Watch the review videos to gain more understanding of a particular topic
- Take notes in your notebook or in the margins of this book

After you've read through everything, go back and review any sections that you highlighted or that you drew an asterisk next to, referencing your notes along the way.

Week 4: Practice Tests

Your success on test day depends not only on how many hours you put into preparing, but also on whether you prepared the right way. It's good to check along the way to see if your studying is paying off. One of the most effective ways to do this is by taking practice tests to evaluate your progress. Practice tests are useful because they show exactly where you need to improve. Every time you take a practice test, pay special attention to these three groups of questions:

- The questions you got wrong
- The questions you had to guess on, even if you guessed right
- The questions you found difficult or slow to work through

This will show you exactly what your weak areas are, and where you need to devote more study time. Ask yourself why each of these questions gave you trouble. Was it because you didn't understand the material? Was it because you didn't remember the vocabulary? Do you need more repetitions on this type of question to build speed and confidence? Dig into those questions and figure out how you can strengthen your weak areas as you go back to review the material.

Practice Test #1

Now that you've read over the instructional content, it's time to take a practice test. Complete Practice Test #1. Take this test with **no time constraints**, and feel free to reference the applicable sections of this guide as you go. Once you've finished, check your answers against the provided answer key. For any questions you answered incorrectly, review the answer rationale, and then **go back and review** the applicable sections of the book. The goal in this stage is to understand why you answered the question incorrectly, and make sure that the next time you see a similar question, you will get it right.

Practice Test #2

Next, complete Practice Test #2. This time, give yourself **4 hours** to complete all of the questions. You should again feel free to reference the guide and your notes, but be mindful of the clock. If you run out of time before you finish all of the questions, mark where you were when time expired, but go ahead and finish taking the practice test. Once you've finished, check your answers against the provided answer key, and as before, review the answer rationale for any that you answered incorrectly and then go back and review the associated instructional content. Your goal is still to increase understanding of the content but also to get used to the time constraints you will face on the test.

As you go along, keep in mind that the practice test is just that: practice. Memorizing these questions and answers will not be very helpful on the actual test because it is unlikely to have any of the same exact questions. If you only know the right answers to the sample questions, you won't be prepared for the real thing. **Study the concepts** until you understand them fully, and then you'll be able to answer any question that shows up on the test.

Behavioral Competencies: Leadership

Leadership and Navigation

Leadership Theories

Situational Leadership

Situational leadership is rooted in adaptability as the theory purports that there is no universally applicable way to lead. A leader should consider the circumstances and his or her followers when planning and making decisions. To remain effective, a leader's style must adapt with the situation. Depending on the circumstances and the maturity and ability of the team, a leader may lead by directing, engaging, collaborating, or delegating.

Inclusive Leadership

Inclusive leadership is promoting an atmosphere of respect, in which all employees have equal ability to share and utilize the skills they bring to the organization. It requires a willingness to listen with understanding and an ability to communicate with diverse populations across differences. Inclusive leadership involves being conscious of cultural values while bridging behavioral gaps and leveraging differences to increase performance. Some leadership traits that encourage inclusion are empowerment, accountability, courage, and humility. Inclusive leaders will do the following:

- Support staff development
- Demonstrate confidence
- Hold employees accountable
- Set personal interests aside
- Act on convictions and principles
- Admit mistakes
- Learn from criticism
- Seek contributions from others

Participative Leadership

Participative leadership allows all employees to be more informed and involved in the operations of the organization. This can be achieved by supporting them when they make mistakes, treating them with consideration and respect, inviting them to recommend innovative ideas and suggestions, and providing training and development opportunities to help them advance.

Transformational Leadership

Transformational leadership involves championing a shared vision with employees. It requires changing the attitudes and assumptions of the team while building commitment for the organization's mission, objectives, and strategies. Leaders inspire awareness of and dedication to the group's mission. Followers are empowered by facts, resources, and support so that they can then approach work in a committed, concerned, and involved way.

Defining characteristics of a transformational leader include the following:

1. **Charismatic**: gains buy-in for the vision and mission, earns respect and trust, and instills pride
2. **Inspirational**: communicates heightened performance expectations and encourages big-picture thinking

3. **Intellectually stimulating**: promotes learning and development and advocates for the use of logic and rationality to solve problems
4. **Individualized consideration**: coaches followers, treats each person individually, and gives personal attention

Theory X + Theory Y of Leadership

Douglas McGregor said that there are two ways for leaders to view employees—either through Theory X or Theory Y. When a leader subscribes to Theory X, he or she sees employees as lazy and only motivated by disciplinary action. Conversely, when a leader believes in Theory Y, he or she views employees as willing, hard workers who need to be shown the importance of their work to facilitate continued motivation.

People Management Techniques

People management can be separated into four phases: directing, coaching, supporting, and delegating. **Directing** involves limited flexibility for the employee and is characterized by defining, planning, teaching, and monitoring. Individuals in this learning stage have high commitment but minimal skills and need clear standards, goals, and timelines with regular feedback. **Coaching** involves supportive direction characterized by praise, encouragement, prioritizing, and feedback. Individuals in this stage have some commitment and skills but still need recognition and feedback while they try to develop more effective ways to perform tasks. **Supporting** involves even less specific direction and is characterized by listening, collaborating, and appreciating. Individuals at this innovative stage are more confident, skilled, and self-reliant problem-solvers. **Delegating** involves lots of flexibility with little direction and is characterized by trusting, empowering, acknowledging, and challenging. Individuals at this final stage have high commitment and excellent skills. They are ready for trust, responsibility, authority, variety, and challenges.

Motivation Theories

Extrinsic vs. Intrinsic Motivation

Motivation is what propels someone to behave in a certain way.

Extrinsic motivation is derived from external factors. People can be externally motivated by money, gifts, and recognition.

Intrinsic motivation is derived from thoughts and beliefs a person has within. People can be internally motivated by the feeling of achievement, the excitement of learning something new, or by their competitive nature.

Taylor's Scientific Management

Frederick Taylor ran a series of experiments within a manufacturing setting to better understand the nature of work. He found that people could be motivated by their working conditions and noted that employers should provide adequate safety measures, lighting, and tools to do the work. Further, he concluded that employees will change their behavior when they know they are being observed.

Skinner's Operant Conditioning

B. F. Skinner concluded that motivation is based on extrinsic factors such as reward and punishment. Employers can influence behavior through positive reinforcement or negative reinforcement, which results in employees acting in certain ways to receive prizes or to avoid discipline.

Maslow's Hierarchy of Needs

Abraham Maslow said that people have a variety of needs that must be met in a certain order. Human needs, presented in order, are physiological, safety, social, esteem, and self-actualization. Physiological needs are tied to the body functioning, like taking care of thirst. Safety needs are based on having adequate shelter from harm. Social needs involve feeling a sense of acceptance by peers. Esteem needs entail feeling respected by peers. Last, self-actualization needs are tied to feeling fulfilled by one's life. Maslow contended that lower-level needs have to be met first. For example, if someone was unsafe, he or she wouldn't be concerned with feeling respected.

Herzberg's Motivator Hygiene Theory

Herzberg concluded that an employee's motivation is affected by both hygiene factors and motivators. **Hygiene factors** are extrinsic and include salary, benefits, and work environment. **Motivators** are intrinsic and include growth and recognition. Both hygiene factors and motivators play roles in job satisfaction or dissatisfaction. Hygiene factors are known as job dissatisfiers, and motivators are known as job satisfiers.

Herzberg learned that job satisfaction and dissatisfaction are independent of one another. In other words, removing causes of dissatisfaction doesn't necessarily equate to job satisfaction. And, adding causes of job satisfaction doesn't necessarily negate job dissatisfaction. For example, if an employee is being underpaid and the work is dreadfully boring, the employee will still be dissatisfied even if given a substantial raise. The employee, although better paid, will still work in a role that has no room for growth. In essence, to keep employees satisfied with their jobs, employers need to eliminate the hygiene factor issues and increase the presence of motivators.

McClelland's Acquired Needs Theory

David McClelland saw motivation as primarily intrinsic and said that it arose from three main needs: achievement, affiliation, and power. The need for achievement involves embracing challenges, being goal oriented, and taking calculated risks. The need for affiliation involves wanting to belong, yearning to be liked, and focusing on collaboration over competition. The need for power involves wanting to influence others, being competitive, and striving to attain a high status. Employees could be motivated by a blend of these needs. For example, an employee may be achievement oriented and still want to be liked.

Locke's Goal-Setting Theory

Dr. Edwin Locke developed a goal-setting theory for motivation in the 1960s. His research concluded that employees are driven by explicit, measurable **goals** that are challenging but attainable. Locke suggested that if the employees take part in **collaboratively** setting the goals and objectives, they will be more vested in attaining them. However, those who have an internal drive may be more likely to succeed. He also noted that providing **feedback** to employees is critical. Locke tied goal setting to task performance because it energized employees and assisted them with handling specific situations that arose. Finally, Locke stated that attaining the goal should provide both intrinsic and extrinsic **rewards** that result in employee satisfaction.

Vroom's Expectancy Theory

Victor Vroom's expectancy theory assumes that rationality will drive employees toward the option that provides *maximum pleasure* and *minimal pain*. Although he noted that performance strength may be determined by an individual's personality, knowledge, experiences, skills, and abilities, Vroom believed that increased effort would eventually lead to better performance as long as employees have the necessary tools to get the job done. Moreover, employees will be motivated if they believe that favorable performance will return a desired reward, which will satisfy an important need and thus make the effort worthwhile. There is a calculation that reflects the **expectancy theory**: *Expectancy x Instrumentality x Valence = Motivation.* **Expectancy** is the belief that one's best efforts will yield good performance. **Instrumentality** is the belief that the good performance will yield a particular result. **Valence** is the value of an outcome to a given employee. (This will fluctuate as not all employees are motivated by the same things at the same time.) If any of the multipliers are low, then motivation will be low.

Attribution Theory

The attribution theory was first introduced by Fritz Heider and further developed by Bernard Weiner. It identifies ability, effort, task difficulty, and luck as the most important factors for achieving success. This theory can help identify the root causes of an individual's behavior or performance. **Attribution** consists of **three stages**: 1) behavior observation, 2) determining if the behavior is deliberate or consistent, and 3) concluding if the behavior is due to internal or external factors. The **locus of causality** identifies outcomes based upon internal controls such as ability and effort as well as external factors such as task difficulty and luck. The **locus of stability** identifies outcomes based upon fixed, stable factors such as ability and task difficulty as well as variable factors such as effort and luck. Correctly identifying the source or rationale behind an employee's behavior can help leaders effectively motivate them.

Self-Determination Theory

This theory identifies three core intrinsic motivators: autonomy, competence, and relatedness. **Autonomy** in this context focuses more on self-initiation and regulating one's behavior toward task selection, organization, and completion. **Competence** involves the mastery of skills required to complete the work and interact with the environment effectively. **Relatedness** involves attachment to and a sense of belongingness within a group. Leaders should give employees the opportunity to make decisions about their work, sharpen their skills, and connect with others in the organization whenever possible. Doing so will increase their internal drive and promote psychological wellness.

Job Characteristics Model

Hackman and Oldman found that the following job characteristics affect job performance and satisfaction: task identity, task significance, skill variety, autonomy, and feedback. Task identity is when employees can see how their roles affect the entire organization so that they no longer feel like they operate in isolation. This knowledge can lead to greater job satisfaction. Task significance is when employees can understand the larger impacts of their work on other people or society, which can also lead to greater job satisfaction. Skill variety is when employees can use many different skills in their work, which reinforces that the job is important. Autonomy is when employees receive their manager's trust and have leeway in decision-making. This empowerment typically leads to higher levels of employee engagement and job satisfaction. Feedback is when employees receive commentary on their performance, enabling them to improve or encouraging them to stay the course. Regular feedback can also lead to higher levels of employee engagement and job satisfaction.

Influence and Persuasion Techniques

Personal Appeal

This technique involves eliciting emotion to prompt behavior. It entails using strong language that conjures up specific imagery designed to lead the communication's recipient into making a certain decision or taking a certain action. If the recipient is more factually driven, this technique may not be as effective.

Forming Coalitions

This technique is useful when a shared goal is identified. Like-minded people within an organization can come together to fight for or against a current cause. Their individual voices will carry more weight as a unified group, increasing the chance that they'll achieve the desired outcome.

Rational Persuasion

This technique employs facts, figures, and logic as the basis for an argument or case. It appeals to someone on a cognitive, rational level and tries to garner consensus based on what's factually correct. If the recipient is more emotionally driven, this technique may not be as effective.

Leading by Example

This technique involves a leader modeling the attitudes, words, and behaviors that they would like to see exhibited by their followers. It shows the followers that the leader is not "above" doing what they are required to do and, in fact, personally endorses it. Although this technique is somewhat indirect, followers may emulate the leader for a variety of reasons. They could admire the leader, fear retribution for not following, or desire to be on the "right" side of corporate law, to name a few. Regardless of individual motivations, leading by example sets the tone for the team.

Trust and Relationship-Building Techniques

Emotional Intelligence

Emotional intelligence describes an individual's ability to be sensitive to the feelings of others, to manage one's own emotions or impulses, and to use this knowledge to motivate others. The four main **fundamentals of emotional intelligence** are self-awareness, self-management, social awareness, and social skills or relationship management. Important social skills include empathy, compassion, and the ability to motivate. Emotional intelligence is used in the moment to make quick assessments and adjustments. For example, if Sam sees Bob frowning during a meeting, Sam can use his emotional intelligence and deduce that Bob is not pleased. Sam can either try to change the course of the meeting, ask Bob what's bothering him on the spot, or talk to Bob after the meeting.

Social Intelligence

Deciding how to handle Bob is a product of social intelligence. **Social intelligence** is an understanding of the best way to behave in both general and specific contexts. For example, someone with social intelligence knows that it's impolite to interrupt a speaker giving a presentation. In the specific case with Bob, because Sam knows Bob's tendencies, Sam has the social intelligence to ask Bob why he looked upset after the meeting. Changing the course of the meeting may not have been a good thing to do as Bob may have been upset about something unrelated. Trying to ask Bob about his mood in the middle of the meeting would make Bob feel singled out and would worsen any issue going on.

Emotional and social intelligence set outstanding leaders apart. Employing these techniques result in a more holistic leadership style that takes both people and profit into account. Because leadership is a social method of influencing others, it can be enhanced by emotional intelligence. However, having a lack of emotional or social intelligence among company leaders can be detrimental.

Ethical Practice

Ethics are the moral principles, values, and accepted standards of behavior that determine whether an action is right or wrong. The Society for Human Resource Management (SHRM) Competency Model defines **ethical practice** as "the knowledge, skills, abilities, and other characteristics needed to maintain high levels of personal and professional integrity and to act as an ethical agent who promotes core values, integrity, and accountability throughout the organization."

Ethical Agent

Ethics and compliance officers ensure that business is conducted in accordance with rules, legal regulations, and industry standards of practice. Additionally, an **ethical agent** makes moral judgments based on fundamental ethical principles that are rooted in their personal character, not based on a situation's potential gains. **Ethical dilemmas** occur when a corporation or individual is faced with a conflict of interest or actions that are blatantly wrong, deceptive, or may have uncertain consequences. Many ethical conflicts value profit over moral principles. Over the past few decades, ethics and business conduct have received increasing attention that has led to more stringent **compliance regulations**, like the Sarbanes-Oxley Act.

Personal Integrity

Personal integrity comes from developing and sticking to an internal code of ethics that deems what is right and what is wrong. It is strengthened by choosing thoughts and actions that are based upon an individual's moral principles and personal values. Some character traits of those with high **personal integrity** might include honesty, trustworthiness, kindness, courageousness, respect, and loyalty. An example of personal integrity in action would be helping an elderly neighbor with yard work or home repairs, even when it might not be convenient. It is these types of behaviors that develop an individual's personal integrity and reputation. Those with high personal integrity are not generally motivated by popularity, nor are they compelled to seek ill-gotten gains. The stronger one's sense of personal integrity, the less likely one is to succumb to corruption.

Professional Integrity

Professional integrity involves choosing actions that adhere to moral principles and codes of ethics (both internal and organizationally imposed) while at work. It originates from an individual's personal integrity. Professional integrity avoids corruption or any potential conflicts of interest and develops professional credibility. An example of professional integrity in action would be telling the CEO that you've made a major mistake, even though you will likely face sanctions. Professional integrity often leads to high professional standards, resulting in an increased quality of work. Moreover, leaders who demonstrate unyielding professional integrity frequently have a greater following of employees and customers.

Ethical Business Principles and Practices

Transparency

Transparency is the free sharing of nonconfidential information. It results in better-informed and more engaged employees. Most employees appreciate it when management is transparent with information, such as healthcare costs, pay increase schedules, or future changes on the horizon. **Transparency** may be a tool for removing obstacles to diversity as employees will be better able to understand one another. Being transparent and openly communicating with staff during decision-making processes can also build employee trust and be leveraged as a recruiting or retention tool. The internet now provides job seekers with transparent information about a company's culture, benefits, average pay, and interview process. It's always better for employees to hear this information directly from the employer so that the firm can ensure accuracy and address any questions or concerns head-on.

Confidentiality

Confidentiality is vital in human resources practices. Maintaining the confidentiality of all **employee records** is imperative. Information to be safeguarded includes, but is not limited to, social security numbers, birth dates, addresses, phone numbers, personal emails, benefits enrollments, medical or leave details, garnishments, bank account information, disciplinary actions, grievances, and employment eligibility data. When employee record information is requested for legitimate purposes, a written release signed by the employee should be obtained and kept on file. Examples of these requests include employment verification for bank loans or mortgage applications.

Further, human resources should internally disclose this sensitive data only to those who are authorized and based on the scenario at hand. For example, a supervisor should have knowledge of employees' disciplinary histories so that they can manage them more effectively. However, that supervisor doesn't need to know what benefit plan the employee elected or that the employee has a tax lien.

However, human resources cannot always promise complete confidentiality. For example, if an employee makes a harassment allegation, human resources will move to investigate immediately. Human resources should inform the complainant and anyone involved in the investigation that the situation will be handled as discreetly as possible; however, the nature of an investigation dictates that information obtained during the process may be shared with those on a need-to-know basis, to include the accused.

Anonymity

Anonymity is similar to confidentiality. It provides employees with the ability to partake in activities without their names being disclosed. Employers may have employees take a survey or evaluate their managers under anonymity to eliminate any fear of retaliation. Individuals may also anonymously report any complaint or ethics violation.

Conflicts of Interest

A **conflict of interest** occurs when someone with a responsibility to act in the best interest of the company may also be in the position to derive personal benefit at the expense of the company. Some examples include: utilizing company resources for personal financial gain; forming relationships or obligations that compromise objectivity when conducting duties; disclosing company information to interfere with bidding, negotiating, or contracting; exerting influence in business transactions that benefit the individual or a relative; traveling at vendors' or customers' expense; or accepting gifts, services, or favors from company stakeholders. Conflicts of interest should be avoided. Clear policies should be in place, and all employees should be held to them.

Privacy Principles

With technology now a part of every business transaction, it is essential that companies and employees adhere to strict confidentiality practices and **privacy principles**. From employee monitoring to asking interview questions, employers need to take care to avoid invading personal privacy. Legal regulations that inform best practices and internal privacy policies should be consulted regularly for guidance. On the other hand, companies should consider implementing **confidentiality or nondisclosure agreements** so employees are aware that databases, client lists, and other proprietary information must be protected and that the sharing of these records externally is strictly prohibited.

Code of Conduct

A **code of conduct** is a set of behavioral rules rooted in moral standards, laws, and best practices that a company develops, adopts, and communicates to employees. It outlines expected behavior as well as defines what behavior won't be tolerated. The document should also state what disciplinary actions employees could face if they violate the code.

Employee involvement in the development of a code of conduct will lead to greater employee buy-in and adherence. The code should be written in ambiguous language that can be applied to specific situations as they arise. Upon finalization, the code should be shared with all employees. Employees should then be required to sign a document acknowledging receipt and understanding of the new code.

Review Video: Ethical and Professional Standards
Visit mometrix.com/academy and enter code: 391843

Behavioral Competencies: Leadership Chapter Quiz

1. Which type of leadership promotes an atmosphere of respect in which all employees have the equal ability to share and utilize the skills they bring to the organization?

a. Situational leadership
b. Participative leadership
c. Transformational leadership
d. Inclusive leadership

2. Which of the following is a theory of leadership in which leaders can view their employees?

a. Theory E
b. Theory M
c. Theory W
d. Theory X

3. Which of the following is NOT one of the four phases of people management?

a. Directing
b. Monitoring
c. Supporting
d. Delegating

4. Who of the following constructed the motivation-hygiene theory?

a. McClelland
b. Herzberg
c. Maslow
d. Locke

5. Vroom's expectancy theory states that

a. Rationality will drive employees toward the option that provides maximum pleasure and minimal pain.
b. Employees are driven by explicit, measurable goals that are challenging but attainable.
c. Motivation is primarily intrinsic and arises from three main needs: achievement, affiliation, and power.
d. Motivation is based on extrinsic factors, such as reward and punishment.

6. Which of the following is NOT one of the three core intrinsic motivators of self-determination theory?

a. Autonomy
b. Wellness
c. Relatedness
d. Competence

7. When employees can see how their roles affect the entire organization so that they no longer feel like they operate in isolation it is called?

a. Task significance
b. Task identity
c. Autonomy
d. Skill variety

Behavioral Competencies: Interpersonal

Relationship Management

Types of Conflict

Task Conflict vs. Relationship Conflict

Task-related intergroup conflicts are cognitive in nature and are typically over goal definition or how work should be performed. Low to moderate levels of task conflict with sufficient levels of trust and safety are functional and may stimulate healthy competition or creative ideas. High levels of task conflict can be harmful to productive work processes and diminish team cohesiveness.

Relationship-related intergroup conflicts are emotional in nature and based on discord within interpersonal relationships stemming from differences in personal values or style. These conflicts carry a perception of interpersonal incompatibility and often involve tension, animosity, and aggravation among team members. Relationship conflicts are almost always dysfunctional, volatile, and destructive. Left unchecked, they can put a big damper on both productivity and morale.

Inter- and Intra-Organizational Conflict

A conflict between two groups, such as union and management, often results in undesirable outcomes for the organization. Each group is driven to pursue their own goals, and often there is little regard for the other or the organization's success. Thus, an **intergroup intervention** should be sought before the situation turns the parties into lasting enemies. These interventions can be selected from the following strategies:

- **Finding a Common Enemy**—This strategy brings both groups together by finding an outside party that both groups dislike. Groups must coordinate efforts to fight the outsider and achieve success.
- **Joint Activities**—This strategy forces members of each group to interact and communicate together to achieve a shared objective. As increased activities foster more positive attitudes and sentiments, ill feelings toward one another should dissipate.
- **Rotating Membership**—Often useful in international relations, this strategy involves moving members from one group to the other group. Group attitudes are strongly influenced by its members, and transferring people between groups may help build awareness and perspective.
- **Conflict Resolution Meetings**—This strategy begins with a meeting of group leaders to share feelings and gain commitment to establishing cooperation. Each group independently identifies their internal feelings and those they perceive from the other group. Then, the groups meet to share and discuss, allowing only for clarification inquiries and not drawn-out explanations. This step is repeated until hostility has been diffused.

Conflict Management Methods

Managing conflict properly can increase trust, cohesiveness, and engagement levels. Human resources and leadership should partner to ensure that functional conflict, which can result in better problem-solving and more innovation, has a place in the organization. However, they should work to minimize dysfunctional conflict resulting from personal differences as it is always counterproductive. All employees should take part in conflict management training so that everyone can do their part to keep the office productive and professional, regardless of personal beliefs. To ensure consistency in addressing conflict, human resource practitioners should evaluate conflict trends within the organization and create a **resolution policy**. Finally, human resources and leaders should model how conflict resolution should be handled to include dealing with their own interpersonal issues diplomatically.

Conflict Resolution Styles

Avoidance

With the avoidance style, conflict goes ignored. Those who employ this method generally dislike confrontation. If the issue isn't urgent, avoiding it likely won't have any noticeable ill effects. The situation may even resolve itself. However, if the matter is truly important, conflict avoidance can lead to the problem getting bigger. If it festers long enough, it may become unmanageable. It's critical to nip real issues in the bud whenever possible to prevent this from happening.

Competition

With the competition style, whoever has the most clout determines how the conflict is resolved. For example, a conflict over how to complete a task is likely going to be won by the supervisor over the employee because the supervisor holds a higher position of authority. This type of resolution can also occur when one voice within the conflict becomes more dominant than the other(s) even if he or she doesn't have a formal position of power. This resolution style can be effective when decisions need to be made fast. Its drawback is that it can make people feel trampled on, negatively affecting morale.

Cooperation

With the cooperation style, preserving relationships is viewed as more important than being right. The conflict is resolved via accommodation or collaboration (discussed in the next section). This style can be effective when there is enough time to come to a consensus or when maintaining harmony is critical to organizational success.

Conciliation

With the conciliation style, one party attempts to gain favor with the other party. He or she may try to overcome differences of opinion and reestablish trust to persuade a person to adopt his or her view. Those who resolve conflict with this style seek to get their way. However, they are less aggressive than those who favor the competition style.

Conflict Resolution Techniques

Accommodate

When **accommodation** is employed, one party decides to give in to the other. Once the other party has what it wants, the conflict should be over. This technique can be useful when the accommodating party wants to preserve the relationship, end the conflict, or isn't that personally invested in the outcome of the situation.

Avoid

When **avoidance** is employed, one or both parties ignore the conflict at hand. Depending on the severity of the issue, this can lead to the concern resolving itself (or at least becoming less important over time) or the concern festering into a much larger problem. This technique can be useful when trivial matters can be safely ignored or when one party needs more time to reflect. In general, however, this technique is likely to yield unresolved conflict that could result in decreased productivity and morale.

Collaborate

When **collaboration** is employed, both parties meet to determine an outcome that is favorable (or at least palatable) for everyone involved. Ideally, this technique strengthens the relationships within the parties and results in an amicably resolved conflict. Collaboration is an effective technique when there is adequate time available to come to an agreement. It is inefficient for conflict that needs to be resolved on the spot.

Negotiation

Negotiation is a vital technique for every business professional. New or expired contracts and changing behaviors require skillful **negotiations**. Human resource practitioners must know how to handle negotiations to successfully avoid conflicts, improve relations, secure pay rates, and evaluate contracts. It is paramount to note that negotiations are possible only when all parties are open to compromise and finding solutions that are mutually satisfying.

Negotiation Tactics, Strategies, and Styles

Perspective Taking

Perspective taking involves deeply understanding the position of the other party. If the negotiator understands where the other party is coming from, he or she will be better able to offer a deal that works well for both parties.

Principled Bargainer

The **principled bargainer** views negotiations as fluid, exploratory conversations, guided by principles, to ultimately achieve mutually beneficial solutions. Rather than viewing the other party as an adversary or a negotiation is something to be won, a principled bargainer sees all parties involved as problem-solvers looking for the most efficient outcome for everyone. This is commonly known as a win-win form of negotiation.

Interest-Based Bargaining

A principled bargainer will utilize interest-based bargaining to establish a win-win deal for all parties involved. The parties begin the negotiation process by plainly stating their main interests. The process involves coming to an agreement that satisfies those interests while minimizing the pain of any concessions to be made.

Auction

An auction can be a great bargaining strategy when a decision needs to be made quickly and will solely be based on price. However, if service and value are important to the parties involved, and time permits, entering into a negotiation process may be a better solution. Negotiations can account for more nuances and can be handled discreetly.

Relationship Building

Relationship building involves establishing strong networks of customers, candidates, vendors, and business professionals. A few key elements to **relationship building** include: 1) connecting with others to find shared interests or goals, 2) fostering a sense of community, and 3) supporting others to solve problems or achieve goals. First, understand your personality, style, and motivations. Then, listen. Try to understand the other person's style of communication and needs, but be sure to value his or her time. Despite the competitive data a company might have, many people will still choose to do business with the strongest personal relationship. This may be a recommendation via word of mouth or an employment referral. Moreover, relationship building is an absolute necessity when trying to connect with passive candidates or create a pool of potential future candidates.

Professional Networking

Professional networking has become a powerful tool in today's business world. **Networking** involves creating a large group of business contacts and staying active with regular communications that are mutually beneficial. It is vital to use network connections to help others and not just to seek help for yourself. Nurturing these relationships through communication is the lifeblood of networking and can be done by providing recommendations, referrals, or advice. Some essential principles of networking include the following:

- Create an engaging elevator speech about yourself.
- Smile and be positive.
- Differentiate yourself.
- Set goals and achievement plans.
- Strive to share information and facilitate opportunities for others.
- Build up your personal reputation and credibility.
- Follow up on all meetings and referrals.

Teamwork

Teamwork encompasses any group of people working cooperatively toward a common goal. It is important that all members of the team be familiar with the plan for achieving goals and feel valued and respected. Each individual should feel important and as though their contributions are validated. Creativity, innovation, and differing viewpoints can be fostered for new ideas. Strong, unified teams are often more efficient and productive due to the fact that members support one another and work collaboratively. Moreover, successful teams distribute work evenly, and everyone shoulders the burden when roadblocks are encountered. This synergy encourages employee engagement and makes businesses more competitive.

Communication

Elements of Communication

Communication is defined as the practice of exchanging information, data, ideas, and opinions. There are many models that depict complex **communication processes**. However, almost all communications will include some variety of these fundamentals: source, sender, encoding, message, channel, receiver, decoding, and feedback. The **sender or source** chooses, creates, and encodes the message. The **receiver** decodes and interprets the message. In between, the message must be **transmitted** through some communication channel or medium like phone, text, email, video, or broadcast. Communication messages often pass through **noise barriers** such as environmental sounds, people speaking, traffic, and construction. Removing these barriers can decrease instances of misunderstanding and confusion. **Feedback** allows the model to be interchangeable, allowing for communication to flow both ways.

General Communication Techniques

Planning Communications

Delivering messages can be difficult, especially if the context is serious in nature. The message content should be tailored to fit the audience. This requires understanding the roles, expectations, and perspective of recipients. First, focus on eliminating any **barriers** or vague wording that may interfere with interpreting the message. Once the proper channel for delivery is selected, it may be important to focus on **nonverbal signals** and ensure that they coincide with the mood of the message content. Finally, messages should allow for **feedback** that will lead to follow-up discussions. If the message is complex in nature, such as a business change or new benefits offering, it may be critical to share repeated reminders and have open lines of communication to reduce confusion and ensure success.

Active Listening

Active listening is an important component of communication that requires paying close attention to what is being said. It often involves making eye contact and appropriately nodding to show engagement. To gain a better understanding, try to understand things from the speaker's point of view, or visualize what he or she is saying. It is important to be considerate, avoid distractions or interruptions, and respond appropriately. Additionally, try to pick up on emotional cues beyond the literal words that are used. Even if the message differs from your own opinion, try to focus on accepting what the other person has to say rather than being critical. Make sure to fully hear what the other person is saying before formulating your own response. When compared to passive listeners, it has been noted that **active listeners** are more connected and conscientious.

Communication Techniques for Specialized Situations

Giving Feedback

Feedback can be written or verbal and should be based upon factual data. Although the process can be emotional, it's important that feedback be constructive in nature, detailing the quality of someone's performance or conduct without judging on a personal level. Effective feedback should be delivered in a timely, consistent, and positively framed manner. If informal, feedback can be used to give advice or to provide clarity. If disciplinary, the feedback should also include required improvements to be made and potential consequences for not meeting the standard. When receiving feedback, take the time to carefully consider it and implement it as appropriate. The most important thing to remember about feedback is why it's being given: to facilitate an improvement.

Facilitating Focus Groups

Focus groups can be used to investigate ideas, opinions, and concerns. **Focus groups** can be beneficial for clarifying supplemental research because they are relatively timely and inexpensive. The topic and objectives of the group should be clearly defined before potential participants are identified. Participants should be notified that their identities will be anonymous and that all information will be confidential. Once a **pool of participants** has been selected and separated into groups, a trained **facilitator** should be chosen, and a guide of discussion questions should be constructed. Most studies will contain three to 10 focus groups, each with five to 12 voluntary participants. A private location is ideal, and many discussions will last approximately 90 minutes. Finally, all collected information will be analyzed and reported.

Facilitating Staff Meetings

There are three core elements to a successful **staff meeting**: 1) invite all attendees to share a little, 2) focus on the group and any outcomes that might need adjustment or improvement, and 3) allow time for feedback in the decision-making process. Staff meetings are an excellent way to increase organizational communication and alignment, offering an open floor for staff to give feedback on recent messages or events. They are also a low-budget way to promote staff recognition, wellness programs, employee referral programs, and employee surveys. Moreover, staff meetings have a history of improving productivity, workplace conflicts, team synergy, and employee relations. It is important to consider religious holidays when scheduling staff meetings, seminars, or training events. For example, staff meetings scheduled on Ash Wednesday, Good Friday, Passover, Rosh Hashanah, or Yom Kippur might have low attendance.

Communications Media

Communication can be transmitted through a wide variety of **channels or media**, such as phone, email, face-to-face, reports, presentations, or social media. The method that you choose should fit both the *audience* and the *type* of communication. **Information-rich communication channels** include phone, videoconferencing, and face-to-face meetings or presentations. **Information-lean channels** include email, fliers, newsletters, or reports. If you are trying to sell a product or service, you might use a series of phone calls, face-to-face meetings, and presentations. This is because information-rich media are more interactive, which is more appropriate for complex messages that may need clarification. Rich and oral communications should be used when there is time urgency, immediate feedback is required, ideas can be simplified with explanations, or emotions may be affected. Lean and written communications should be used when you are simply stating facts or need information permanently recorded.

Global and Cultural Effectiveness

Cultural Intelligence

Cultural intelligence is a measure of one's capability to interact suitably with people from other cultures and to behave appropriately in multicultural situations. It involves the following:

- **Motivational drives**: personal interests and confidence in multicultural situations
- **Knowledge and attitudes**: learning and accepting how cultures are similar or different
- **Cognitive or strategic thinking**: awareness and ability to plan for multicultural interactions
- **Behavioral actions**: talent for relating and working with others of differing backgrounds

Learning about one's own culture is vital to cultural intelligence because it provides a more objective model when gaining familiarity about other cultures. Exploring diverse cultural values and expectations may help address insecurities and introduce new attitudes or behaviors that appreciate differences. Some considerations when comparing cultures may be how relationships are viewed, local laws, societal norms, and so on. **Cultural intelligence** is much more than knowing what kinds of gifts are appropriate, when to bow, and which nonverbal gestures to avoid. Cultural intelligence can be increased by learning a different language, attending a holiday celebration, or spending time in a cultural setting different than your own while sincerely asking questions about habits, attitudes, and beliefs. The key is to always concentrate on valuing and showing respect for others.

Cultural Norms, Values, and Dimensions

Hall Model of Organizational Culture

The Hall model, developed by Edward T. Hall, investigates cultural relationships and separates them into two classes: high contrast and low contrast. **High-contrast relationships** tend to last longer and have more defined patterns of behavior or boundaries of entry, such as families, religious congregations, or on-campus relations. In high-contrast environments, there may be more implicit communications, body language interpretation, shared values, and a great deal of commitment. **Low-contrast relationships** tend to be short term and require more rules and structure, such as a cafeteria line or making your way through a large, international airport. In low-contrast environments, there may be more explicit communications, diverse beliefs, and limited commitment. It should be noted that every culture will demonstrate a combination of both high- and low-contrast interactions.

Hofstede Model of Cross-Cultural Differences

The following are the six values identified by the Hofstede model of cross-cultural differences:

1. **Power distance** is the social acceptability of power distinctions, such as rich versus poor. In *lower-power distance societies,* high-power distance is regarded as undesirable, and inequalities are kept to a minimum. In *high-power distance societies,* power differences or castes are generally accepted, and those of particular status receive privileges.
2. **Uncertainty avoidance** is the acceptability of ambiguity and the unknown. Societies that practice *strong uncertainty avoidance* attempt to avoid risk and impose structure. Societies that practice *low uncertainty avoidance* view risk as unavoidable and are more tolerant to ambiguity.

3. **Individualism versus collectivism** is the relationship between society as a whole and the individual. *Individualistic cultures* believe in self-reliance and acting in the best interest of the individual. Power is more evenly distributed, and economic mobility is attainable. *Collective cultures* believe in cohesiveness and are loyal to the best interests of the entire group. Power is contained within the in group, and economic mobility is limited.
4. **Masculinity versus femininity** is the societal perception of the value of typical male and female traits. *Low-masculinity societies* accept the blending of male and female roles and tend to favor traits like cooperation and modesty. *High-masculinity societies* accept clearly defined gender roles, and traits like achievement, assertiveness, and competition are championed.
5. **Long-term orientation versus short-term normative orientation** describes a society's propensity to remain traditional or change with the times. Low-scoring societies are skeptical of change and hold steadfast to their norms. High-scoring societies are likely to prepare for the future.
6. **Indulgence versus restraint** is whether a society values fun and gratification or regulation. Those societies that favor indulgence allow members to give in to their desire for enjoyment. Those that favor restraint suppress these desires.

Schein's Model of Organizational Culture

Edgar Schein developed his well-known **model of organizational culture** in the 1980s. Many of Schein's studies indicate that culture is rooted with the CEO and developed over time. The model separates culture into three core layers: 1) artifacts, 2) values and beliefs, and 3) underlying assumptions. The first layer, **artifacts**, is the most visible. This includes the vision and mission, office dress codes, and generally accepted behaviors. Employee **values**, thought patterns, and organizational goals make up the second layer. The deepest layer is the **underlying assumptions**, ideologies, and perceptions of the organization. These cannot be easily measured but can greatly affect the organizational culture.

Trompenaars's Model of Organization Culture

Fons Trompenaars designed a model of organizational culture that divides people and cultures into seven dimensions:

- **Universalism versus particularism**—what's more important (rules vs. relationships)?
- Individualism versus communitarianism—who comes first (me vs. community)?
- **Specific versus diffuse**—how much separation (work/life balance vs. work/life blend)?
- **Neutral versus affective**—what's appropriate (reason vs. emotion)?
- **Achievement versus ascription**—do we need to prove status or title (accomplishments vs. identity)?
- **Sequential time versus synchronous time**— how do we work (focused vs. multitasking, punctual vs. flexible schedule)?
- **Internal direction versus outer direction**—what's in control (autonomy vs. circumstance)?

Techniques for Bridging Individual Differences and Perceptions

Barrier Removal

Global and cultural barriers are increasing as businesses spread across oceans and countries. When two different cultures clash, gestures can be misinterpreted, and communications can be misunderstood. For example, although we shake hands when meeting new people, other countries might bow, hug, or kiss. Moreover, making eye contact or expressing emotional sensitivity might be found offensive in some cultures. As operations grow and outsourcing or manufacturing is sent overseas, language barriers can make finding the best resources difficult and delay communications. **Inclusive cultures** are key to **removing these barriers** because they welcome individuals regardless of culture, age, race, ethnicity, sexual orientation, religious belief, disability, or any other factor. Inclusive cultures foster understanding and ensure that appropriate accommodations are made in the workplace as needed. They also provide team members with regular training to underscore the value of cultural diversity and instill accepting beliefs.

Assimilation

During the **transition process**, people are first separated from their previous roles and gradually initiated into their new roles. **Assimilation** is the final stage of the transition process in which people overcome any initial shock and are successfully integrated into the new role and company culture. During this stage, people become part of the group and begin to fit in while new expectations are formed. To ensure the process is a success, new employees should be partnered with long-tenured staff who can show them the ins and outs of the organization. The new employee should be given ample time to ask questions, make and correct mistakes, and adapt to the new environment. They should also be immediately included in office events and meetings.

Best Practices for Managing Globally Diverse Workforces

Diversity fosters the potential for more perspectives, creative ideas, and innovation. **Inclusion** involves realizing and accepting the benefits and competitive advantage to be had when everyone feels welcome and respected. This environment can be developed with openness, cultural sensitivity, and equal support. Human resource practitioners can advocate for a diverse and inclusive workplace by reflecting how it can align with business objectives. Building diverse teams can improve problem-solving and productivity and may increase customer satisfaction by providing better representation of an employer's stakeholders. Once buy-in has been gained from upper management, a **diversity committee** can collaborate to design and communicate initiatives.

Human Resource practitioners should identify if there are any areas of concern or need in the organization. Do current employees fairly represent the available talent pool? Human resources should work to address any unconscious biases or prevailing attitudes in policies or practices that do not support diversity initiatives. Human Resource practitioners can further support diversity by drawing attention to and eliminating discriminatory perspectives or prejudices. They should train managers how to fairly and consistently conduct interviews and to supervise employees from various backgrounds. Moreover, providing appropriate **accommodations** to employees in need can increase safety, efficiency, and team morale.

Human resource practitioners should create programs that outline and reinforce organizational core values and ensure that employees who embody those values are recognized and rewarded. Training programs can educate managers and employees about work values, regardless of national origin or home culture. **Behavioral norms** that are consistent with company values can then be cultivated.

Human resource departments need to adjust their strategies when the **company structure** evolves to international, multinational, or global levels. This might involve learning about new cultures, religious customs, foreign labor laws, safety regulations, union activity, or economics. Knowledge of expatriation, repatriation, and global compensation are additional assets for human resource practitioners. Some companies may choose to seek consultation with a local specialist in payroll laws and taxation to assist in-house human resources.

INTERACTIONS AND CONFLICTS OF PROFESSIONAL AND CULTURAL VALUES

Research suggests that one's home national culture has a greater impact on thought processes and behaviors than the culture of the current organization. As such, if the cultural values of one's home nation and the cultural values of one's workplace aren't in alignment, conflict may arise. Because organizations are becoming much more diverse and globally dispersed, this type of conflict is common. The conflict may arise due to differences in things like communication style, perceptions of hierarchy, decision-making processes, the need for physical space, adherence to timelines, and many others. Leaders need to develop their cultural intelligence and work with these differences to reduce conflict. They can also try to facilitate constructive conflict, where employees and leaders collaborate through their cultural differences.

Behavioral Competencies: Interpersonal Chapter Quiz

1. Which of the following is NOT an intergroup intervention?

a. Finding a common enemy
b. Joint activities
c. Conflict resolution meetings
d. Static membership

2. Which of the following conflict resolution styles views preserving relationships as more important than being right?

a. Avoidance
b. Competition
c. Cooperation
d. Conciliation

3. What is it called when one party decides to give in to the other?

a. Accommodation
b. Avoidance
c. Collaboration
d. Compromise

4. Which of the following is NOT an element of relationship building?

a. Connecting with others to find shared interests or goals
b. Setting firm boundaries and establishing rules
c. Fostering a sense of community
d. Supporting others to solve problems or achieve goals

5. All of the following are essential principles of networking EXCEPT

a. Differentiate yourself
b. Set goals and achievement plans
c. Create an emotional and lengthy story of triumph about yourself
d. Build up your personal reputation and credibility

6. Motivational drives, strategic thinking, and behavioral actions are all part of which of the following?

a. Social intelligence
b. Emotional intelligence
c. Cultural intelligence
d. Business intelligence

7. Schein's model of organizational culture separates culture into how many core layers?

a. Six
b. Five
c. Four
d. Three

Behavioral Competencies: Business

Business Acumen

Business Terms and Concepts

Return on Investment (ROI) is usually reflected as a percentage that measures how beneficial a new tool or practice has been compared to its initial investment. The **ROI** can be calculated as net return on investment/cost of investment X 100 percent. Human resource professionals may be asked about ROI to determine the effectiveness of training programs, recently implemented software, or supplementations to the workforce. However, it is important to consider all associated costs. For example, if you are considering the ROI of a harassment training seminar, you want to include the travel costs to get employees to the seminar. Total costs associated with the seminar can then be compared to alternatives, such as videos or webinars. Another strategy is to compare your firm's ROI with the ROI of other companies. If there is a competitive return, strategic plans should not be drastically changed. But, if the ROI is much lower than competitors, a new strategy is in order. It should also be noted that when making decisions among investments, an estimated ROI is used.

Return on equity (ROE) is the amount of money made compared to the average investment of each shareholder. Return on equity is usually the foundation of an organization's strategic plan. This is because the primary goal of any business is to offer its shareholders the largest possible return on their investment. A for-profit organization's ROE is an indication of overall performance.

Analyzing and Interpreting Business Documents

Balance Sheets

A balance sheet conveys financial position and reports a company's assets, liabilities, and equity over a specified period of time. The **balance sheet** reflects the following balanced equation:

$$\text{Assets} - \text{Liabilities} = \text{Equity}$$

An **asset** is any resource possessed by the company as a result of previous actions and from which future gains are expected. A **liability** is a current obligation as a result of previous actions expected to result in an outflow of resources. **Equity** is the residual interest and assets after deducting all liabilities.

Budgets

The **budget** for many businesses involves collecting relevant or historical data and often stems directly from the organizational vision and the strategic plan. The **strategic plan** should ensure that resources are used to support achieving the organizational objectives. Fixed costs, variable costs, and revenue estimates can be developed to establish the budget. The **budget performance** should be monitored on a monthly, quarterly, and annual basis. Any **budget variances** should be investigated to determine the cause of the variance. Some variances may be caused by unforeseen situations, such as a change in compliance regulations or training requirements. Furthermore, some businesses will provide individual departments with a budget. Some factors to consider when constructing the budget for a human resources department might include the number of employees, benefit cost projections, training needs, and any anticipated legal expenses.

Budgeting helps ensure that future financial costs are coordinated and controlled. There are two basic methods for creating budgets: a bottom-up approach and a top-down approach. **Bottom-up**

budgeting requires department supervisors to forecast departmental expenses and payroll costs for the coming period. This method relies heavily on lower-level supervisors, with assistance from human resources and final approval from top managers. **Top-down budgeting** involves estimating expenses and payroll costs for an entire organization and then allocating a set amount to each department manager, leaving them responsible for managing their funds.

Cash Flow Statements

Cash flow refers to the amount of money taken in compared to the amount of money spent during a given period. Profits, credits, or loans would reflect an **inflow** of cash, whereas expenses, purchases, or payments would reflect an **outflow** of cash. Most businesses prepare and rely heavily upon a **cash flow statement** to monitor business performance. One obvious key factor of cash flow is **profits**. An organization can sustain itself with additional funds or reserved savings in spite of profits but not for long. The other obvious key factor is **expenditures**, which must be kept within budget and sustained. Many businesses will utilize cash flow **forecasting** and then compare forecasted figures to actual amounts. Businesses should always strive for positive cash flow. Negative cash flow can be an indication of poor company health. Whereas debt in certain cases is necessary for growth, negative cash flow forces the business to take on debt just to operate.

Profit and Loss Statements

A **profit and loss statement** reports a company's income, expenses, and profits over a specified period of time. **Income or profits** increase in the form of inflows, expansion of assets, or reducing liabilities, resulting in an increase in equity, not including contributions. **Expenses** include declines in the form of outflows, depletion of assets, or undertaking of liabilities, resulting in decreases in equity, not including distributions.

Elements of a Business Case

A **business case** is a document produced to explore solutions to a business problem. Based on objective data, it facilitates decision-making for scenarios such as committing to large purchases, choosing vendors, or implementing new initiatives. A properly written business case clears up potential confusion or disagreements early on in the project timeline, helping the firm complete its objectives more effectively. Although the content requirements of a business case will vary due to leader preferences, there are common elements that should typically be included.

- **Problem statement**—The business case should begin with identifying the problem that needs to be fixed.
- **Background**—The problem background will help readers understand the causes of the issue. It should also state what's required to combat the issue in general terms.
- **Objectives**—The business case should list how solving the issue will help the firm.
- **Current status**—The business case needs to describe how the solution will affect current operations.
- **Requirements**—This section should clearly define the resources that the project will need to be successful such as capital, staffing, time commitment, software, and so on.
- **Alternatives**—The business case should list, describe, compare, and contrast several alternatives to the proposed solution. This gives leadership options and demonstrates that human resources has done their due diligence in their research.
- **Additional considerations**—The business case must account for potential risks and anything else that may be affected by the project.

- **Action plan**—The action plan should spell out specific steps that will be taken both in the short (first three months) and long (beyond three months) term. Project milestones need to be established and measurements for success defined. It should also be clear who would oversee the project.
- **Executive summary**—This should be a high-level, one-page document showing how the information gathered culminates in the business case.

Business Intelligence Tools and Techniques

Businesses are constantly generating data, and they need an effective way to utilize it to become and stay competitive. Previously, businesses would simply construct reports with their data, using them for decision-making. Although that still happens every day, data is now being used in more advanced ways.

Online Analytical Processing (OLAP)

OLAP is on demand and facilitates decision-making. It's capable of reporting, what-if planning, and trend spotting, to name a few. OLAP also allows the user to view data from different angles, which provides a deeper understanding of the subject at hand.

Advanced Analytics

Although advanced analytics includes reporting, it goes way beyond that. By way of data mining, formulas, and algorithms, advanced analytics can be used for forecasting, pattern detection, and demonstrating correlation. Keeping up with technology, advanced analytics is also a part of machine learning and artificial intelligence. Although advanced analytics is a powerful business intelligence tool, there is a caveat. Using data for reporting produces straightforward, typically accurate results. Analyzing the data, however, requires interpretation. Those handling the task should be trained to do so and prepared to continuously refine their approach.

Business Intelligence Portals

A **business intelligence portal** is a centrally stored collection of firm data that's accessible on demand across the organization. The portal has a user interface that allows employees to run a number of analytical processes. The portal will show the results of queries in a visual format, making it easier to spot trends and answer business questions.

Financial Analysis Methods to Assess Business Health

Financial ratios can be broken down into relevant categories for management, stakeholders, and auditors. **Profitability ratios** analyze a business's ability to generate earnings in comparison to expense costs. **Liquidity ratios** measure the business's available cash or ability to pay off short-term debts. **Operational efficiency and employee productivity ratios** measure the efficiency of employees and business resources to generate a profit. **Leverage or capital structure ratios** assess how the business uses debt to finance operations. Although being able to calculate financial ratios is important, being able to interpret financial ratios is more valuable.

Marketing and Sales Metrics

Three of the most common sales and marketing business metrics are the number of customers or orders for the period, the average amount received for each order, and the gross profit margin. The **number of customers or orders** is an exact or estimated count of the number of people purchasing products from the company or the number of orders the company has received during a specific period of time. The **average amount received for each order** is the total amount in dollars received for a particular period divided by the number of orders. Finally, the **gross profit**

margin is the total revenue for a certain period of time minus the cost of sales for that particular period divided by the total revenue for that period.

The number of customers or orders received is usually used to identify problems with current marketing and sales strategies. If the number of customers or orders for a specific period is significantly lower than previous periods, or the number of customers or orders is significantly lower than the numbers estimated from competitors, there may be a problem with the marketing strategy. For example, owners of a fast-food restaurant may decide to change their menu by adding and marketing healthier options to expand their customer base. If there is a sudden drop in the number of customers, the strategy is not working.

The average amount received per order is usually used to determine the effectiveness of marketing and sales strategies from the current customer base. The average amount received per order helps identify how much each customer is contributing to the organization's cash flow. This helps determine if the focus should be on expanding the customer base or encouraging the current customer base to spend more through marketing initiatives such as special sales, discounts, reward programs for frequent shoppers, and so on.

The gross profit margin is usually used to help determine whether a particular marketing or sales strategy currently in effect is profitable. For example, a fast-food restaurant chain may have instituted a new less-than-a-dollar menu and a marketing campaign focusing on this menu a year ago. Comparing the gross profit margin for the current year with the previous year is helpful in determining if the new campaign is increasing sales or if a new strategy is needed.

Operations and Business Development Metrics

Three of the most common operations and business development metrics used to measure performance are the number of activities, the opportunity success rate, and the innovation rate. The **number of activities** is an exact or estimated count of how many tasks the organization is attempting to do at one time. The **opportunity success rate** is the number of opportunities taken advantage of divided by the total number of opportunities available. Finally, the **innovation rate** is the gross revenue from new ideas, products, and services divided by the total gross revenue.

The number of activities is usually used to determine whether the company is taking on a larger workload than what it can normally handle. Multitasking is an important part of any enterprise, but it is important to identify how much work is too much. For example, if an old-fashioned toy manufacturer that prides itself for handcrafting toys wants to start building a large array of modern toys, they may find that it is not possible to expand without drastically increasing costs or eliminating other activities. This is because each old-fashioned toy takes a significant amount of time to construct, and the company may not be able to expand its modern toy-building activities without eliminating some of the old-fashioned toys from its product line.

Innovation rate is useful for developing a strategic plan because it helps determine if new ideas, products, and services are profitable. If the innovation rate is equal to or higher than competitors' rates, the current innovation strategy is appropriate, and the focus should be on designing products and services similar to those recently placed on the market. On the other hand, if the innovation rate is significantly lower than competitors' rates, a new innovation strategy should be implemented focusing on developing products and services not similar to those recently placed on the market. The innovation rate is not a measure of how innovative a company is but rather a measure of how profitable each group of new innovations has been for the firm.

Information Technology Metrics

Three of the most common information technology metrics an organization might use are the number of online orders, the availability of information resources, and the number of views per page or listing. The **number of online orders** is a count of how many orders have been placed by customers using the company's website. The **availability of information resources** is the percentage of time the company's servers, websites, email, and other technological resources are accessible at the time those resources are needed. The **number of views per page or listing** is a count of how many times customers have looked at a particular web page or online product.

The number of online orders placed using an organization's website can be useful for developing a strategic plan because it measures the effectiveness of the website. If the number of orders made online through the website or by email is equal to or greater than the number of orders placed through traditional means (such as in a store or by phone), the focus should be on maintaining or expanding online services. On the other hand, if the number of orders placed online is significantly lower than the number of orders placed through more traditional means, strategies should be implemented to improve online services. It is also useful to compare the number of online orders made through the website to the number of online orders made through websites belonging to competitors to determine the effectiveness of the website in relation to the rest of the industry.

The availability of the organization's information resources is an essential factor to consider for any organization's strategic plan because technology is useful only if it is working. If the computer systems, websites, email services, or other pieces of technology used by employees or customers are frequently inaccessible, the organization will not be able to function properly. Identifying problems with information technology (IT) systems and IT personnel minimizes future problems.

The number of views per page or views per listing for an organization's websites, ads, or other information resources is an important factor for an organization to consider during the strategic planning process because they measure the effectiveness of its websites and ads. If a listing receives a large number of views and results in many orders, it's performing well. However, if a listing is not receiving a large number of views, or it is receiving a large number of views but not resulting in many sales, website marketing and design should be rethought.

General Business and Economic Environment Metrics

Three of the most common metrics related to the general business and economic environment an organization might use are the current number of competitors and the average number of new competitors entering the market per year, the organization's current market share, and the average income of customers in the target market. The **current number of competitors** is the number of other businesses within the same market. The **average number of new competitors** is the average number of businesses entering the same market during a year. The **current market share** is the percentage of the local or overall market the business controls or the percentage of the market with which the organization usually does business. The **average income of customers** in the target market is the amount an average customer would normally earn in a given year.

The current number of competitors in the market and the average number of new competitors entering the market per year is a useful set of statistics for organizations attempting to develop a strategic plan. The current number of competitors in the market measures how much competition is present in a particular market. The average number of new competitors entering the market per year is a good way to measure how that competition will change. In other words, these statistics help determine how much competition is in the market now and how much there will be in the near future. These statistics help in planning for the amount of competition likely to be faced and serve as a warning for potential problems in the market.

The organization's current market share is an important factor to consider during the strategic planning process because it measures success and growth in a particular market and compares that success and growth with competitors. As a result, the current market share is ultimately an indication of how the organization as a whole is performing in the current business environment for each specific market the organization is doing business in. If an organization's market share is continuing to grow or it is maintaining a large, stable market share, it is usually an indication that current strategies are working. However, if market share is beginning to decline or is stable, but low when compared to competitors, the firm needs to review its current marketing strategies.

The average income of customers in the target market can be an important piece of information to consider during the strategic planning process because it analyzes the current economic environment. Because the amount of money individuals within the target market earn can vary greatly, it is essential to ensure customers can afford to purchase the firm's products or services. For example, if a car dealer is attempting to sell a new car that costs $35,000, it will be much more difficult to convince someone who makes $40,000 a year to purchase the car than someone who makes $70,000 a year.

Key Factors Influencing Business and Competitive Awareness

Business and competitive awareness covers a broad range of areas, especially on a global scale. **Business and competitive awareness** reflects an understanding of the organization's operations, products, and services while considering the economic, social, and political environment in which the business may operate. The organization must be knowledgeable of other practices in similar industries while keeping up with internal, external, and local factors. This can be done through benchmarking or following news and trends. Moreover, organizations can ensure they are competitive by focusing on human development, the current labor market, financial policies, level of business sophistication, and overall quality of products, services, and work environment.

Business Analysis

Business analysis methodology works as a vehicle for introducing change into an organization, the product of which is often a series of proposed solutions that align stakeholder needs and business capabilities. Human resource practitioners might assist with business analysis in the form of being strategists, identifying leadership goals, or acting as change agents. Business analysis comes in many forms and involves collecting data, analyzing it, and investigating any gaps. One popular method of business analysis is the SWOT analysis, which looks at the **strengths, weaknesses, opportunities, and threats** of the enterprise. Business analysis may be used to investigate business processes, management styles, team collaboration, employee engagement, information systems, or organizational communication and culture, to name a few.

Strategic Alignment

Strategic alignment involves coordinating business resources and practices with the organizational mission and environment. Business partners should investigate both potential internal and industry challenges. The goal of **strategic alignment** is to optimize performance and competitiveness and meet strategic goals. Human resource practitioners might support strategic alignment by following these steps:

1. Outline **departmental objectives** that support business success.
2. Establish **departmental goals** such as reducing costs or increasing engagement and retention.
3. Develop an **action plan** for meeting goals.
4. **Collaborate** with others, and set the plan into motion.
5. **Report** and **monitor** results.

Consultation

Organizational Change Management Theories and Models

Gene Dalton's Theory of Lasting Change

Many change efforts struggle to produce **lasting and sustainable results**. Although initial goals may be met, the ability to stick to the efforts or behaviors needed to prolong the success proves to be more difficult. **Gene Dalton** argued that change would not occur without a feeling of loss or pain to motivate it and that people will continue old patterns of behavior unless they feel a need for change. He also noted that those initiating and supporting organizational change should be perceived as trustworthy facilitators.

Lewin's Change Management Model

Kurt Lewin's theory of change describes three stages for planning change: unfreezing, change, and refreezing:

- **Unfreezing** is the first step. It occurs when current values, attitudes, and behaviors are challenged, and people understand the need for change.
- **Change** occurs during the action phase, whereby the situation is examined, and a new equilibrium is created. People develop new values, attitudes, or patterns of behaviors.
- **Refreezing** is the final step in which the change is stabilized, and new patterns are solidified. Refreezing requires that people experience positive consequences to strengthen their continuing commitment to the change process.

McKinsey 7-S Model

The McKinsey 7-S Model is frequently used in strategic planning and change management. The model is founded on the principle that each company has seven **elements** or key factors. Strategy, structure, and systems are more easily identified. Shared values, style, staff, and skills can be more difficult to describe and may be continuously changing. However, each element is interconnected and may affect one another. The seven key elements of the McKinsey 7-S Model include the following:

1. **Strategy**—plan for competitive advantage and growth regarding business, products, and markets
2. **Structure**—structure of reporting hierarchy
3. **Systems**—everyday procedures and processes
4. **Shared values**—core concepts and work ethic, organizational mission, and goals
5. **Style**—leadership approach and operational culture
6. **Staff**—employee development and empowerment
7. **Skills**—competencies and capabilities

John Kotter's 8-Step Change Model

John Kotter's 8-Step Change Model identifies eight steps for implementing effective change:

1. **Create a sense of urgency**—examine the competitive market, identify threats or opportunities, articulate importance of speed, and make the case for change.
2. **Build a guiding coalition**—establish support from executives, and design a group with credibility and power to lead change efforts.
3. **Develop a shared vision and strategy**—create a plan to direct change efforts, and develop success metrics.

4. **Communicate the change vision**—readily and persistently communicate the new vision and strategy from the top down.
5. **Empower action**—eliminate obstacles, systems, or structures that undermine the new idea, and reward creativity.
6. **Generate short-term wins**—recognize and reward visible improvements in performance.
7. **Capitalize on momentum**—take advantage of small wins, reinvite those who have resisted, and become reenergized.
8. **Make the change stick**—continue to encourage new behaviors and leadership development.

Review Video: US Employment Law: Employee and Labor Relations (NLRA)
Visit mometrix.com/academy and enter code: 404217

Organizational Change Processes

Leadership Buy-In

Buy-in is support or endorsement for something. In the case of change, leadership buy-in is critical. Often, their support is necessary to get the change movement started because they may need to approve the use of resources or major modifications to business operations. If the change requires their endorsement, and they will not give it, then the change is defeated before it can get started. Additionally, leadership buy-in is necessary to champion the change across the organization. If the leaders believe in the effort, they can communicate their enthusiasm for it and model the new desired behavior, making it easier for the change to take root.

Building a Case for Change

One useful way to approach organizational change activities is the **action research model**. Once a problem has been identified, there are six basic steps that follow: data gathering, feedback of data to the target group, data discussions and diagnosis, action planning, action, and recycling. **Data gathering** involves collecting information about the problem from sources such as observations, interviews, surveys, and archived data. **Feedback of data to a target group** involves making the gathered data openly available and sharing it with a group through presentations. **Data discussions and diagnosis** involve a roundtable conversation and analysis by the target group to diagnose a root cause and to explore alternatives or viable solutions. **Action planning** involves creating a plan to implement solutions, which may require outside parties. **Action** involves the execution of new changes. Finally, **recycling** involves reviewing and repeating the processes to ensure problems do not reoccur.

Engaging Employees

For changes to be implemented successfully, the employees need to embrace them (or at least understand them). This can be accomplished by engaging them in the change process and ensuring that they remain engaged overall as employees. Engaging them in the change process includes asking for and using their feedback (when possible) before, during, and after the change. Doing this shows that the organization values their opinion and places an importance on collaboration and transparency. When employees can help shape the change, they are far more likely to go along with it. Additionally, when employees are truly engaged at work, they will have an easier time adapting to change (even if unpleasant) because of their strong emotional commitment to the company.

Communicating Change

Provide clear communication to employees and all stakeholders as early as possible. Keep communications simple, and explain both the necessity and the timeline for the change. Let employees know what will be staying the same and proactively counter any negative reactions that can be anticipated. Develop opportunities for **two-way communications**. This provides employees with the chance to ask questions. Then, repeat communications, and explain how employees will be kept informed throughout the process to manage expectations. Finally, have leadership get involved to advocate for the change, and lead by example to keep morale high.

Removing Barriers

Human resource practitioners must be cognizant of any barriers to organizational change. Change actions can be thwarted by barriers such as staff attitudes or behaviors that discourage implementing new ideas, insufficient skills or technologies, and distances or obstacles between formal structures. These barriers can be eliminated by regularly communicating the rationale and timeline of the change, implementing new training programs or technologies, involving employee advocates in decision-making processes, and welcoming feedback from all levels.

Ensuring Change Management Is Successful and Avoiding Failures

These tactics are recommended to accomplish a successful change effort:

- Have a change sponsor lead the initiative.
- Communicate a clear need for the change.
- Create a shared vision of the organization post change.
- Rally commitment or request participation from all involved.
- Integrate past systems, structures, policies, and procedures into the new normal.
- Monitor progress and benchmark results against other successful companies.
- Make change sustainable by having a clear plan and rewarding desired behavior.

Some important reasons that **change efforts fail** include the following:

- Change was not strategically aligned with organizational goals or mission.
- Change was not communicated meaningfully or was perceived as a superficial, quick fix.
- Change was unrealistic given the current economic and political environment.
- Change leaders were inadequate or lacked the necessary commitment.
- Measurable goals and timelines were not established.
- Resistance to the change thwarted change efforts.

Consulting Processes and Models

Discovery

Discovery is the first step of the consultation process. During the **discovery phase**, the consultant should begin by getting all relevant information through an audit process and reviewing the facts. In this phase, the consultant will hear business and user requirements. This may be done through methods like content analysis and employee interviews. The consultant should start each potential project with an open mind and consider all perspectives to build trust.

Analysis and Solution

After all the information has been gathered, analysis can begin. The consultant should conduct a SWOT analysis as well as utilize any other methods that are appropriate for the situation. The consultant should investigate industry best practices and strive for solutions that fit the staff and customers. Once the organizational culture and any potential barriers have been considered, a diagnosis can be made, and solutions can be created. It's a good idea to engage stakeholders in the development of solutions when possible. This will lead to increased satisfaction with the consulting process and outcome.

Recommendation

Following the analysis, recommended actions and goals should be detailed in a **strategic project plan**. During this stage, it is important to clearly document how the solution will develop from the current state to the desired state and how the process will be managed.

Implementation

Once the strategic project plan has been accepted, successfully **implementing** the recommended solution is critical. Human resource consultants must manage all logistics to include staffing, scheduling, procuring needed supplies and equipment, and communicating the project status to stakeholders. Clear processes and procedures to support and utilize the solution should be established, and training opportunities should be available as needed. Throughout the implementation process, the consultant must maintain brand image, integrity, and a good working relationship with stakeholders. Once the implementation is complete, the consultant should schedule follow-ups with affected stakeholders to ensure satisfaction and to make any necessary adjustments.

Effective Consulting Techniques

Understanding Organizational Culture

The organizational culture is essentially how and why an organization operates. Consultants must understand and factor in the organizational culture as they craft their strategic plans. If the consultant tries to implement change that doesn't fit the culture, the change will not take root. Knowing the culture will enable the consultant to see potential roadblocks to and opportunities for developing and facilitating new strategies.

Understanding Areas and Limits of One's Own Expertise

Consultants must recognize the **areas and limits of their expertise**. Knowing this, they will be able to enjoy greater success because they can get involved with projects that play to their strengths. Ignoring this may lead consultants to get in over their heads and underperform, which damages their credibility and reputation. When the needs of the client fall outside the realm of the consultant's areas of expertise, the consultant should recommend other resources or consultants. This will help strengthen relationships with clients and build more meaningful networks with other consultants whose strengths might offset existing limitations.

Setting Reasonable Expectations

Customer satisfaction and understanding **client expectations** are vitally important to the success of the consultant. Managing client expectations and establishing needs, priorities, and timelines early in the relationship will save both the consultant and the client from future headaches. Be honest. Do not make any unrealistic promises. Do explain what is realistic and why. Once both parties are in agreement, outline specific and measurable goals, objectives, and timetables to establish credibility. Then, revisit with regular discussions to review how the project is advancing. Keep the lines of communication open to include any necessary changes to the schedule. This will help avoid inconsistencies and misunderstandings.

Avoiding Overpromising

Although we all want to guarantee the best service, consultants should **avoid overpromising** in an effort to gain a client or please everyone. Don't overpromise and under deliver. The end result will likely be a lot of frustration and dissatisfaction. Setting reasonable expectations, while being transparent and honest with clients, can help avoid any difficulties or misunderstandings. In fact, you are far better off setting goals and objectives that are attainable and overachieving.

Key Components of Successful Client Interactions

- **Listening**—the consultant should truly listen to stakeholders involved in the process. This will go a long way in terms of relationship building and satisfactory outcomes.
- **Empathy**—the consultant should display empathy when working with stakeholders. They need to understand where the stakeholders are coming from as they design and implement solutions. By being sensitive to stakeholder thoughts and feelings, the consultant can make them feel heard and valued. This positive working relationship will ensure a smoother overall process.
- **Communication**—the consultant should continuously communicate with stakeholders. Effective and consistent communication reduces confusion, frustration, and errors while promoting unity and positive project outcomes.
- **Follow-Up**—the consultant should follow up after project completion to ensure satisfaction and to see how else they can be of service.

Methods for Design and Delivery of Human Resource Functions and Processes

Issue Tracking

Issue tracking comes in many forms, some more complex than others. In its simplest form, **issue tracking** is like pulling a ticket at the deli counter—there is one single channel that leads to one single point of service. In larger corporations, issue tracking may come from various channels and span across many service centers. For example, customer service or support centers may be an initial contact for issue tracking. Customers open cases or ticket requests through communication channels like phone, chat, and email. Once a case or ticket is created, it can be assigned to individual users or departments. More complicated tickets may also be escalated through service level ranks, assigning involved tasks to senior-level staff and simpler tasks to new or lower-level staff. Tickets may also be flagged by priority, such as low, medium, or high. Robust tracking systems show the status of issues and include helpful notes regarding what has been discussed and done. This allows more than one person to easily be involved in the resolution. It also creates a historical record.

Client Service

Whether human resource professionals are working as an outside consultant or as an internal member of an organization, they should be service minded. They are there to balance the needs of the organization with the needs of the employees, trying to keep them in alignment whenever possible. Although often tasked with duties that will make them unpopular, human resource professionals strive to keep people satisfied if it's in their power to do so. Everything that human resources does should be done with effective client service in mind.

Critical Evaluation

Survey and Assessment Tools

Development

Human resources can either create the survey or assessment tool in-house or use a third-party solution. In either case, human resources needs to have a clear understanding of the survey's purpose and what it's supposed to measure. If historical survey or assessment results exist, they should be reviewed as they can provide context and potential survey items. Further, human resources could elect to use employee focus groups to help clarify questions before the survey is administered.

Human resources should ensure that the survey is short (takes less than 30 minutes to complete) to encourage participation. To help keep the survey concise, only the most relevant questions should be asked. Further, the survey should ask clear questions about single topics to avoid skewing results. For example, the survey should contain separate items for compensation and benefits as an employee could be satisfied with one but not the other. Additionally, closed questions often work better as they make analysis and trend detection much easier. Finally, the survey must be written using neutral and balanced language to mitigate bias.

Administration

Human resources should communicate about this survey before, while, and after participants take it. Management and employees alike need to understand why the survey is happening, what the survey process looks like, and when results will be shared. Human resources should provide ample notice to any unions, if applicable, so they can determine what union participation will look like.

Although times of stress within the organization could provide useful results to human resources, ideally, surveys should be administered during slower periods of production. This allows employees to have enough time to participate. Human resources should avoid administering a survey around the time of a holiday as staff absence will affect the participation rate.

Survey participation should be completely anonymous and voluntary. This allows employees to provide their feedback freely as they know they can't be identified, reducing the fear of retribution. In terms of how to administer the survey, electronic means have several benefits. It's often faster to click than to select an answer by hand. Additionally, electronic survey systems tabulate the results, saving human resources from the task of manually counting them. However, because not all employees may use a computer, human resources should ensure that a paper version is easily accessible.

Finally, human resources needs to make good on their promise and release the survey results by the announced date. They should also work closely with management to implement solutions for problems uncovered in the survey. Additionally, human resources can use employee focus groups to explore dominant themes brought up in the survey and solicit their input for how to address concerns.

Validation

If HR uses a third-party vendor for their employee survey, they need to research the credibility of the vendor to ensure that the survey instrument is valid. Unfortunately, some companies will violate copyright laws by compiling bits and pieces of other surveys. Not only are their actions illegal, but the survey may not produce valid results. If HR creates the survey in-house, they should be prepared to discard questions with low response rates or that come across as poorly phrased.

Sources of Data

Observations

Observations are sometimes the only way to answer some research questions. For example, the best method to assess a job redesign proposal is to observe a work group and determine if efforts flow smoothly and cooperatively. The disadvantage of observations is that they are invasive, which could lead employees to behave differently. They can also be time-consuming.

Surveys

Carefully designed surveys may be administered to large groups to gain insight about a particular topic. Surveys are often used because they are easy to implement and disseminate. However, they may be time-consuming to develop, and data collected is restricted only to the questions that are asked.

Interviews

Interviews are an effective way to understand employee perspectives and feelings about issues. The advantage to interviews is that they provide richer data than surveys. They also allow for follow-up questions. Interviews can be time-consuming, however, and human resources should note that not all employees will be comfortable sharing feedback in this way.

Focus Groups

One method for making interviews less time-consuming is by using focus groups in which more than one person is interviewed by a single moderator. Although more perspectives can be captured in less time with this technique, human resources should bear in mind that not all employees will feel comfortable discussing issues in front of their peers.

Basic Concepts in Statistics and Measurement

Descriptive Statistics

Descriptive statistics are used to summarize data that has been collected. **Descriptive statistics** can measure central tendency, dispersion, variability, frequency distribution, and proportions. The most common numerical descriptive statistic is the average or mean. The **mode** is the value of data that occurs most frequently. Other forms of descriptive statistics include frequency count, range, standard deviation, and correlation coefficient.

First the data is collected through primary methods such as surveys, observations, or experiments. Then, the data is analyzed or characterized by variable and presented using graphs or charts, such as the histogram. As samples get larger, the sample distribution often begins to appear more like the population distribution, which may result in a bell-shaped curve.

Correlation

A **correlation** is the relationship between two variables. There can be a positive relationship or a negative relationship. The strength of this relationship, or the **correlation coefficient**, is reflected as a range from –1.0 to 0 for negative correlations and 0 to 1.0 for positive correlations. The numbers closer to 0 represent a weaker relationship, whereas the numbers closer to –1.0 or 1.0 represent a stronger relationship.

Regression Analysis

Regression analysis is another statistical measurement that is used to find relationships among a set of variables. It is frequently used for predicting and forecasting. **Regression analysis** estimates or predicts the unknown values of one variable (dependent variable, labeled as Y) from the known or fixed value of another variable (independent variable, labeled as X). When there is only one independent variable to consider, a **linear regression** is used. When there is more than one independent variable to consider, a **multiple regression** is used. Regression analysis is also used to recognize which among the independent variables are related to the dependent variable and to what degree. There can be a **positive relationship** in which the line moves upward from the bottom left to the upper right. There can be a **negative relationship**, in which the line moves downward from the upper right to the bottom left. Finally, there can be **no relationship** in which plots are scattered all over.

Reliability

Reliability refers to the consistency of a particular measure. A research tool is said to be **reliable** if it produces consistent and repeatable measures every time. For example, measuring tapes and stopwatches provide consistent and reliable measures. Surveys should be reliable if the questions are clear and straightforward, but ambiguous questions might return unreliable results.

Validity

Validity refers to whether an instrument accurately measures what it is supposed to be measuring. The validity of a survey may be more difficult to interpret. For example, can a survey accurately measure company commitment or employee satisfaction? For an instrument to be deemed as valid, it needs to go through and pass rigorous statistical testing.

Interpretation of Data and Charts

Data interpretation involves drawing conclusions from data sets with the goal of answering a question and spurring meaningful action. Data can be qualitative or quantitative. **Qualitative data** is descriptive and focuses on categorizing concepts based on making observations, conducting interviews, or reviewing documents. **Quantitative data**, on the other hand, involves a numerical, statistics-driven approach, in which data is derived from surveys and other quantifiable media.

Using Data to Support a Business Case

When human resource professionals present a business case to senior leadership, they must show a compelling need for the allocation of resources that they're requesting. They can accomplish this by incorporating relevant data into their business case. For example, if human resources wants to hire an additional maintenance technician per shift, they should include things like the average machine downtime (and the resulting cost of lost productivity) and how long the average repair ticket stays open. Additionally, human resources could add more descriptive data in the form of complaints from production management and current maintenance staff, who are experiencing major disruptions in productivity or are feeling overworked, respectively.

Behavioral Competencies: Business Chapter Quiz

1. Any resource possessed by the company as a result of previous actions and from which future gains are expected is known as what?

a. Asset
b. Liability
c. Equity
d. ROI

2. The element of a business case that describes how the solution will affect current operations is known as?

a. Current status
b. Objectives
c. Problem statement
d. Executive summary

3. OLAP is an acronym that stands for?

a. Online analytical processing
b. Objective learning and processing
c. On-demand licensing and production
d. Operational logistics and processing

4. Which type of ratio measures the business's available cash or ability to pay off short-term debts?

a. Profitability
b. Operational efficiency and employee productivity
c. Liquidity
d. Leverage or capital structure

5. All of the following are common sales and marketing business metrics EXCEPT

a. Number of customers or orders
b. Number of market competitors
c. Average amount received for each order
d. Gross profit margin

6. All of the following are common information technology metrics EXCEPT

a. User interface (UI) feedback
b. Number of online orders
c. Availability of information resources
d. Number of views per page or listing

7. Which of the following is a popular method of business analysis?

a. OLAP
b. SWOT
c. CLAP
d. HIIT

Human Resources Expertise: People

Human Resources Strategic Planning

APPROACHES TO PROJECT MANAGEMENT

Project management is the process of creating, implementing, and facilitating a plan that will lead to the completion of a particular task within defined constraints. It refers to the process of planning how to complete a project that meets quality standards, achieves predetermined milestones, and is completed within the time allowed and the financial limitations established. Project management ultimately makes it possible for a firm to prioritize a long list of large undertakings.

The three main factors project managers traditionally have been expected to control while completing a project include the cost of the project, the time spent on the project, and the scope of the project. The **cost of the project** is the total amount of money spent on the project including raw materials, supplies, human capital, and other expenditures. The **time spent on the project** is the total amount of time spent by employees to complete the project tasks. The **scope of the project** refers to the requirements needed to complete the project in an appropriate fashion. In short, project managers must make sure the project is completed within all of the parameters set and the end result is of high quality and meets the organization's requirements.

Project managers may also be expected to control for risks associated with a project. Most projects carry some risk of failure such as overspending, missing deadlines, putting out inferior work, or never being finished. It is essential for a project manager to find ways of minimizing these risks to avoid significant negative impacts to the organization.

Whereas the project manager is in charge of overseeing and orchestrating the project, the tasks required to complete the project are carried out by their project team. Therefore, the project manager needs to ensure that the team has (or can develop) the right mix of skills—both technical and interpersonal—to get the job done effectively. The project manager must provide clear guidance to the project team and hold each member accountable for completing assigned work.

LEAN SIX SIGMA

Lean Six Sigma is a data-driven, results-oriented method for increasing speed and improving efficiency while solving problems, minimizing costs, and maximizing profits. Most often used in manufacturing, **Lean Six Sigma** streamlines processes and eliminates activities identified as waste. There are eight types of waste: defects, overproduction, waiting, non-utilized talent, transportation, inventory, motion, and extra processing. This allows companies of all sizes to do more with fewer resources. There are **five basic phases** of Lean Six Sigma:

1. Identify general problems with efficiency. (Production line speed has decreased after a change to the product.)
2. Map and measure current steps in a given process to gather data. (Carefully observe the production line, and note how the people and equipment perform.)
3. Analyze the data, and identify specific issue(s). (Conclude that a better conveyor belt is needed to move the heavier product faster.)
4. Improve and standardize processes to solve the issue(s). (Purchase and install the new conveyor belt.)
5. Implement controls and procedures to maintain results. (Document the conveyor belt purchased so that it can be easily reordered as necessary.)

AGILE

Agile is a software development methodology that is known for developing code in small chunks in a collaborative, team-oriented environment. Developers continually work in cross-functional teams to review and adjust their development process to meet the project needs. The team is held accountable for completing the project on time while meeting quality and functionality requirements. At the foundation of the project, there are development best practices that must be adhered to. Ultimately, the software solution must meet customer needs and align with company goals.

CRITICAL CHAIN

Critical chain is a form of project management that reduces the likelihood of the project's completion being delayed. The project is scheduled backward from the date the deliverables are due, and time buffers are added to protect the tasks that ultimately drive the duration of the project. These tasks are known as the critical chain. This form of project management is also known for identifying and mitigating bottlenecks, which helps expedite project completion.

PROJECT MANAGEMENT PROCESSES

Project management process groups are created when assessing and logically grouping related processes and activities into collective groups that support achievement of specific objectives in the project. Although project phases follow a more time-based flow, process groups are not necessarily chronological and may draw from tasks in points in the project. **Process** can be classified into five major groups: monitoring, planning, executing, initiating, and closing.

- **Initiating:** grouped activities that define the charter, team, working rules, new phases, and project authorization.
- **Planning:** activities that create the project scope, objectives, and project work breakdown and schedule.
- **Executing:** activities that perform the planned work in the project.
- **Monitoring:** processes that oversee the use of time, resources, quality, and change management.
- **Closing:** processes used to complete phases or the project itself.

SYSTEMS THINKING

A system is a group of interdependent, related parts that form a unified whole designed to carry out a specific purpose. The system must maintain stability by getting regular feedback. Because all parts of a system affect one another, the feedback occurs in a loop. Systems thinking, the opposite of linear thinking, is the discipline of seeing things as interrelated instead of looking at each in isolation.

The **input-process-output (IPO)** model involves putting information or resources into a process to achieve a result. In human resources, an example of this could be collecting résumés (input), screening them (process), and scheduling interviews (output).

PROJECT PLANNING, MONITORING, AND REPORTING METHODS AND TOOLS

GANTT CHARTS

A Gantt chart is a date and time-based bar chart that is frequently used in project management. It depicts critical deadlines for planning, scheduling, and monitoring project timelines. It reflects all of the start and end dates of each element or task and measures the timeframes and relationships between tasks. **Gantt charts** have dates listed along the top and tasks listed along the left side. The anticipated time for completing each task or subtask is reflected as a bar, and shading conveys progress. The end result looks almost like a staircase. **Milestones** are frequently represented as diamonds, and small arrows indicate **dependencies**.

Critical Path Analysis (CPA)

Critical path analysis (CPA) is a project management scheduling and planning tool that allows project managers to track project goals and make course corrections as needed. CPA pinpoints which tasks must be finished on schedule for the project to meet its overall deadline. It also identifies which tasks can be deferred to catch up on the more critical tasks as needed. CPA denotes which tasks are sequential (need to be completed in a certain order) and which are parallel (can be done at any point or after a certain milestone has been met). CPA shows project managers and stakeholders the minimum amount of time required to finish a project. CPA workflows are illustrated using circles (events in the project, like starting and finishing certain tasks) and arrows (actions and time required to finish tasks).

Project Evaluation and Review Technique (PERT)

The project evaluation and review technique (PERT) is another method of determining how much time is required to complete a specific project. The **PERT** process consists of breaking the larger project into a series of smaller, separate tasks and then organizing each of these smaller tasks into a chart. Each task in the PERT chart is represented by a line or arrow drawn from a circle representing an event or goal (such as the project beginning or completing a task and moving onto the next task) to a circle representing the next event or goal. Each event or goal circle is assigned a number, and the circles are arranged based on the order in which they are to be completed. The organization can then estimate the amount of time each task will take and note that estimate above the corresponding task line or arrow in the chart. PERT is a type of CPA. However, it assumes that tasks will take longer to complete.

Work Breakdown Structure (WBS)

A **work breakdown structure (WBS)** is a method for breaking a project down into a series of separate, smaller tasks. It's based on the **100 percent rule**, which states that the smaller tasks must total 100 percent of the work necessary to complete the project. WBSs are usually depicted in a tree chart that starts off with the main project goal and then branches out to the smaller tasks. These smaller tasks are then broken down even further into subtasks. Each subtask is then assigned a percentage that denotes how much of the overall project is completed by doing that task.

Outcome Monitoring

For a project to be successful, the project manager must constantly keep informed of the project's status and monitor progress toward the desired outcome(s). If the project isn't meeting preestablished key performance indicators (KPIs), the project manager must decide whether to stay the course or make adjustments to the project plan. Rooted in systems thinking, **outcome monitoring** is a continuous cycle that spans the entire project's timeline.

Variance Analysis

Often, an organization's actual performance will be different than its projected performance. For example, an organization may sell fewer products, bring in less revenue, or spend more on labor than they had planned. When this occurs, it's important for leadership to try and explain why the variance exists. It's possible that the firm lost a large customer due to service issues or that a new product launch caused employees to work a significant amount of overtime. Having this knowledge will enable a company to make course corrections so that they can get back on track with their goals and make more accurate projections going forward.

Organizational Mission and Vision Statements, Values and Impact on Strategic Management, and Planning

Mission and vision statements are similar in that they are both intended to clarify the objectives of the organization. However, a **mission statement** is intended to define only the broad mission an organization is attempting to carry out on a daily basis. A **vision statement** is intended to define the specific goals an organization hopes to achieve in the future.

A mission statement is a declaration of the reason an organization exists. This is important in determining standards, values, strategies, and other organizational aspects and serves as a guideline for establishing the processes needed to achieve goals. For example, the mission statement of a retail chain might be "to provide the best shopping experience possible for our customers." As a result, a decision might be made to implement standards and practices that promote high levels of customer service.

A vision statement is a declaration of the goals the organization wishes to achieve at some future point, which is important in designing and implementing the strategies necessary to meet those goals. For example, the vision statement of a retail chain might be to become the largest retail chain in the United States. As a result, the decision might be made to implement strategies that allow for rapid expansion, like finding and purchasing new locations and training new personnel quickly.

Role of Strategic Planning and Management in Creating and Sustaining a Competitive Advantage

Strategies Identified by Michael Porter to Maintain a Competitive Edge

The three grand strategies outlined by Michael Porter include cost leadership (being the low-cost manufacturer or servicer, like Southwest Airlines or Walmart), differentiation (having a unique service or product in a large market, like Apple or Porsche), and focus (having a unique service or product in a niche market). Gaining a competitive advantage through **cost leadership** can be obtained by providing your goods at a lower cost than competitors. Often, this is achieved by using low-cost labor or production materials and implementing technological innovations that improve efficiency of operations. A **differentiation strategy** involves providing unique services or products that offer innovative designs, are of exceptionally high quality, and/or possess remarkably high brand image. Regardless of the attribute, the company's marketing must convey exclusivity to validate premium pricing. A **focus or niche strategy** targets either a cost advantage or a differentiation advantage in a narrow, niche market segment. This could be a select geographic location, a predefined channel of distribution, a particular end-user, or a specific product.

Michael Porter's Five Forces Model of Competition

The five forces model suggests that profit potential is a function of the interactions among suppliers, buyers, rival firms, substitute products, and potential entrants. Organizations can analyze these factors to determine profit potential and create a secure, competitive position. Each of the five forces affect the competitive market:

- **Suppliers**—organizations depend on the availability of suppliers to provide materials.
- **Buyers**—buyers can be powerful if they purchase large quantities of a firm's goods, are one of the firm's few potential customers, or have the ability to buy the firm.
- **Rival firms**—competition is stimulated when one or more companies identify an opportunity to improve market position or a need to differentiate against mutually competitive pressure.

- **Substitute products**—organizations compete against other businesses that sell similar, substitute products or services, which places a limit on the prices organizations can charge.
- **Potential entrants**—new entrants can threaten existing companies by providing additional production capacity and shifting the market supply, resulting in less demand and price cuts.

Strategic Planning Analysis Frameworks

SWOT Analysis Process

The SWOT analysis involves scanning both internal and external factors to identify potential sources of competitive advantage. There are six steps to the process:

1. The first step is to define the organization's **mission and objectives**.
2. The second step is to analyze the external environment for prospective **opportunities or threats**.
3. The third step is to analyze the organization's resources for **internal strengths or weaknesses**. Unique skills that set the firm apart from others and support a competitive edge are called **core competencies**.
4. The fourth step is to combine both the external and internal analysis and formulate a stable **strategy**.
5. The fifth step is to establish **trust** in leadership and encourage **involvement** from all levels of the organization to implement the new strategy.
6. The final step is to **evaluate and monitor** organizational results to preserve the competitive advantage.

PESTLE Analysis

This form of analysis is an extension of the SWOT analysis and looks at how the following factors impact a business:

- **P**—political: Changes made by the government can affect a business in the form of tariffs, tax policy, and fiscal policy.
- **E**—economic: Changes to inflation, interest rates, and foreign exchange rates can affect the firm's finances and operations.
- **S**—social: Cultural trends affect consumer purchases, which affect an organization's revenue and profit.
- **T**—technological: Technology used in a business can enhance or detract from a company's innovation level and competitive advantage.
- **L**—legal: External laws and internal policies affect a firm's day-to-day operations.
- **E**—environmental: Climate, weather, and geographic location all have an impact on a company's performance.

Industry Analysis

Industry analysis is a process in which a company figures out how it ranks among its competitors so that it can find a way to differentiate to gain a competitive advantage. The examination should be completed in the context of the PESTLE analysis as those factors will likely affect the entire industry similarly. Companies should understand the potential for new entrants to the industry (more competition), substitute goods available (substitutes limit profits and promote competition based on price), the power of suppliers (having fewer suppliers puts pressure on firms), and the power of buyers (having fewer buyers puts pressure on firms).

SCENARIO PLANNING

Scenario planning makes assumptions about what the future will look like, anticipates how the future will affect the company, and creates a strategic plan to address that impact. The four-step process begins by forecasting upcoming major societal, political, economic, and technological shifts. These are identified as driving forces. Next, the company must choose two of the most pertinent driving forces to work with. Then, the company should create a conceivable range of potential situations it may face based on the selected driving forces. Finally, the potential impacts of those situations must be assessed, and the company must create a new business strategy that accounts for them. Although the subjective scenario planning process isn't meant to be a stand-alone strategic planning method, it provides another layer of information to be used in conjunction with other business analysis techniques.

GROWTH-SHARE MATRIX

The **growth-share matrix** is a long-term planning tool used to evaluate a company's products (or services) to determine if the company should continue investing in them. The matrix is a quadrant labeled market share along the x axis and market growth along the y axis. Products can be classified as stars (top left: high market share, high growth), question marks (top right: low market share, high growth), dogs (lower right: low market share, low growth), or cash cows (lower left: high market share, low growth). Because dogs don't bring in a lot of money and don't have a lot of potential, the company may want to stop investing in them. Stars, on the other hand, are making money and have a lot of potential upside. The company will likely want to invest in them to try and turn them into cash cows. Cash cows are the most profitable products, but because that market isn't growing, companies need to consider how much to invest in them. Finally, question marks have potential, but they could either become stars or dogs, so companies need to think carefully before investing a lot into them. The growth-share matrix has some limitations. It's best suited for larger firms. Additionally, there are always exceptions to the rules, so companies should use other forms of analysis and their knowledge of their firm to supplement what they've learned from using the growth-share matrix.

STRATEGIC PLANNING PROCESS

FORMULATION

To set the foundation for the strategic plan, the company must perform analyses such as SWOT, PESTLE, industry, and so on. Once the company understands its current position both internally and externally, it can move into the goal-setting phase of the process.

GOAL SETTING

There are a variety of ways to ensure specific goals are well-defined, valid, and useful. The most effective way is to use the acronym SMART: specific, measurable, achievable, relevant, and time bound. Valid goals should be specific and well-defined, able to be accurately measured, feasible considering present resources and environment, and relevant to overall objectives. A valid goal should also have a specific deadline to ensure it is completed efficiently and can be compared accurately with other goals.

IMPLEMENTATION

Once goals are established, the company must take action to enact change that supports them. Changes, or interventions, could include modifications to policies, workflows, or personnel, to name a few. The changes may be scheduled to occur all at once or at set intervals. All interventions need to remedy a concern or help the organization achieve its strategic goals.

EVALUATION

To see which changes help and which changes don't, the strategic plan needs to be evaluated regularly. The company should have methods of measurement available to gauge the effectiveness of the interventions. If the changes aren't working as intended, the plan should be modified so the company can get back on track.

Talent Acquisition

Approaches to Employee Onboarding

There are many approaches to **onboarding** newly hired employees, from the interview to the orientation and through the 90-day review. However, all companies do things a bit differently, and the size or engagement from the welcoming committee will vary. A majority of the responsibility will fall upon human resources in most cases, but the hiring manager and information technology personnel often share some responsibilities as well. Here are a few steps that might appear on an onboarding checklist for new hires:

- **Phone interview**—a brief 10- to 30-minute screening of applicants (human resources)
- **Live interview**—more in-depth discussion often lasting one to three hours (human resources/hiring manager)
- **Offer letter**—formal written offer to finalist (human resources)
- **Computer access**—workstation set up with email, phone, and systems access (information technology)
- **Keys, equipment, and business cards**—order/log equipment usage (operations)
- **Welcome email**—introductory email welcoming new hires with tips for success (human resources)
- **Federal paperwork**—employment eligibility and tax forms (human resources)
- **Company paperwork**—handbook, policies, nondisclosure agreements, and benefits acknowledgments (human resources)
- **Orientation**—thorough company and policy overview and required training (human resources/hiring manager)
- **Position overview and mentoring/training**—buddy assignment, job expectations, and process manual (hiring manager)
- **Introductions**—site tour, staff introductions, and icebreaker questionnaires or games (human resources/hiring manager)
- **30-/60-/90-day reviews**—summary of how the new hire is assimilating into the new role (human resources/hiring manager)

Approaches to Sourcing

When a job opening has been identified, human resources must determine whether to recruit externally or internally. Often, unless human resources is certain that the position will be filled internally, both methods will be used. Recruiting **internal candidates** allows the employer to encourage loyalty and reward high performance and is less expensive. A **job posting** notifies employees of available positions. **Job bidding** allows qualified employees to apply for opportunities.

Recruiting **external candidates** can be accomplished through several avenues. **Referrals** are often touted for being relatively quick and inexpensive while returning high-quality candidates. **Online job posting** reaches the largest audience, but it can be time-consuming to review the number of applications. **Employment agencies** are viable resources for locating executive or highly skilled candidates, fulfilling temporary needs, or evaluating performance prior to extending an employment offer through temp-to-perm opportunities. However, employers should consider that the average fee charged by employment agencies falls between 10 and 25 percent of an employee's annual salary. **College recruiting** can return a large pool of professional candidates, whereas vocational schools and associations are usually good sources for technical or trade skills. Other common external recruiting sources include job fairs, social media, state workforce websites, and the company's own applicant tracking system.

When common recruiting avenues do not provide an adequate number of candidates, more unusual sources may be needed. Some of these are looking for individuals leaving vendors and suppliers who may make good employees, restructuring the position to accommodate remote workers if top talent isn't local and doesn't want to relocate, and offering sign-on bonuses. Recruiters can also build **talent pipelines** by networking both on and offline with professionals that possess critical skills. That way, when a job vacancy occurs, the recruiter already has a short list of people that they can contact regarding the position.

Employment Categories

Exempt and Nonexempt Employees

The Fair Labor Standards Act (FLSA) separates employees into two main categories: exempt and nonexempt. Nonexempt employees must be paid minimum wage and overtime rates that meet both state and federal regulations.

- **Exempt**: those who generally paid an annual wage are exempt from overtime provisions of the FLSA, such as administrative or outside sales workers, information technology specialists, professionals, and executives. To be classified as exempt, employees must be paid at or above the threshold for exempt workers ($23,660 annually as of 2019) as well as meet certain job duty requirements.
- **Nonexempt**: those generally paid an hourly wage and covered by minimum wage and overtime provisions of the FLSA, such as blue-collar workers, maintenance workers, technicians, laborers, and novice workers.

Temporary or Contract Workers

Sometimes, employers may have a temporary need for contingent or contract workers. Temporary worker assignments are generally entry level and are often short in duration (such as a seasonal role at a retailer).

These workers are eligible for unemployment insurance and workers' compensation from their employer of record (generally a staffing agency). Moreover, nonexempt workers must be paid at least the federal minimum wage and are eligible for overtime provisions under the **FLSA**.

Interns

Employing interns can be a win for all parties involved. A well-designed internship program will allow the intern to gain practical experience to reinforce their studies, learn new skills, prepare for their careers, and expand their networks. The firm will benefit from inexpensive labor and a pool of potential hires for their entry-level roles. Having an effective internship program also fosters goodwill with local colleges and the community.

However, human resources must be careful that the internship program is compliant with labor laws. In most cases, interns must be paid at least minimum wage and are eligible for overtime pay. Nonprofit and public sector organizations can generally offer unpaid internships, though. However, for a for-profit firm to do so, the intern must receive academic credit for the internship and be the primary beneficiary of the experience. This means that the firm cannot have the intern complete actual work. The intern could be involved only in training and purely educational exercises.

Importance of Correctly Classifying Workers

Organizations must be diligent when classifying workers as **employees** versus **independent contractors**. Courts are more likely to favor employee classifications than independent contractor relationships to be sure that employers are not inappropriately avoiding income taxes, social security matches, unemployment or workers' compensation protection, and healthcare costs. The difference between an employee and independent contractor is determined by the entire working relationship. The Internal Revenue Service (IRS) looks at several factors when evaluating a worker's classification: behavioral control, financial control, and type of relationship.

If the company directs the workers on how to act or perform their work, the court is likely to label them as employees. If, on the other hand, the company allows the worker to reach a mutually agreed-upon objective in the manner that they see fit, they're more likely to be classified as an independent contractor. In terms of financial control, if the firm provides the worker with the necessary equipment to perform the work, that worker is more likely to be an employee. Conversely, if the workers purchase their own tools and supplies, they are probably independent contractors. In terms of the relationship, if the company offers the worker benefits, that worker is an employee. However, if the firm does not provide any benefits, the worker may be an independent contractor. The IRS views the relationship between the parties holistically and weighs every detail before making a determination.

Job Analysis and Identification of Job Requirements

A job analysis is an essential part of any workforce planning process because it identifies specific skills, knowledge, and traits required to meet staffing goals and organizational objectives. It outlines what a worker needs to be successful in a given role and also establishes the relative importance of each role to the company.

The three main products of a job analysis include job competencies, job specifications, and job descriptions. **Job competencies** are a detailed list of all broad skills and traits (such as leadership ability) needed for a particular position. **Job specifications** are detailed descriptions of all specific qualifications (such as experience or education) an individual must have to perform the role. A **job description** is a detailed written breakdown of all tasks that a worker in that role must complete as well as the job competencies and job specifications required to be qualified for that role. Equal Employment Opportunity Commission (EEOC) guidelines encourage employers to prepare written job descriptions listing the essential functions of each job.

Some of the major uses of **job analysis** include the following:

- Human resources planning, to develop job categories
- Recruiting, to describe and advertise job openings
- Selection, to identify skills and criteria for selecting candidates
- Orientation, to describe activities and expectations to employees
- Evaluation, to identify standards and performance objectives
- Compensation, to evaluate job worth and develop pay structures
- Training, to conduct needs assessments
- Discipline, to correct subpar performance
- Safety, to identify working procedures and ensure workers can safely perform activities
- Job redesign, to analyze job characteristics that periodically need updating
- Legal protection, to identify essential functions that must be performed and protect the organization against claims

Job Analysis Methods

To determine what a job entails, human resources needs to do research using their existing workforce. They can observe people perform work, ask them to fill out questionnaires about their jobs, look at work logs kept by employees, or interview staff for deeper insights.

Job Offer Contingencies

Many employers will conduct **preemployment background checks** on candidates to ensure that employees have sound judgment and are unlikely to engage in improper conduct or don't have a criminal record. Human resource departments often order credit checks or criminal record searches through online service providers and then review results. However, drug screening may either be administered by staff or conducted at a local or national site. The **Fair Credit Reporting Act**, like many legal regulations, requires that employers not only notify applicants that they administer background checks, but applicants must also sign a written release consenting that the employer may receive their personal information. Furthermore, when implementing a preemployment background check, employers must consider if doing so may be discriminatory and, as such, must validate the business necessity. Many states have joined the Ban the Box movement, which prohibits employers from asking about an applicant's criminal history at the time of application. If an offense is found, employers are urged to consider the severity of the offense, the amount of time elapsed since the offense, and if the offense is related to the nature of the job. Applicants must also have the opportunity to contest or explain adverse results before officially being turned down for employment. The prospective employer must furnish a copy of the report to the applicant. The Federal Trade Commission advises employers to give the applicant five days to respond before sending them an official letter of rejection.

Job Offer Negotiations

Written Employment Contracts (Offer Letters)

Many employment details may be explained in **written contracts or job offer letters**. The contract should summarize what position is being offered, rate of pay, benefits, perks, expectations regarding performance, probationary periods, and proprietary information. Written employment contracts will frequently include some combination of these elements:

- **The length of the contract**—if agreement is for a specified period of time
- **Duties and responsibilities**—if not included in a job description
- **Career opportunities**—succession planning or likelihood of advancement
- **Compensation**—hourly or salary rate and sign-on bonus inclusions
- **Benefits and bonus incentives**—relocation assistance, commissions, bonus potential, stock options, and paid time off
- **Restrictive covenants**—limitations such as confidentiality and noncompete disclosures
- **Severance payments**—if employees can expect any promised pay at the end of an assignment
- **Dispute resolution**—arbitration requirements and payment of legal fees
- **Change of control**—in the event of a merger or acquisition

Review Video: Written Employment Contracts
Visit mometrix.com/academy and enter code: 407808

Human resource professionals should be prepared for a candidate to try to negotiate a better job offer. Before officially extending the offer, human resources should determine what, if anything, can be negotiated. This will facilitate a smoother offer conversation and increase the chance of a mutually beneficial outcome.

Methods for Creating and Maintaining a Positive Employer Value Proposition and Employment Branding

Employment branding is the act of marketing an image that makes people want to work for the organization. This image stems from the organization's **employer value proposition (EVP),** which is what they have to offer as compared to other firms. The EVP may include the work environment, internal opportunities, benefits, and compensation. Employers should consider **active branding** because it can increase the talent pool, firm productivity, and team morale while reducing the turnover rate.

An organization can showcase a positive EVP and brand in the following ways:

- Describing their benefits, perks, and culture on their website, in their job ads, and in other promotional materials
- Sharing current employee testimonials about how great it is to work there
- Doing charity work in the community and demonstrating a commitment to corporate social responsibility

Methods for Selection Assessment

Selection methods and tools are an essential part of an organization's hiring process because the goal is to find groups of acceptable employees and then choose the best candidate from that group. However, even if an organization has located a suitable group of potential employees, it can be extremely difficult for an interviewer to separate the most qualified individual from the rest of the group based on applications and résumés alone. As a result, it is necessary to have a set of well-defined selection tools and methods that are both valid and reliable.

Eliminating unqualified candidates saves money and time and focuses resources on those individuals most suited for each position. The screening tools most commonly used include employment applications, résumés, and interviews. **Employment applications** include any form designed by an employer requiring an individual to give personal information, previous experience, education, and so on. **Résumés** are usually one to two pages and list experience, education, and references qualifying an individual for a particular position. Résumés are not usually a premade form to be filled out but rather a document designed and written by the individual seeking employment.

Selection Process

The **selection process** is sequential and includes a series of steps; each systematically screens out unsuccessful individuals who will not continue to the next round. The order of steps is often organized based upon a cost/benefit analysis, with the most expensive steps at the end of the process. Steps of selection process may include introductory screening, questionnaires, initial interviews, employment testing, final interviews, selection decisions, reference checks, drug testing, post-offer medical exams, and placement. The **two basic principles of selection** that influence the process of making an informed hiring decision are 1) past behaviors and 2) reliable and valid data. Past behavior is the best predictor for future behavior, and knowing what was done in the past may be indicative of future actions. **Reliable data** is consistently repeated, whereas **valid data** measures performance.

PREEMPLOYMENT TESTS

Two of the most common types of preemployment tests are aptitude tests and in-box tests. An **aptitude test** is an examination designed to determine if an individual has the basic knowledge to perform the tasks associated with a particular position. For example, an aptitude test for a bank teller might consist of a series of basic math problems related to specific banking activities (e.g., determining an account balance after several deposits and withdrawals).

During an **in-box test**, the individual must determine the appropriate way to handle particular problems. For example, a person applying for a position as head bank teller might be asked to describe the appropriate way to handle a check deposited into the wrong account.

The two main advantages associated with preemployment tests are that they allow the organization to have more control over the information gathered and they make it easier to gather information in a consistent way. Preemployment tests comprise premade questions that assess an individual's ability to use specific skills and areas of knowledge. The results will either support or refute the information gathered during the interview. Preemployment tests provide consistent results as long as each applicant takes the exam under the same conditions.

There are some disadvantages associated with using a preemployment test. First, it is easy to unintentionally cause a disparate impact to a protected class if questions are not relevant to the position for which the individual is applying. A series of poorly worded or irrelevant questions may make it more difficult for members of a particular group of people to get the job, which may make the organization legally liable. Second, preemployment tests do not allow for flexibility because the same questions are asked of every applicant. An interviewer is able to ask questions specifically related to each individual applicant, whereas a preemployment test cannot.

ASSESSMENT CENTERS

An **assessment center** is a standardized system of tests designed to gauge candidates' knowledge, skills, abilities, and behaviors in relation to the position for which they are being considered. The assessment center may include interviews, psychological tests, simulations of scenarios typical to the role, and other forms of measurement. A firm employing this screening approach may use live raters. However, technological advances, such as objective computerized tests, have made it possible to rate candidates without human intervention, resulting in a more cost- and time-effective process.

INTERVIEWS

After making it through the résumé and job application review round, and possibly a phone screening, the applicant advances to the interview phase of the selection process. Some reasons for conducting interviews are to obtain information about the applicant, to sell and provide information about the company, and to build relationships.

There are many different types of interviews. A **structured, or patterned, interview** allows the interviewer to ask a series of prepared questions and may even contain a list of multiple-choice answers. A **semi-structured interview** allows the interviewer to follow a guide of prepared questions but allows for follow-up questions to evaluate qualifications and characteristics. Situational interviews that gauge responses to hypothetical problems and behavioral interviews that question previous or anticipated behavior are frequently semi-structured in nature. An **unstructured, or nondirective, interview** is more conversational and allows more freedom so the applicant may determine the course of the discussion. To be successful, the interviewer should listen carefully without interruption.

Due to technological advancements and the rise of telecommuting, the number of **virtual interviews** has increased. These may involve the candidate sitting in front of a webcam and answering recorded questions or both the candidate and the interviewer speaking in real time from their respective locations. These interviews are often less expensive and more convenient and can provide both personality and standardized evaluations.

Sometimes interviews involve many parties. **Group interviews** involve multiple candidates, whereas **panel interviews** and **board interviews** involve multiple interviewers. Finally, candidates may be required to go through additional screening, such as preemployment testing, a physical examination, drug testing, a background investigation, academic achievement verification, and/or reference checking.

There are two main disadvantages associated with a selection interview. First, it can be heavily affected by the interviewer's own biases. Regardless of how much experience or training an interviewer has, preconceived ideas of a particular candidate or a particular type of candidate can influence the evaluation. Second, even the best planned interview can be rendered useless when intelligent applicants, wanting to cast themselves in the best possible light, control the interview. Further, when the interviewer does not ask the right questions, the applicant may appear to be a viable candidate even though he or she lacks the necessary skills or traits to do the job.

Concerns with Using Behavioral or Personality Assessments in the Hiring Practice

When evaluating the potential use of behavioral or personality assessments in the hiring process, human resource practitioners should focus on what they are trying to achieve and research options carefully to ensure they are not **unethical** or violate any employment regulations. If human resources decides to use such assessments, they must ensure that they are designed specifically for making employment decisions and that they have undergone rigorous reliability and validity testing.

Ensuring Validity and Reliability of Screening and Selection Methods

One reason valid and reliable screening tools are important is to avoid unintentionally causing a disparate impact to a particular group of individuals by using screening measures that are not necessarily related to the actual position. Because disparate impact is unlawful discrimination, an organization using questionable screening procedures may unintentionally open itself to liability. Another reason valid and reliable screening tools are important is to ensure the employee hired for a position is suitable. When a screening procedure does not relate to the position or provides inconsistent information, highly qualified candidates might be eliminated.

A good rule of thumb is if the procedure used to gather information from the applicant does not actually assess the basic qualifications of the job or the information is not relevant to the specific position being applied for, the procedure is probably inaccurate or unfair. A valid screening tool should provide information that is well-defined, relevant, and job related.

The three main types of validity a human resources professional may employ to determine if a screening or selection tool is valid are construct validity, content validity, and criterion validity. **Construct validity** assesses the specific traits shown to indicate success for a particular position. It must test for specific characteristics shown to be indicators of job performance. **Content validity** assesses the skills and knowledge necessary to perform the tasks associated with a particular position. **Criterion validity** is used to predict how an individual will behave in the workplace based on written or verbal test scores.

The two types of criterion validity a human resources professional may evaluate to determine if a screening or selection tool is valid are concurrent and predictive validity. **Concurrent validity** indicates that the individual currently possesses the desired trait or will behave in the desired fashion. For example, a test might be considered valid if test scores indicate the individual remains calm in stressful situations, as indicated by a stressful situation the organization places the individual into at the time of the test. **Predictive validity** indicates that the individual will possess the desired trait or will behave in the desired fashion at some point in the future.

Talent Acquisition Metrics

Organizations of all shapes and sizes should regularly review recruiting processes and try to make them more efficient. When evaluating recruitment efforts, it is important to consider these two main metrics: the average cost per hire and the average time to fill.

Time to fill: Total Days Elapsed Since Job Posted ÷ # Hires

Cost per hire: (External Costs + Internal Costs) ÷ # Hires

Human resource professionals should also ensure that their job ad spend is effective.

Employee Engagement and Retention

Types of Organizational Culture

Organizational culture refers to the system of beliefs and values established by a firm that guides the behavior of the individuals within it. In essence, it's the work environment that the employees and managers of the organization have created and continue to create as time passes. Companies typically attempt to control the culture to some degree to make sure that employee motivation stays high and organizational objectives are met. However, the culture is usually heavily influenced by the specific experiences of its members and by external forces. As a result, it can sometimes be difficult for an organization to shape its culture, especially when prominent figures become unhappy or outside influences begin placing a great deal of stress on employees. Shared vision is the discipline of creating a culture that encourages employees to work toward a common goal.

Authoritarian

An **authoritarian culture** is extremely focused on efficiency and productivity. In this culture, employees produce out of fear or anticipation of rewards. Characterized by micromanagement, this culture can be appropriate during times of uncertainty, when one strong leader takes the helm and makes all of the decisions. This culture can result in low morale as employees have zero input, autonomy, or ability to be creative.

Mechanistic

A **mechanistic culture** is characterized by organization, specialization, and strong guidance from leadership. Focused on productivity, employees in this culture operate like a well-oiled machine. This culture's decision-making can be bogged down by an overly bureaucratic structure. In addition, this culture does not foster collaboration or creativity, which could result in low morale.

Participative

A **participative culture** features open communication and shared power. In the spirit of democratic decision-making, employees may have the opportunity to voice opinions, give input, or take ownership of decisions completely. This culture is characterized by training, collaboration, empathy, and empowerment. Although morale may be high, the drawback is that it can be hard to get anything accomplished quickly.

Learning

A **learning culture** aims to use knowledge, abilities, and innovation to adapt to an ever-changing business environment. Characterized by creativity, initiative, experimentation, and collaboration, knowledge is shared freely. This culture earmarks a lot of resources for training and development. In a learning culture, failure is not feared. It's merely another learning experience. This culture encourages employees to solve problems and improve workflows whenever they see an opportunity to do so.

High Performance

A **high-performance culture** promotes goal achievement by setting clear objectives, clearly spelling out employee responsibilities, encouraging continuous development, and fostering trust. This culture is characterized by innovation, collaboration, communication, leadership support, and accountability. To sustain high levels of productivity, this culture promotes employee wellness so that workers can continue to operate at their best.

Approaches to Developing and Maintaining a Positive Organizational Culture

Learning Strategies

Organizational culture should be a focal point beginning with new hire orientation. Introductory training materials should discuss the culture and provide examples of it in action within the firm. From there, managers should regularly coach and train staff so that the culture stays top of mind. Finally, leaders should live the company culture in all that they do. Employees may be influenced by their behavior.

Communication Strategies

Organization culture should be communicated often, clearly, and consistently. If employees see inconsistencies in this communication, they may distrust leadership or be less engaged at work.

Building Values

An organization's values are the foundation of its culture. Therefore, leadership must establish them early on. Human resources should hire candidates that embody the firm's values. Additionally, any policies and procedures developed should reflect the same principles. Finally, discipline and rewards systems should be built upon these core values.

Maintaining Organizational Culture

Culture encompasses every facet of an organization and comprises four **key elements** including norms, artifacts, values, and core assumptions. Shared **norms** are not always defined or obvious but often inferred by specific situations. For example, punctuality and professionalism are reflected by group practice. Likewise, the collective beliefs, ideals, and feelings of the members of an organization construct its cultural **values**. Alternatively, cultural **artifacts** are tangible traits that portray core beliefs such as behaviors, language, and symbols. An organization's shared **assumptions** reveal the basis of how people think. This can be reflected by the measure of controls management imposes upon line staff. Organizational culture can be maintained through employee selection and disciplinary procedures, rewards systems, recognition ceremonies, stories, symbols, and leadership reactions to achievements and problems.

Modifying Organizational Culture

The following are the six core steps for modifying organizational culture:

1. Conduct a **culture audit** by performing interviews to identify current values and beliefs.
2. Assess the **need for change** by evaluating whether the current culture is appropriate for the company's size and mission. Determine whether it solves or creates problems for the firm.
3. **Unfreeze** the current culture. This often happens during times of extreme events, such as the loss of a partner, a merger, or the announcement of drastic operational or technological changes. Modifications to the culture are often most successful when the need is well communicated, and organizational members believe the changes are important.
4. Encourage support from the **leadership team**; they establish the code of conduct and are the cultural elite of an organization.
5. Implement an **intervention strategy** that might include frequent communications, revised training policies, revised rewards programs, restructuring or defining new roles, team-building and involvement activities, or even announcing a new slogan or mission statement.
6. Monitor and evaluate the **transitional change process** over an extended period of time.

Approaches to Recognition

Employee recognition programs will vary from firm to firm. However, they are most often used to motivate and reward achievements. The most common types of recognition include verbal praise, performance acknowledgements, employee of the month awards, length of service awards, or certificates for other achievements. **Rewards** may include thank-you notes, business paraphernalia, spot bonuses, gift cards, or extra time off. A combination of **tangible and intangible incentives** will ensure that the program is valuable to all participants. Almost all employees have an innate desire to be **valued and appreciated** for their contributions. Employee recognition programs can also be used to reinforce organizational expectations, attract and retain talent, increase productivity, improve quality and safety, and reduce absenteeism and turnover. Regardless of the methods chosen by an employer, a **formal written policy** should be published to reflect what rewards will be given, how they can be earned, and when they will be doled out. This policy will ensure fairness and consistency and will increase the likelihood of desired behaviors being repeated.

Employee Lifecycle Phases

- Recruitment: initial phase that encompasses the entire process of finding and acquiring new talent, from creating job descriptions through onboarding a new hire
- Integration: subsequent phase of getting the recent hire fully acclimated and functioning well in his or her assigned role
- Development: third phase when employee grows as a professional via training programs, promotion opportunities, and so on
- Departure: last phase of the employment relationship when the employee leaves the organization and human resources processes him or her out of company systems

Employee Retention Concepts and Best Practices

Causes of Absenteeism and Turnover

Absenteeism is when employees miss work temporarily. **Turnover** is when employees leave permanently.

Poor morale, frustration, and conflict are some factors that lead to absenteeism and turnover. **Involuntary absenteeism and turnover** are caused by situations beyond the employee's control, such as illness, family concerns, relocation, layoffs, and terminations. **Voluntary absenteeism and turnover** occur when employees have a choice and intentionally miss work or resign. Absenteeism can be further categorized as planned absences, unplanned absences, intermittent absences, or extended absences. Employees may also permanently leave their jobs for higher-paying work, better benefits, a promotion, to start a business, or for other reasons.

Retention and Turnover Metrics

Retention Rate: (number of employees who were employed for entire measurement period / number of employees at start of measurement period) x 100

Turnover Rate: (number of employees who left during the measurement period / average number of employees during the measurement period) x 100

Employee retention programs

An employee retention program is a set of policies, procedures, and practices designed to encourage employees to stay with the organization. This program can be an essential part of a staffing strategy because it decreases employee turnover, which is especially important for positions that are difficult and costly to replace. An employee retention program may offer extra benefits or compensation (such as vacation time and bonuses), which can help the organization retain key staff and function effectively.

Realistic Job Previews

A **realistic job preview (RJP)** refers to any activity that helps give applicants an idea of the specific day-to-day tasks and responsibilities that they will need to perform if hired. These activities can include watching videos about the organization, observing current employees, or looking at illustrations of the job being performed.

Job Attitude Theories and Basic Principles

- **Engagement**: Although there is no universally accepted definition for engagement, it can be viewed as the level of connection employees feel to their work and their employer. This connection affects the amount of effort that they will put into fulfilling their roles.
- **Satisfaction**: Satisfaction is a measure of how happy employees are with their work and their employer. It can also be viewed as their level of gratification or fulfillment derived from their employment.
- **Commitment**: Commitment is a measure of how dedicated employees are to their employer and their employer's goals. It can also be viewed as their sense of obligation to be loyal and perform at their best.

Equity Theory

Equity theory strives to address motivation problems and levels of job satisfaction. According to **equity theory**, individuals tend to feel satisfied and report fair conditions when they perceive a state of equity. Attitudes toward pay can be influenced by the rate of pay, the work done to earn pay, and whether the ratio of pay to work appears to be fair in comparison to the pay-to-work ratio of others. Individuals ultimately evaluate if what they get from a job is commensurate with what they put into a job. There are six methods that individuals may utilize to **reduce inequality**:

1. Altering inputs, such as time effort, hard work, loyalty, commitment, and trust
2. Altering outcomes, such as salary, benefits, recognition, and achievement
3. Cognitively manipulating inputs or outcomes by rationalizing or self-justification
4. Distorting the inputs or outcomes of others
5. Changing objects of comparison
6. Leaving the field

Methods of Assessing Employee Attitudes

Focus Groups

Focus groups can be used to glean employee views and concerns. They may be used to assess a new benefit plan or organizational change. Most **focus groups** contain five to 12 voluntary **participants**, with three to 10 groups in total. Participants should be informed about the subject of the focus group, about who will benefit, and that the information will be kept confidential. Participants may be selected at random or through the use of certain applicable filters. Focus group organizers should ensure that power differentials within the group are avoided. It's also important to involve participants from various levels of staff so they can fully represent the affected population. A neutral **facilitator** should be chosen to lead the discussion and ask open-ended, guided questions. Following the meeting, collected data should be analyzed and reported.

STAY INTERVIEWS

A **stay interview** is a purposeful yet casual conversation between an employee and a company leader regarding the employee's propensity to leave the organization. The leader will ask the employee questions such as the following:

- What keeps you in your current role?
- What might cause you to leave the company?
- What's important to you professionally?
- What can I do to improve your overall work experience with the firm?

The objective is to increase the employee's engagement and prevent turnover.

SURVEYS

Employee surveys can be valuable when examining employee engagement levels and job satisfaction. These surveys, whether created externally or internally, may be completed on a number of websites and platforms. Employee participation should be voluntary and anonymous. If they want to participate, employees should be provided with time during the workday to complete the survey. The survey should be available long enough to give all departments and shifts ample time to participate.

Many third-party vendors and national agencies conduct regular surveys and publish statistics. Human resource practitioners should benchmark their own survey results against these results or those of similar organizations before presenting findings to the executive leadership team. Generalized survey results and plans to address concerns raised should be shared with the employees as soon as practically possible after the survey period ends. **Employee engagement** should be analyzed on a regular basis, and survey results should be kept on file for data comparison over time. Moreover, survey items should be measured against organizational **key performance indicators (KPIs)** like quality, productivity, and customer satisfaction.

INTERVENTIONS FOR IMPROVING JOB ATTITUDES

There are several ways that a company can improve the job attitudes of their employees. First, they should conduct a survey to get a baseline reading and identify areas of concern. The company should make every effort to address attitude issues revealed as appearing to ignore them will further disgruntle staff. In general, doing the following can go a long way toward fostering positive employee attitudes:

- Make the work interesting and meaningful.
- Offer opportunities to learn and grow.
- Provide regular feedback on performance.
- Recognize a job well done and above and beyond effort.
- Communicate expectations, changes, and overall firm performance clearly and consistently.
- Be transparent whenever possible.
- Foster respect and fairness.
- Ensure that the compensation and benefits package is competitive and strategically designed.

JOB ENRICHMENT, ENLARGEMENT PRINCIPLES, AND TECHNIQUES

Job enrichment involves redesigning roles so that they have more meaning, are less monotonous, and are more challenging to employees. To achieve this, employees may be asked to take on additional planning, decision-making, and controlling responsibilities. The goal of **job enrichment** is to provide employees with greater opportunity for autonomy, responsibility, recognition, achievement, and advancement. Ideally, job enrichment should create a greater sense of belonging to the organization as well as develop a multitalented workforce.

Depending on the employee's capabilities, employers may also consider **job enlargement**. Job enlargement is adding more duties to the role that are at the same level of difficulty as the employee's current tasks. Although employees are not able to exercise more discretion with job enlargement, they can learn new things and add variety to their workday, which may stave off boredom and increase engagement.

Key Components and Best Practices of Performance Management Systems

Performance management is the human resource function concerned with setting performance standards, evaluating employee effectiveness against those standards, identifying any problem areas, and implementing interventions to correct said problems. Performance management is vital because an organization can't thrive if individuals, teams, and departments aren't effective in their roles.

The performance management process can vary from organization to organization, but most firms follow three basic steps:

- Through activities like goal setting, needs analysis, and the creation of a corporate value statement and code of conduct, company leaders and human resource professionals establish organizational goals. They then identify the knowledge, skills, behaviors, and tasks required to achieve those goals and inform employees how to best work to meet the company's objectives.
- The firm's management then needs to monitor employee performance, document any problems, and help employees correct those problems, if possible.
- At predetermined intervals (typically once a year), managers will conduct in-depth performance appraisals for each employee. The appraisals measure performance during the preceding period (usually a year). Often, the manager and employee will set goals for the employee to work toward in the new appraisal period.

Principles of Effective Performance Appraisal

Performance appraisals serve four main organizational functions:

1. **Guide human resource decisions**—performance data is required for supporting and justifying promotion or termination decisions.
2. **Reward and motivate employees**—pay rate, status, and recognition should be based on performance.
3. **Promote personal development**—performance feedback will help employees identify strengths and improve weaknesses.
4. **Identify training needs**—a well-designed appraisal process establishes necessary skills and abilities for each role and identifies individuals, areas, or departments that could benefit from additional training.

Each employee's **performance** appraisal should assess the following:

1. Progress toward goals set at the last appraisal meeting
2. Completion of normal job duties
3. Organizational behaviors, such as cooperation, innovation, motivation, and attitude
4. Any notable achievements

Performance Appraisal Methods

There are many different performance appraisal methods; some involve feedback only from the immediate supervisor, and some involve the feedback of peers, clients, or subordinates. Many organizations begin the process with self-appraisals. **Self-appraisals** are most beneficial when used for personal development and identifying training needs but less beneficial when they are used as a basis for the formal evaluation process. Good supervisors are able to evaluate performance and give meaningful feedback. Hence, it should not be surprising that **supervisor appraisals** are typically required as at least one major component of the overall performance appraisal process. One type of appraisal that considers feedback from multiple sources is a **360-degree appraisal**. These appraisals have rapidly grown in popularity and are expected to share a broader perspective of performance because they include feedback from everyone the employee interacts with—managers, peers, clients, and subordinates.

Ranking Techniques of Appraisal

Ranking procedures put employees in order from highest to lowest based upon evaluation characteristics, such as performance. There are three main forms of ranking: straight ranking, alternate ranking, and paired comparison. **Straight ranking** involves listing all employees in order with number one being the best, number two being second best, number three being third, and so on. **Alternate ranking** entails choosing the best and the worst from a list of all employees, removing these names from the list, and repeating until there are no names left. **Paired comparison** consists of evaluating only two employees at a time, deciding which is better, and continuing until each employee has been paired against every other employee. Ranking procedures assist with distributing budgeted pay increases that are more clearly tied to performance and eliminate some of the biases found in traditional review criterion. The forced-distribution method, also known as **forced ranking**, uses a bell curve in which the majority of employees will receive an average score and a small group will receive extremely high or extremely low performance scores.

Rating Techniques of Appraisal

There is a variety of rating appraisal methods, but the two most common are the checklist method and the rating scale method. The checklist method is a series of statements describing a certain level of performance. The performance evaluator can then check a box next to the statement that best describes the individual's performance in each performance area. The rating scale method rates an individual's performance on a point scale, usually a 1–3, 1–4, 1–5, or 1–10 scale, with lower numbers representing poor performance and higher numbers representing superior performance.

Behaviorally Based Techniques of Appraisal

Greater focus on accountability and results has led to new approaches for appraising performance. Three main **behaviorally based appraisal methods** include management by objectives, behavioral anchored rating scale, and behavioral observation scale. **Management by objectives** is proactive rather than reactive. It focuses on predicting and shaping the future of the company, accomplishing results rather than simply following directions, improving competence and effectiveness, as well as increasing participation and engagement of employees. **Behaviorally anchored rating scales (BARS)** assign numerical values to performance based upon a given range, for example, five-star systems or scales from 1 to 10. The BARS method analyzes the job description for a particular position and identifies the tasks that must be performed for the organization to function effectively. Once the tasks are identified, a determination is made about the specific way the individual should behave to perform each task. For example, if communication is identified as a necessary skill for a management position, an individual in that position must be able to keep others "in the loop." A series of statements that are ranked is then designed that describe how effectively the individual performed. Performance appraisers can then choose the statement that best describes the employee's behavior. The key benefits of behaviorally anchored rating systems are that they create agreement by being less subjective and more based upon observations, whereas characteristics are more carefully considered. **Behavior observation scales** are similar to behaviorally anchored rating scales but with greater focus on frequency of behavior than on quality of performance, for example, a sliding scale of always, sometimes, and never.

Narrative Techniques of Appraisal

The three most common narrative appraisal techniques are the critical incident method, the essay method, and the field review method. The **critical incident method** documents each performance problem related to an employee occurring during a set period so the evaluator can discuss problems with the employee at the end. The **essay method** requires performance evaluators to write a short essay about each employee describing the employee's performance during the performance period. The **field review method** is a method in which an individual other than the employee's direct supervisor or manager performs the appraisal and writes down a series of assessments and observations about that particular employee's performance.

Common Performance Appraisal Problems

Performance evaluations are meant to measure performance of job objectives, but they can be tainted by a number of criterion problems. One dilemma is whether to focus evaluations on **outcomes and results** or **behaviors and activities**. Many will advocate that outcomes are more important than behaviors and will base performance on the measure of results. However, focusing only on outcomes can lure individuals to achieve results by unethical or adverse means. Evaluations should also measure performance results without contamination by factors that are beyond an individual's control, such as improper materials, poor equipment, or economic conditions. Furthermore, even performance evaluations that are consistent and reputable may be influenced by biases. The absence of standards to assist with grading performances can lead some evaluators to judge too harshly, some to inflate scores, and some to judge all performers concentrating in the middle. The best method ensures that group results form a **bell curve.**

Performance Appraisal Training

It is important for an organization to train performance evaluators to use appropriate appraisal methods because a performance appraisal is useful to the organization only if it is fair and accurate. This is because an organization's performance management process relies heavily on the ability of the organization to identify and eliminate performance problems. As a result, a performance appraisal must offer an accurate view of an individual's performance so the organization can accurately identify problem areas or performance issues and then improve these problem areas or handle these issues appropriately. However, there are a number of different factors, such as the evaluator's own biases or the appraisal process that the evaluator uses, that can influence a performance appraisal, so it can often be extremely difficult for a manager or supervisor to conduct an appraisal that is completely fair and accurate. Therefore, to make sure that each manager or supervisor conducts each appraisal as effectively as possible, the organization must train each manager or supervisor to use the appropriate set of appraisal methods.

Workplace Flexibility Programs

There have been many benefits touted in favor of **workplace flexibility**, such as increased morale, attendance, and productivity. Flexibility might involve either the **work location**—where work is performed—or the **work schedule**—when work is performed. However, the practice is gaining momentum slowly due to many employers embracing traditional viewpoints despite technological advances creating lower overhead costs for remote workers or greater employee engagement and satisfaction when allowed schedule flexibility to accommodate family or personal responsibilities. Workplace flexibility allows employees greater autonomy and empowerment as well. Flexibility can also be used to encourage brand recognition, attract talent, and support retention strategies.

Learning and Development

Learning Organizations

A learning organization is a company in which employees are encouraged to develop their knowledge, skills, and abilities so that the organization will remain competitive and profitable as the business environment changes. This happens by promoting the open exchange of ideas, rewarding individuals for exceptional performance, and rewarding or allowing employees to try out new ideas for solving problems or improving the way certain tasks are performed.

According to Peter Senge, the five disciplines essential to a learning organization are personal mastery, mental models, shared vision, team learning, and systems thinking. Personal mastery is the discipline of having an area of expertise and the ability to increase their knowledge in that area. Mental models are all the assumptions and beliefs affecting perception and acts based on those perceptions. Shared vision is the discipline of creating a culture that encourages employees to work toward a common goal. Team learning refers to the idea that a team must be able to openly exchange ideas and put in as much effort as possible to achieve its goals. Systems thinking is the discipline of seeing problems as parts of broader systems instead of looking at each problem in isolation.

Approaches to Coaching and Mentoring

Coaching

Coaching in business is a method of training in which an experienced individual provides an employee with advice to encourage his or her best possible performance and career. Having a strong **coaching culture** among strategic goals often leads to increased organizational performance and engagement. Coaching is a personal, one-on-one relationship that takes place over a specific period. Coaching is often a technique used in performance management, but it can be applied to many business objectives. For example, coaching may be used to prepare individuals for new assignments, improve behavior, conquer obstacles, and adapt to change. Coaching might also be used to support diversity initiatives, such as generational differences, behavioral styles, or awareness and inclusion.

Mentoring

Mentoring is a career development method in which a new or less experienced employee is paired with an experienced leader for guidance. **Formal mentoring programs** need to be measurable and integrated into the culture, without being seen as a rigid, forced system. These programs typically establish goals at the onset and track progress throughout. Similar to coaching, mentoring is a partnership relationship that takes place over a specific period—and both need a customized approach that fits the receiver. However, mentoring carries a history of recognition for having considerable impact with the power to positively transform career trajectory. Successful mentors are able to support, encourage, promote, and challenge while developing deep connections. Mentoring can also happen more informally where the mentee looks up to and takes the advice of the mentor without there being defined goals or objectives. This happens naturally, and often the people involved don't know the mentor–mentee relationship existed until later reflection.

Career Development

Stages of Working and Professional Career Development

Professional careers and trade careers both involve four stages of career development. For **professional careers**, the stages are internship, independent contributor, mentor, and sponsor. **Interns** are individuals who are continuing learning under the supervision of experienced professionals. **Independent contributors** are autonomous workers whose success is based upon how well they take initiative, meet objectives, and exceed expectations. **Mentors** have displayed their ability to perform, supervise, and coach others. **Sponsors** make strategic decisions while providing organizational guidance, influence, and accountability. For **trade or working careers**, the stages are exploration, establishment, maintenance, and decline. The **exploration stage** describes individuals who are just beginning their careers, often between the ages of 15 and 24, who are still working on trade programs or courses and who may be prone to frequently changing positions while trying to explore interests and abilities against job demands. The **establishment stage** describes individuals, often between the ages of 25 and 44, who are striving to create a more stable position within their chosen occupation to establish work and build a reputation. The **maintenance stage** describes individuals, often between the ages of 45 and 64, who are concerned with job security and survival. The **decline stage** describes individuals, often older than 65, who are approaching the ends of their careers and entering retirement.

There are a variety of methods to further a person's career development. Commonly used methods include coaching programs, employee counseling and support programs, and training workshops. Coaching programs are designed to provide each employee with a specialist to help learn new skills or understand how to handle work-related problems or situations. Employee counseling and support programs are designed to provide help if the employee is experiencing problems that may be affecting performance or the ability to seek other opportunities. Training workshops that offer employees the opportunity to learn the knowledge and skills associated with other positions within the organization can also be helpful.

There are a variety of methods a manager or supervisor can use to further an individual's career development. Some methods commonly used are coaching, counseling, mentoring, and evaluating. Employees can be coached to perform new tasks, handle certain problems outside of the scope of their current positions, and develop communication and leadership. Employees can also be offered counseling, advice, or emotional support. Managers or supervisors can act as mentors by helping employees apply for promotions, suggesting them for promotions, and offering guidance about other positions. Finally, managers or supervisors can help further an employee's career by candidly evaluating and discussing strengths and weaknesses.

There are a variety of methods individuals can use for their own career development. Some of the most important methods include attending training workshops, networking, and seeking additional education. Many organizations offer training workshops to help individuals seek management positions or positions in other departments, but most of these workshops are optional, so they will only help if an individual takes the time to attend the program and learn the material. Networking is an essential part because it is nearly impossible to progress in an organization if there is unwillingness or an inability to establish relationships with managers, supervisors, coworkers, or customers. Finally, when the knowledge or educational background required for a particular position is lacking, the best way to develop a career is to seek additional education from colleges, universities, or seminars.

Techniques for Career Development

Career pathing or mapping is a plan for employees to progress within the organization. It involves a management-guided employee self-assessment of interests, motivations, knowledge, and skills. Potential matching roles within the organization will be identified and may be a promotion or lateral move. Plans will be created to fill gaps in skills and knowledge needed for the potential roles. When the identified opportunities arise, employees will further explore and pursue them if ready.

Developmental Assessments

360 performance appraisal is a developmental assessment technique that involves getting feedback from customers, coworkers, managers, and subordinates. It can be an effective tool as it results in broad and varied input, with the goal of painting a more holistic picture of employee performance. However, human resources must take note of the potential pitfalls of this method. Raters may not be adequately trained to provide effective feedback. They also may not agree on what areas of performance to review. Further, office politics could get in the way of meaningful and fair input. For these reasons, human resources should be careful about making any employment decisions based on the results of a 360 assessment.

Knowledge-Sharing Techniques and Facilitation

Knowledge management is a system of initiatives, practices, procedures, and processes used to ensure that each member knows or can access all the information necessary to perform his or her responsibilities. Knowledge management can be important when there are many employees working in different departments at different times. It is designed to ensure that everyone has the same basic training and access to information from other departments to avoid performing the same task multiple times.

Knowledge retention is a collection of strategies designed to keep important information in-house so that a firm doesn't lose valuable insight or critical skills as employees leave the organization. It can be accomplished in several different ways such as sharing information via mentoring programs and cross-departmental collaboration. Additionally, employees should be encouraged to reflect after each project completion and to document procedures and lessons learned for future reference. Companies should also make it easier to access subject matter experts so that other employees know who to seek out when they need specialized information. This results in a more educated workforce over time.

Learning and Development Approaches and Techniques

Main Kinds of Learning and Best Processes

There are three main types of learning, each with different suitable training methods. If teaching **motor responses**, such as physical acts that involve muscle groups, a training method that involves exploration, demonstration, activity practice, and corrective guidance works best. If teaching **rote learning**, such as memorization, a training method that involves familiarity, patterns or associations, repetition, and timely feedback works best. If teaching **idea learning**, such as operant conditioning or learning complex ideas, a training method that involves sequential concepts, with practice or exhibition, progressive mastery, and reinforcement at each step works best.

Employee Development Methods

A few methods of employee development include the following:

- **Literacy training**: basic education programs offered by companies such as English-as-a-second-language training, how to interpret engineering designs, or how to make basic computations.
- **Competency training**: teaching skills, abilities, and behaviors essential for executing responsibilities effectively and successful performance.
- **Mentoring**: when a more experienced individual teaches valuable job skills and provides encouragement or emotional support.
- **Attitude change**: group communications through lectures, video presentations, or similar methods to accomplish increased customer service, diversity training, ethical behavior, or harassment training.

On-the-Job Training Methods

On-the-job techniques are used more frequently due to the lesser cost and immediate production compared to off-the-job trainings, which are designed more for education and long-term development.

Some **on-the-job training techniques** include the following:

- **Job-instruction training**, the most popular method of training, involves introductory explanation and demonstration or shadowing before given the opportunity to try alone.
- **E-learning** is generally on-demand training (sometimes learners can log on live) that can be taken anywhere with an internet connection at a time that's convenient for the learner. E-learning modules can cover a range of topics such as company policies, job-related how-tos, and more. E-learning is extremely cost-effective. The main drawback is that those watching a recording can't provide or receive any real-time feedback.
- **Apprenticeships** are a process of working alongside and under the direction of a skilled professional, such as trade electricians, plumbers, and carpenters.
- **Internships, cooperative education, and assistantships** are similar to apprenticeships but are often paired with colleges or universities.
- **Job rotation and cross training** involve a rotating series of job assignments in departments for specified periods of time to expose individuals to a number of skills and challenges.
- **Coaching and counseling** act as providing an identifiable and virtuous model, setting goals, providing timely feedback, and providing reinforcement and encouragement.

Off-the-Job Training Methods

A few **off-the-job techniques** include the following:

- **Independent study**: people self-motivated to take individual responsibility toward learning and attempting to train themselves by reading books, taking courses, or attending seminars
- **Corporate universities**: where employees attend classes taught by corporate trainers, executives, and consultants
- **Vestibule training**: similar to on-the-job training but occurs in a separate training area identical to the actual production area
- **Lecture**: an efficient way to transfer large amounts of information to a large audience

Management and Leadership Development

Management development is ensuring individuals have all the knowledge, skills, and abilities necessary to manage effectively. **Leadership development** is ensuring individuals have all the knowledge, skills, and abilities necessary to lead effectively. Management development is designed to teach an individual how to ensure each function is carried out as expected, whereas leadership development is designed to teach an individual how to predict change within the business environment, identify the way the organization needs to change to meet those needs, and encourage other individuals to meet the changing needs of the organization.

ADDIE MODEL OF TRAINING

The assessment, training and development, and evaluation (**ADDIE**) model of training reflects these three primary phases of learning in greater detail:

A	Analysis—gather data and identify problems, needs, or discrepancies between current capacities and desired performance.
D	Design—determine learning objectives and goals, decide course content or exercises, and plan delivery methods.
D	Development—create training materials or purchase materials, and modify them to meet objectives.
I	Implementation—deliver the training program tools to the target audience and observe changes.
E	Evaluation—compare training program results of knowledge and behavior to the course objectives.

NEEDS ANALYSES

It is important for an organization to perform a needs analysis before designing a training program for several different reasons. First, an organization should accurately identify problems. Second, even if a particular problem is known prior to the analysis, it can be difficult to identify the cause of that problem. Third, and most importantly, it is impossible to design an effective training program without first identifying the specific knowledge, skills, and abilities required to achieve goals or to correct a problem. A **needs analysis** can be an essential part of the training development process because it helps to identify and detail problems so possible solutions can be found.

There are a variety of steps that might be taken during a needs analysis, but most begin by collecting data related to the performance of each part of the organization. This information is usually gathered from surveys, interviews, observations, skill assessments, performance appraisals, and so on. Once this information is collected, problems are identified within specific areas of the organization and solutions proposed. Advantages and disadvantages of each solution are then identified and the plan chosen that seems to provide the greatest benefit for the lowest cost.

COST/BENEFIT ANALYSIS

Although training and development programs should be viewed as an extremely valuable capital investment, they should also provide measurable returns. Simple calculations can be used to measure the costs and benefits of training. **Costs** should include both direct costs (e.g., materials, facilities, etc.) and indirect costs (e.g., lost production time). The overall costs of training and development programs might contain staff hours, program materials, hardware or software, videos, and production losses such as training time and respective salaries. **Benefits** of training should be evaluated according to how well the training will increase productivity, advance product quality, reduce errors, improve safety, or reduce operating costs. One calculation for measuring training is the cost per trainee, in which the total cost of training is divided by the total number of trainees. Regardless, the long-term benefits of training should outweigh the costs, and this can be determined through a **cost/benefit analysis**. There are creative adjustments that can be used to reduce training costs. The size of training classes can be increased, and materials can be reused when not violating copyrights. Expenses can be further eliminated by making training available online or using videoconferencing.

Learning Evaluation

Kirkpatrick's Four-Level Learning Evaluation Model

It's important to analyze the effectiveness of training programs so you don't waste resources. Donald Kirkpatrick introduced a **four-level training evaluation model** for planning, evaluating, and preserving. The four levels of the evaluation model include 1) reaction, 2) learning, 3) behavior, and 4) results:

- **Reaction**: measures how people react to the training, often a survey upon completion that asks for feedback or satisfaction levels on the subject, the material, the instructor, and so on
- **Learning**: measures what objectives people have learned from the training program (could be in the form of a questionnaire, assessment, etc.)
- **Behavior**: measures how far the performance or behavior of people that received the training has changed and observes how they apply what has been learned to their environment
- **Results**: analyzes noticeable effects of training, such as changes in production, efficiency, and quality

The Learning Curve

A learning curve is a representation of the rate at which an individual learns. It is referred to as a curve because the rate changes over time. Learning curves are useful tools for instructors, human resource professionals, managers, and other individuals who are overseeing training or evaluating training programs. Sudden changes in the learning curve may indicate a new training program is working effectively or that a change in the work environment is slowing the learning process.

A **negatively accelerating learning curve** is the most common type of learning curve. Negatively accelerating learning occurs when an individual rapidly acquires information in the beginning and then makes smaller successive achievements as time progresses. Some examples of this learning behavior include everyday tasks such as walking, talking, or riding a bike.

Some people are slow to pick up and absorb material in the beginning, then everything gradually "clicks," and they are able to ramp up learning speed. This would be a **positively accelerating learning curve.** Positive accelerating learning curves are most common when the material is highly complex, when the individual doesn't have the standard background, or when motivation or confidence is low to start.

A combination of positively accelerating in the beginning and negatively accelerating down the road creates an **S-shaped learning curve**. S-shaped learning curves occur most frequently when an individual is learning a new problem-solving task. Initially, there will be a gradual success, then rapid comprehension, followed by a slowdown to "polish" the new skill. A period in which no learning takes place and performance remains stagnant is often referred to as a **plateau**.

Learning Theories

Training vs. Education and Explicit Knowledge vs. Tacit Knowledge

Although both training and education programs enable people to acquire new knowledge, learn new skills, or conduct behaviors in a new way, they are distinct and different processes. **Training** can be described as the more narrow acquisition of specific knowledge or skills. Most training programs try to teach students how to perform a particular activity for a specific job. **Education** is broader and attempts to provide students with general knowledge that may be applied to a variety of settings. Distinguishing between two kinds of knowledge can assist with the design of training and education programs. **Explicit knowledge** can be formalized, communicated, or found in job specifications and manuals. **Tacit knowledge** is personal, based upon past experience, and is more difficult to explain to others.

Principles of Learning

Research from both operant conditioning and social cognitive theory suggest **principles of learning** that are critical to the architecture of training programs. These principles of learning include the following:

- **Stimulus**—should be easily perceived and meaningfully organized in a local or systematic way
- **Response**—providing students with opportunities for practice and repetition
- **Motivation**—reinforcements to facilitate extrinsic rewards, intrinsic satisfaction, and active participation
- **Feedback**—performance feedback is necessary for learning, change, and knowledge of results
- **Transfer**—occurs when students can apply the knowledge and skills learned to their jobs

Bloom's Taxonomy of Learning

Learning occurs at different levels. **Bloom's taxonomy of learning** is sometimes reflected as a pyramid containing six **domain levels**. **Knowledge** forms the base of the pyramid and is the stage in which learners can recall previously learned facts. Learners then graduate to the **comprehension stage**, in which they are able to grasp the meaning of the material. The **application stage** comes next. In the application stage, learners can apply information to solve problems in new situations. Following application is the **analysis stage**, in which learners are capable of understanding the context and structure of material. The tip of the pyramid comprises synthesis and evaluation. During the **synthesis stage**, learners are capable of drawing from existing knowledge or sources and processing to form conclusions. Finally, at the **evaluation stage**, learners are capable of judging the value of materials.

Andragogy and Pedagogy

Andragogy and pedagogy are both sciences of how individuals learn. **Andragogy** is the study of how adults learn and focuses on making it easier to teach adults. **Pedagogy**, on the other hand, is the study of how children learn and focuses on making it easier to teach children. They are different fields because studies have found that children and adults learn in different ways. An instructor who understands these differences is able to identify the most effective teaching methods. However, there is a noteworthy debate as to whether there is a great deal of difference between pedagogy and andragogy.

Malcolm Knowles's Assumptions of Learners

According to Malcolm Knowles, there are five assumptions typically made about adult learners. The first assumption (motivation) is that they are internally motivated to learn by understanding why they need to learn. The second assumption (self-concept) is that they want to direct their own learning. The third assumption (adult experience) is that they want to apply what they already know as they learn and use their experience to help others learn. The fourth assumption (readiness) is that they are willing to learn if what they learn will help them in some way. The fifth assumption (orientation) is that they learn so they can apply knowledge to current rather than future problems.

According to Malcolm Knowles, there are five assumptions that can typically be made about child learners. The first assumption (motivation) is that they are externally motivated to learn due to other's expectations. The second assumption (self-concept) is that they want teachers, parents, and so on to guide their learning. The third assumption (child's experience) is that they learn more effectively by being taught because they do not have enough knowledge yet to apply it. The fourth assumption (readiness) is that they are willing to learn because society tells them to learn. The fifth assumption (orientation) is that they learn to be able to apply the information in the future.

Learning Styles

A **learning style** refers to the way an individual learns most effectively. Because each person learns information differently, some teaching methods are more effective than others. The three main learning styles are auditory, tactile, and visual. Training programs need to be designed to take different learning styles into consideration so participants will learn the material as efficiently as possible.

Review Video: Adult Learning Processes and Theories
Visit mometrix.com/academy and enter code: 638453

An **auditory learner** learns most effectively by hearing information rather than seeing it or using it. They usually learn most effectively by hearing descriptions or instructions such as lectures, group discussions, demonstrations of a particular sound (such as an alarm that might indicate a problem with a piece of machinery) or by listening to themselves read aloud.

A **tactile learner** learns most effectively by touching or using something rather than hearing it or seeing it. They usually learn most effectively by using a new tool or process, by actually being able to touch or move an object, or by physically applying the information in a controlled situation. They will have difficulty learning through verbal instructions (lectures or explanations) and visual methods (reading a handout). Learning activities include practicing techniques, role-playing, simulations, and other activities that allow the individual to learn through a hands-on approach.

A **visual learner** learns most effectively by seeing information rather than hearing or using it. They learn most effectively by seeing the information on a flashcard, chalkboard, handout, or book; seeing a representation in a picture or diagram; watching videos or presentations; or taking detailed notes and then rereading those notes. They have difficulty learning through verbal instruction (lectures and explanations) or by performing a task without written instructions or handouts.

Total Rewards

The concept known as **total rewards** refers to all of the compensation and benefits received for performing tasks related to each position. It is important to have an effective total rewards program for two main reasons. First, it encourages employees to join and then stay with the organization. Second, there are legal concerns associated with the minimum amount of compensation an individual can receive for a certain amount of work, making it essential to consider these concerns to avoid unnecessary fines or litigation.

Types of Rewards

The two main types of rewards used to compensate employees are monetary and nonmonetary. **Monetary compensation** is any tangible reward provided as payment for work, including salary and wages, paid sick days, paid vacation time, retirement plans, and stock options. **Nonmonetary compensation** is any intangible reward provided to encourage an individual to perform work, including better assignments, employee-of-the-month awards, flexible scheduling, and special privileges.

An organization can issue monetary compensation to employees through direct or indirect compensation. Direct compensation is any monetary compensation paid directly to the employee, including salary or wages, bonuses, overtime, or special pay. Indirect compensation is monetary compensation paid to a third party on the employee's behalf or paid without the employee having to perform work, including health insurance, paid sick days, paid vacation time, retirement plans, and stock options.

Philosophy

A total rewards philosophy is developed to clearly state reward goals and how those goals will be achieved. Identifying this philosophy is necessary to determine if the rewards are reflecting the values and goals of an organization or if they need to be modified.

The two types of total reward philosophies are entitlement philosophies and performance-based philosophies. An **entitlement philosophy** issues rewards based on the length of time a particular employee has been with the organization. It assumes an individual is entitled to certain rewards because of seniority or length of time in a specific position. Entitlement philosophies encourage individuals to stay with the organization but do not necessarily encourage effective performance. A **performance-based philosophy**, on the other hand, issues rewards for good performance.

Strategy

A **total rewards strategy** is a plan used to design a total rewards program. It is based on the organization's total rewards philosophy and is primarily designed to establish the framework for the allocation of program resources. It refers to the ways resources are used to encourage individuals to work for the organization without exceeding limits.

There are a variety of factors to consider when designing an effective total rewards strategy. The four main factors include the competitive environment, the economic environment, the labor market, and the legal environment. The **competitive environment** is the effect competition has on the ability to allocate resources to the total rewards program. For example, if competitors are offering a specific product at a price that is far lower, the organization may need to reduce the amount of funds allocated to its total rewards program to afford a price reduction. The **economic environment** refers to the effect the economy has on the cost of labor. For example, as the cost of living increases, the cost of labor will usually increase as well. The **labor market** is the availability of skilled employees and the **legal environment** refers to taxes and regulations.

Pay Structures

A **pay structure** is the compensation system an organization uses to determine the appropriate base pay for positions by separating each job into categories based on value to the organization. The pay structure is an essential part of any organization's total rewards program because it establishes a guide for appropriate hourly wages or salaries. Specific base pay minimums and maximums for each category are well-defined and allow firms to avoid arbitrarily assigning pay.

Creating a pay structure can vary greatly, but most organizations begin the process by conducting a job evaluation for each position. Once all positions are evaluated and assigned a value, they are categorized based on their value to the organization. The organization will usually gather information from salary surveys to determine the market median for each category and wages an individual would receive at the midpoint of a similar pay category for another organization. Finally, using all of this information as a guide, a pay range is developed for each category.

Pay Levels and Pay Banding

Some compensation structures break out pay grades or ranges into separate **levels** or **bands** so the company can maintain pay equity and stay within budget. This is done by conducting a job analysis and grouping titles into families. For example, those that fall into the first pay grade may have a pay band of $20,000 to $35,000, the second pay grade may have a band of $30,000 to $50,000, and the third pay grade may have a band of $50,000 to $100,000. Jobs may also be evaluated and ranked based upon overall responsibilities and worth to the organization. Although pay bands are broken out based upon job duty and skill level, it is important to recognize whether the company tends to lead, lag, or match current market rates. Matching or leading the market is best for recruitment and retention. The sizes of pay bands tend to grow as you move up the managerial ladder, with executives having the largest pay levels.

Broadbanding

Broadbanding is a type of pay structure design in which an organization creates a small number of broadly defined pay grades into which all jobs are separated, for example, general staff, management, and executives. Organizations usually choose to use a broadbanding approach to encourage teamwork and eliminate problems arising from perceived differences in status between different pay grades. The focus is on performance rather than activities related to achieving promotions.

Job Evaluation or Analysis

It is important to conduct a job evaluation during the total rewards planning process for two major reasons. First, a job evaluation identifies the positions most important to success so rewards can be assigned appropriately. Second, it determines whether there should be a difference in pay between two positions. For example, a secretary and an administrative assistant with the same skills and performing similar jobs should receive equal pay even though they have different titles.

A **compensable factor** is a specific characteristic of a position used to determine the value of that position. They are specific job requirements that are considered important, and individuals are compensated based on their ability to meet these requirements. Compensable factors are commonly used during a job evaluation to compare the requirements of a variety of different positions. Some of the most common compensable factors relate to knowledge, skills, and abilities. These factors include characteristics related to a particular position such as experience required, level of education required, level of responsibility required, and knowledge of specific technology or processes required.

The two main types of job evaluation techniques used to determine the value of a particular position are nonquantitative techniques and quantitative techniques. **Nonquantitative techniques**, also referred to as **whole job methods**, are used to evaluate the skills and abilities associated with a particular position and assign it a value based on whether it requires more or less skill than other jobs within the organization. **Quantitative techniques**, also referred to as **nontraditional techniques** or **factor-based methods**, are techniques of assigning a specific value to each factor in a series of compensable factors identified as important. The organization can then evaluate each position, determine how many compensable factors are required for the position, and can assign a value to the position by using a mathematical formula.

The three most common nonquantitative job evaluation techniques are the classification method, the pricing method, and the ranking method. The **classification method** separates positions into categories based on tasks. Each category is then listed in order of its importance and assigned pay based on its importance. The **pricing method**, also known as the slotting method, assigns a value to a position equal to the value of a similar position or category that already exists. Finally, the **ranking method** ranks each position from lowest to highest based on how the skills and abilities required to perform the position compare with those associated with other positions.

The most common quantitative job evaluation techniques are the factor comparison method and the point factor method. The **factor comparison method** identifies a series of compensable factors and establishes a ranking system to measure how much of a particular compensable factor, such as education, is required for a particular position. Each factor ranking is assigned a specific dollar value, and the value of the position is determined by adding the total dollar value for the rank of each factor required for the position. The **point factor method** is similar, but it assigns a point value to each factor instead of a dollar value, and the pay for the position is determined by comparing the total amount of points to a chart.

WAGE COMPRESSION

Wage compression occurs when an employee is hired at the same or higher wage than existing employees with more experience already in that position. It can also occur when line level employees earn close to what management earns. It is important to avoid wage compression because it leads to employees becoming dissatisfied and unmotivated because of the perceived arbitrary nature of pay decisions. Wage compression can happen in several ways, such as external hires expecting more of a pay bump to change jobs than a normal, internal annual increase (typically less than 4 percent), and companies may be willing to offer inflated salaries in a tight labor market. To combat wage compression, human resources can use strategies such as reviewing existing staff salaries prior to hiring a new employee (and making adjustments if necessary) and promoting from within whenever possible, which should result in a lower salary than hiring externally.

COMPA-RATIO

A compa-ratio is a mathematical formula used to compare a specific employee's pay with the pay at the middle of the pay range. A **compa-ratio** is expressed as a percentage and can be determined by dividing the employee's base salary by the midpoint salary for the employee's pay range (base salary / midpoint salary = compa-ratio). For example, if an individual is in a pay grade that ranges from $25,000 to $45,000 a year and the individual receives $30,000 a year, the midpoint of the range is equal to ($25,000 + $45,000) / 2 or $35,000, and the compa-ratio is equal to $30,000 / $35,000, which is equal to 0.857 or 85.7 percent. Compa-ratios are primarily used to compare an employee's current pay with the pay of other employees in similar positions to determine whether the individual is receiving a fair amount considering seniority, performance, and so on.

Calculating Piece Rates

Piece rates calculate the amount of compensation an employee receives for conducting a specified unit of work. A worker who produces multiple products at different rates would need overtime calculated using a combined weighted average to find the regular hourly rate of pay. First, multiply each rate by the total hours worked, then divide the sum by the total hours worked to find the **blended hourly rate**. This method is industry standard best practice for compliance with **FLSA**. For example, if a worker produced 60 pieces at a rate of $9.00 per piece over 40 hours and another 40 pieces at a rate of $6.00 per piece over 10 hours, the hourly rate for this worker would be $7.80 (60 pieces times $9.00 per piece plus 40 pieces times $6.00 per piece equals $780, divided by 50 hours equals $15.60 per hour). Then, earnings would be calculated as follows:

Regular time = 40 hours × $15.60 = $624.00

Overtime = 10 hours × $23.40 = $234.00

Weekly earnings = $858.00

Using Benchmarking to Design Compensation Initiatives

When organizations and compensation professionals need to make pay decisions or determine whether internal rates are competitive with the industry, most will rely upon **benchmarking** of both internal and external peer groups. Benchmarking is a tool for measuring and comparing current practices or processes against **competition** so that any gaps may be addressed. For example, making changes to incentive plans may be a tough sell. If your business practice involves not providing employees with a bonus plan, benchmarking data might support new initiatives by showing that many in your industry do provide bonus incentives. Thus, not providing this incentive could jeopardize performance or risk losing top performers. However, it is important to consider organizational structure, size, location, industry, and other factors. Compensation rates in San Francisco will differ greatly from rates in Omaha, and smaller companies often pay less than large, national entities.

Using Remuneration Surveys to Ensure Competitiveness

Competitive compensation structures are not only equitable and motivating, but they should also be legal, be cost-benefit effective, and provide security. The most readily available **remuneration surveys** are those conducted by government agencies, such as the Bureau of Labor Statistics (BLS) and wage surveys conducted by private organizations. Government surveys may include local, state, or federal data. BLS regularly publishes reliable data findings on occupational earnings and benefits of blue- and white-collar jobs. Furthermore, professional organizations, journals, and associations may perform sophisticated surveys to obtain remuneration data of top managers, supervisors, and entry-level workers. Some popular publications are *Forbes's* CEO compensation report or those compiled by wage survey companies like PayScale or Towers Watson. However, the U.S. Justice Department has stated that human resource professionals cannot conduct salary surveys on their own. Doing so violates the Antitrust Safety Zone guidelines. Professionals should consider that these surveys frequently consider varying components of compensation, such as base pay, incentives, and benefits.

Pay Practices and Issues

Base Pay

Three of the most important factors involved in determining the appropriate base pay for a new employee are the value of the position, the education and experience of the individual, and the demand for individuals able to fill the position. The value of the position refers to the value identified during the job evaluation process based on the importance of the position to the organization. The education and experience refers to the knowledge, skills, and abilities the individual has beyond the minimum requirements necessary to perform the position. The demand for individuals able to fill the position refers to the ability of the individual to seek employment with another organization and the ease or difficulty the organization would have in replacing the employee.

Differential Pay

FLSA requires that employers pay **time and a half** for overtime hours in excess of a 40-hour workweek. Some regulations may impose additional overtime payments, such as overtime hours in excess of an eight-hour day. Companies may also provide an adjustment for employee transfers to locations with a higher cost of living or in compliance with certain localities that may also require a higher minimum wage. Many organizations use some form of **differential pay** for performing unpleasant or less desirable work. For example, weekends or holidays might be paid at time and a half or even double time. FLSA requires that employers compensate on-call employees if their activities are restricted, and premiums often compensate employees who are called back to work for emergency services due to the inconvenience. Likewise, those who work night shifts or put themselves in harm's way will often receive a shift differential or hazard pay.

Incentive or Variable Pay

Many organizations use some form of **financial incentives** that are tied to productivity as these pay-for-performance plans may increase worker output. One of the most popular methods is **merit pay increases**. Not to be confused with an annual cost-of-living increase, merit pay is an adjustment or one-time bonus awarded to top performers following an evaluation of clearly defined objectives. Some employers prefer to use **bonuses and commissions** to reward performance. Unlike merit increases that can increase annual pay levels, bonuses and commissions must be earned each period. Moreover, bonus payments do not need to be tied to individual performance. Sometimes, they are awarded at management's discretion or based upon company performance. Employers may also choose to pay employees on a **production or piece rate plan**. One example of this plan that also ties in an additional incentive is the Halsey Premium Plan. Under this plan, production standards are determined by past performance, and employees receive a guaranteed hourly rate plus a percentage of the rate for any time saved.

Other common variable pay programs include gainsharing programs and profit sharing programs. A gainsharing program encourages the achievement of certain financial goals by offering a percentage of the money the organization earns or saves from achieving that goal. A profit sharing program encourages the achievement of certain goals by offering a percentage of the profit when goals are met.

Compensation Plans for Common and Special Workforce Groups

Executive Compensation Plans

Executives often receive compensation plans that include both monetary and nonmonetary rewards. **Executive compensation plans** may be influenced by many factors but are most often associated with revenue and responsibility. **Monetary rewards** might include salary, bonuses or commissions, stock options, director's fees, or multiple forms of deferred compensation. **Nonmonetary rewards** might include a company computer, parking, a company vehicle, first-class travel arrangements, car rentals, health club memberships, and more. **Executive bonuses** are frequently much higher than mid-level managers as well. CEOs might receive bonuses that are greater than 100 percent of their base pay, whereas upper-level managers might receive bonuses that are greater than 50 percent of their base pay, and lower-level supervisors might receive bonuses between 10 and 35 percent. Moreover, executives often receive golden parachutes or extravagant bonuses when they leave office whether they do well or are forced to resign. Stock options and deferred compensation plans can vary greatly from one organization to another. Human resource and compensation professionals want to ensure that these plans are in compliance with the **Sarbanes-Oxley Act**.

Sales Compensation Plans

Sales compensation plans are designed to incentivize top performers. Salespeople will earn more if they meet or exceed predefined sales targets. These sales targets could be to hit a certain level of revenue, sales volume, profit margin, market share, or customer satisfaction and should be tied to overall company goals. Typically, salespeople are compensated with a mix of salary and incentive pay, but a company could opt to offer straight salary or straight incentive pay. The incentive pay is usually a mix of commissions and bonuses but may include stock options or other prizes. When designing these plans, human resources must determine the appropriate mix of compensation types based on the industry, product being sold, the salesperson's role, and other factors. They must also determine the territory that each salesperson is supposed to cover. Sales compensation plans must have detailed rules about what sales are counted, if salespeople can share credit, if there is a draw system, and more. Further, human resources must ensure that the compensation plan is compliant with labor laws and that each type of pay gets properly taxed. The compensation plan must be well communicated, and human resources should make sure that the salespeople and management understand it.

Global and Expatriate Compensation Plans

Global employees may be provided additional income in the form of **expatriate allowances**, and these amounts may be as much as three or four times the executives' base salary. Total compensation might include base salary, premiums for foreign service and hardship, and allowances for cost of living, housing, and storage. Tax considerations can make calculating these payments complicated. Some multinational organizations have begun the compensation practice of **localizing** or **mirroring** the local compensation package for employees on assignment in other countries. Most cultures will utilize similar factors to determine compensation and benefits structure or assign jobs to labor grades: skill, effort, and responsibility. Whereas wage levels and benefits may differ a great deal, individual wage decisions are frequently based upon performance and seniority. For example, European remuneration packages consider benefits and perks to be a much larger part of the total compensation package than in the United States, and American executives are excessively overpaid by international standards. Many firms pay a cost-of-living allowance to expatriates to equalize the costs of living in both the host and home countries. Moreover, housing allowances are often considered the single most expensive item in expatriate remuneration packages and must be frequently reviewed (as often as quarterly or even monthly) because of exchange rate fluctuations and inflation.

Other Compensation

Deferred Compensation

Any compensation that is paid out at a specified future date or during retirement is likely a form of **deferred compensation**. These plans may be qualifying or nonqualifying pensions, retirement plan accounts, or employee stock option plans. 401(k), 403(b), 503(c), Individual Retirement Accounts (IRA), or Savings Incentive Match Plans for Employees (SIMPLE) plans are qualifying plans and must adhere to the **Employee Retirement Income Security Act** and IRS limits. **Nonqualifying plans** often involve funds that are withheld and may be invested to be paid out at a later time for tax advantages and potential capital gains. Companies might choose deferred compensation plans, such as top hat plans, restorative benefit plans, or supplemental executive retirement plans to attract and retain business officers. It is important to note that payments for nonqualifying deferred compensation plans must be scheduled for a specified future date, and funds may not be withheld in advance. Additionally, nonqualifying plans can carry concerns about company sustainability or what happens in the event of mergers and acquisitions or bankruptcy.

Company-Wide Incentive Plans

Profit sharing and gainsharing programs reward employees based upon the performance of the entire organization. In **profit sharing plans**, employees receive their regular pay and a share of the company's profits. These may be cash plans, in which payments are made after the close of a specified (quarterly or annually) period, or tax-advantageous deferred plans, in which funds are invested. If deferred, funds are a tax-deductible expense for the company for the year in which they are contributed, and employees are not taxed until their funds are received. In **gainsharing plans**, employees receive bonuses based upon improved productivity as opposed to profits. Gainsharing plans often fall into three categories: Scanlon Plans, Rucker Plans, or Improshare Plans. **Scanlon Plans** are most popular in union environments and combine gainsharing with an employee recommendation system. These plans establish a standard ratio of labor costs as a percentage of revenue. **Rucker Plans** are similar, but the employee gains are based upon production. These plans establish a ratio of labor costs as a percentage of value added or the sales value of output minus the cost of materials. **Improshare Plans**, broken down as improved productivity through sharing, provide bonuses to employees based on the amount of time saved.

ESOP

An **employee stock ownership plan** (ESOP) is created by establishing a trust into which the business makes contributions of cash or stock that are tax deductible. Employees are then granted with the ability to purchase stock or allocate funds into individual employee accounts. The stock is held in an **employee stock ownership trust (ESOT)**, and the business can make regular contributions, typically up to 25 percent of its annual payroll. ESOPs became popular because it is believed that employees who have an ownership interest in the business will work more diligently and also have a vested interest in its efficiency and profitability. Although this logic is debatable, many studies have shown that ESOPs actually do motivate employees and support business growth.

Leave Plans and Approaches

PTO Policies

There are many different **paid time off** (PTO) policies across different businesses, industries, and geographic locations. Many of these all-encompassing PTO plans are available only to full-time employees. Whereas many companies recognize eight to 10 fixed holidays, some companies have implemented policies that provide employees with floating holidays. Trends have shown an increase in organizations of all sizes adopting a collective in which vacation, personal, sick, and sometimes holiday days are kept in a **single pool** of PTO. Many employees and employers report that having flexibility in time-off plans leads to greater employee engagement and retention. However, as more states are imposing sick time regulations, recent trends reflect a number of organizations moving back to traditional buckets of separate vacation and sick time. Additional consideration should be given to state regulations for **termination payouts**. Some states do not require employers to pay out accrued sick time, but many consider PTO pools equivalent to vacation during terminations, so employers must pay out any accrued balances. Companies must also determine whether employees will be gifted with a bank of time immediately or at a predetermined time versus **accrued**. Policies should provide details about carryover provisions and if negative balances are allowed. Having an attractive and well-administered PTO policy can give employers an advantage against growing competition for talent, evolving legal regulations, and an increasingly diverse workforce.

Holidays and Other Pay for Time Not Worked

Whereas the average number of **paid holidays** is around eight per year, most businesses will recognize the following six U.S. holidays: New Year's Day, Memorial Day, Independence Day, Labor Day, Thanksgiving Day, and Christmas Day. Additionally, a majority of employers will pay a set number of days for bereavement and jury duty for eligible employees. However, employees may be required to provide documentation. Other instances in which employees might be paid for time not worked include reporting time guaranteed for minimal work, union activities, and time to vote.

Unpaid Leave

When employees have exhausted all of PTO options and needs to take time away from work, the employer may allow them to take an unpaid leave. This leave may be classified as a personal leave or a work sabbatical. Criteria to qualify and rules that govern the leave will depend on individual firm policies. Policies will need to address items such as how to apply for the leave, length of leave allowed, benefits continuance, the employee's right to return to the same role, the process to return from a leave, and more.

Healthcare Insurance Plans

There are many forms of healthcare insurance plans, and the increasing cost of insurance has forced employers to absorb additional costs, pass more costs to employees, or find affordable alternatives. **Fee-for-service plans** allow employees to decide what services they need from any provider; fees are paid by both the employee and the employee's benefits plan through deductibles and co-insurance. **Preferred provider organization (PPO) plans** allow insurers to contract with providers of the employees choosing with lower fees and better coverage for providers within the organization; fees are paid by deductibles, co-insurance, and co-payments. **Health maintenance organization (HMO) plans** emphasize preventative care through fixed costs regardless of the number of visits, but primary care physicians (PCPs) must refer others, and no other providers are covered; fees are paid by deductibles, co-insurance, and co-payments. **Point of service (POS) plans** are similar to PPO plans with certain elements (PCP referrals) of HMO plans; fees are paid by deductibles, co-insurance, and co-payments. **Consumer-directed health plans** provide tax-favored accounts, such as an FSA or an HSA, to pay for medical expenses, and may allow employees to see any provider of their choosing. However, these plans carry high deductibles and may have low or no co-insurance after deductible is reached.

FSA

A flexible spending account (FSA) is a special account in which an individual can put money in to pay for certain out-of-pocket, non-covered health care costs. FSA users don't have to pay taxes on this money. This means the insured can save an amount equal to the taxes he or she would have paid on the money set aside. Money is placed in the account by the enrollee tax free and is taken out tax free or as tax deductible to pay for qualified medical expenses. FSAs are available only with job-based health plans. Employers and the employees themselves can make contributions to the FSA. Individuals cannot use FSA funds on insurance premiums. FSAs are set up by the employer, but funds can be added by either the employer or employee. FSAs can be used to reimburse an enrollee's—or his or her dependent's—medical, dental, and vision expenses. Funds in FSAs can be used to cover expenses related to prevention diagnosis and treatment of medical illnesses.

Eligible medical care expenses are defined by the IRS and include costs that relate to disease deterrence, diagnosis, or treatment. Expenses for solely cosmetic reasons generally are not expenses for medical care and are not reimbursable. These include procedures and services such as liposuction or Botox treatments and are therefore not eligible under an FSA. Ineligible expenses also include contact lenses and personal trainers, for example. Eligible expenses do, however, include things like service or guide animals and acupuncture. Employees can also open dependent care FSAs, which allow them to use pretax dollars to pay for dependent care, like day care.

The IRS determines FSA contribution limits annually. The main drawback to the FSA is that it requires careful budgeting as there is a lose-or-use provision attached to the benefit. If employees do not use the funds within an account during the given plan year, they may lose the money. Exceptions to this are when the employer opts to offer a grace period (granting an additional 2.5 months to use the funds) or a carryover provision (limited to $500). Employers are not required to offer either and can offer only one of the two. They may also offer a run-out period, which gives employees an additional 90 days to make claims for reimbursement.

HSA

The health savings account (HSA) is an individual, tax-advantaged account, and funds can be deposited by both the employee and employer. The funds added to this account are then used to pay medical expenses not covered by the high deductible health plan (HDHP), including the deductible. An HDHP is a health insurance plan that meets federal guidelines in three benefit areas—deductible, out-of-pocket maximum, and first-dollar coverage. These amounts are adjusted each calendar year by the IRS.

Health Savings Accounts (HSAs) have been growing steadily in popularity since their introduction in 2003 as part of the Medicare, Prescription Drug, Improvement and Modernization Act. This health insurance product consists of two parts: the individual HSA and an HDHP. The HDHP is like a traditional health plan, but its unique feature is that it has higher deductibles giving the insured a higher financial stake and financial incentive in healthcare decisions. Federal law says individuals can open an HSA only if they are enrolled in an HDHP and are not enrolled in other forms of low-deductible health insurance.

The HSA offers a triple tax advantage. The money is not taxed going into the account. If the money is invested and increases in value, those gains are not taxed. And, withdrawals are not taxed so long as employees use them for qualified medical expenses. In addition, an HSA does not have any use-or-lose provision, and funds may be carried over from year to year. Like an FSA, however, there is an annual contribution limit, which the IRS announces each year.

Other Benefits

Workers' Compensation

Workers' compensation provides employees with coverage of medical expenses and a continuation of income for individuals who sustain work-related injuries. The basic concept makes compensation and expenses the employer's responsibility without liability or fault to the employee, assuming that the employee has adhered to reasonable safety precautions. Each state administers its own **workers' compensation** per state and federal laws. There are **three types of benefits** awarded to employees: medical expenses, wage replacement payments, and death benefits. The wage replacement payments are often calculated based upon an employee's average weekly wages and become available after a waiting period. Costs are determined by an experience rating based upon an employer's claim history.

Unemployment Compensation

Unemployment compensation is a national program that is regulated by the IRS as the **Federal Unemployment Tax Act (FUTA)** to provide workers with short-term sustenance while they are looking for new employment. Employers pay FUTA as a payroll tax at a rate of 6.2 percent. Although a majority of the administration is held at the state level, the federal government also administers the programs. FUTA applies to all employers who either employ one or more employees or pay wages greater than $1,500 in any quarter of a calendar year. Employees typically receive about half of their former weekly wages; however, each state regulates the amount and duration of benefits. Eligibility requirements require that individuals be available and readily seeking new employment opportunities, which they must record and present upon request. The company costs vary depending upon the employer's experience rating, which is based on prior claims receiving payments.

Cafeteria Plans

IRS section 125 defines a **cafeteria plan** as a defined employer plan providing participants the opportunity to receive certain benefits on a pretax basis. Funds allocated to these benefits are not included as wages for state or federal income tax purposes and are generally exempt from Federal Insurance Contributions Act (FICA) and FUTA. Qualified benefits under these plans might include the following:

- **Medical healthcare coverage**—plans may include some or all portions of physician services, office visits and exams, prescription drugs, hospital services, maternity services, mental health, physical therapy, and emergency services.
- **Dental coverage**—plans may include some or all portions of routine exams, cleanings, X-rays, fluoride treatments, orthodontic services, fillings, crowns, and extractions.
- **Dependent care**—plans may cover some or all portions of on-site childcare, allowances and flexible spending for childcare, day-care information, or flexible scheduling.
- **Short-term disability**—this provides partial income continuation to employees who are unable to work for a short period of time (three to six months) due to an accident or illness.
- **Long-term disability**—this provides partial income continuation to employees who are unable to work for long periods of time (greater than three to six months) due to an accident or illness.
- **Group-term life insurance and accidental death or dismemberment**—this provides financial assistance to an employee or his or her beneficiaries if the employee has an accident that results in the loss of limbs, loss of eyesight, or death. The cost of group plans is frequently lower than individual plans, and payments are based upon the employee's age and annual salary.

Disability Insurance

Disability income insurance is divided into two categories: short-term disability (STD) and **long-term disability (LTD)**. These private insurance plans replace a portion of employees' wages if they are out of work due to an injury or illness. Contrary to workers' compensation, the injury or illness does not need to be work related to qualify for STD or LTD. Many employers offer disability insurance benefits on a fully paid, partially paid, or ancillary basis. Employers should check state regulations to determine if they are required to provide partial wage replacement insurance coverage to eligible employees. STD typically runs for 90 to 180 days, providing employees with 60 to 75 percent wage replacement following a short waiting period. LTD kicks in after STD is exhausted. Depending on the plan, the LTD coverage may last 24–36 months or run until employees can return to work (whether for the same company or a new one) or until they are old enough to collect retirement or they are able to collect social security disability.

Employee Wellness Programs

Many companies have begun to implement **employee wellness programs** to encourage employees to take preventative measures and avoid illness and accidents. The level of employee wellness programs varies greatly. Some may include physical examinations to assess health and health education to teach nutrition or healthy habits, whereas others might be intended to assist with smoking cessation, but almost all employee wellness programs will include some element of weight management. Moreover, the Patient Protection and Affordable Care Act allows employers to **reward** employees for participating in wellness programs, such as covering a higher percentage of premiums for employees who comply with wellness program requirements like having annual physical examinations and attending trainings. However, rewards should be based only upon participation and not achieving health objectives.

Employee Assistance Programs

Employee assistance programs (**EAPs**) help employees with personal problems, such as seeking guidance through a substance abuse problem and obtaining counsel referrals during a marital separation. An EAP may be categorized as a **welfare plan** and require reports be filed with the Department of Labor and IRS if it provides counseling for substance abuse, stress, anxiety, depression, or similar health and mental problems. Moreover, these programs may be required to comply with reporting and disclosure requirements of the **Employee Retirement Income Security Act (ERISA)**. EAPs must adhere to strict guidelines to avoid legal risks regarding privacy, malpractice, or coercion.

Family and Flex Benefits Programs

In recent years, employees have come to expect benefits that promote work–life balance and support families. To that end, an increasing number of employers offer telecommuting, flex time, and compressed work week options to help workers juggle all of life's different demands. In addition, many workplaces now offer benefits like paid parental leave and designated lactation rooms, making it easier on new parents. Additionally, some employers have started offering paid caregiver leave, which allows workers to care for parents and other relatives without worrying about their paychecks.

Pensions or Retirement Plans

Pensions and company retirement plans fund an individual's retirement by providing deferred payments for prior services. These accounts may be funded by the employer through a variety of means. Retirement benefits are accumulated by the total amount contributed plus interest and market earnings. These **defined contribution benefit plans** are the traditional company-provided plans, such as 401(k)s, 403(b)s, Simplified Employee Pensions (SEPs), SIMPLEs, and IRAs. A defined contribution benefit plan requires separate accounts for each employee participant, and funds are most often contributed by both the employee and the employer. Some employers will implement an auto-enroll policy in which new employees are automatically enrolled and minimum contributions to the plan are withheld from payroll. The contribution rates may even automatically increase on an annual basis. However, the **Pension Protection Act of 2006** provides employees with a 90-day window to opt out of these plans and recover any funds contributed on their behalf.

Social Security

The Social Security Act was first implemented to force workers into saving a fraction of earnings for retirement and making employers obligated to match those funds. These funds are now withheld as a portion of the **Federal Insurance Contributions Act (FICA) payroll taxes** and regulated by the IRS. The benefits have since been extended to cover four types of **insurance benefits**:

1. **Old age or disability benefits**—for workers who retire or become unable to work due to disability, based upon eligibility requirements
2. **Benefits for dependents of retired, disabled, or deceased workers**—paid to certain dependents
3. **Lump-sum death benefits**—paid to the worker's survivors
4. **Medicare**—healthcare protection provided to individuals age 65 and older, consisting of Parts A, B, and D

Total Compensation Statements

Total compensation statements show employees the overall value of their compensation and benefits package. In general, the more benefits included in the statement, the better. However, human resources should ensure that the following are highlighted: year-to-date pay, paid time off, retirement, and insurance. The point of issuing the statement is to demonstrate that the employee gets much more than their base salary and that the employer is making a significant investment in their well-being.

Total Rewards Metrics and Benchmarks

Compensation as a percentage of operating expense: total compensation/total operating expense X 100

Benefits as a percentage of operating expense: total benefits cost/total operating expense X 100

Employee burden: the total cost to employ someone, taking into consideration pay, benefits, and taxes

Utilization review: an audit to ensure the accuracy of the healthcare provider's billing

Human Resources Expertise: People Chapter Quiz

1. How many types of waste are identified in Lean Six Sigma?

a. Seven
b. Five
c. Six
d. Eight

2. Which of the following is a form of project management that reduces the likelihood of the project's completion being delayed?

a. Critical chain
b. IPO model
c. Systems thinking
d. Agile

3. What does a diamond typically indicate on a Gantt chart?

a. Progress
b. Anticipated time for completing each task
c. Dependencies
d. Milestones

4. A work breakdown structure is based on which rule?

a. 80/20 rule
b. 50/50 rule
c. 30/60/90 rule
d. 100 percent rule

5. How many forces are included in Michael Porter's model of competition?

a. Three
b. Four
c. Five
d. Two

6. Which of the following is an extension of the SWOT analysis?

a. PESTLE
b. MORTAR
c. FORCE
d. Growth-share matrix

7. Which of the following laws separates employees into two main categories: exempt and nonexempt?

a. Bifurcation of Exemption Clause
b. Occupational Safety and Health Act
c. Equal Employment Opportunity Act
d. Fair Labor Standards Act

8. How many basic principles of selection that influence the process of making an informed hiring decision are there?

a. Five
b. Four
c. Three
d. Two

9. Which of the following validities assesses the skills and knowledge necessary to perform the tasks associated with a particular position?

a. Construct validity
b. Concurrent validity
c. Criterion validity
d. Content validity

10. A high-performance culture

a. Promotes goal achievement by setting clear objectives, clearly spelling out employee responsibilities, encouraging continuous development, and fostering trust
b. Features open communication and shared power
c. Aims to use knowledge, abilities, and innovation to adapt to an ever-changing business environment
d. Is characterized by organization, specialization, and strong guidance from leadership

Human Resources Expertise: Organization

Structure of the Human Resources Function

Operational Integration and Alignment of Human Resources Management

Human resource policies direct organizational procedures and actions toward integrated goals and objectives. **Human resource policies** are meant to guarantee consistency while assuring employees that they are to be treated fairly, assisting managers with making consistent and at times quick decisions, and providing with confidence problem resolution and the ability to support conclusions. Human resource practitioners and managers must ensure that core goals and objectives are aligned and integrated with **operational standards**. It is also important to maintain organizational culture and compliance procedures. **Operational integration** should take place throughout human resource recruitment, selection, employee relations, communications, and legal requirements. For example, some businesses have stricter policies for reporting to work during inclement weather, more inclusive policies around diversity and inclusion, or learning and development initiatives. Human resource policies and operational practices should be integrated and aligned with the organizational culture to support the **organizational mission**.

Key Elements of Human Resources

There are many elements to the **human resource business function**. Some key elements include the following:

- **Recruiting**—sourcing, interviewing, hiring, and onboarding new employees
- **Organizational culture**—collection of values, norms, and attitudes that support the vision
- **Employee relations**—evaluations, performance management, and grievances
- **Compensation and payroll**—wage earnings, tax withholdings, benefits deductions, and direct deposit processing
- **Benefits**—enrollment and education for medical, dental, vision, life, 401(k), and so on
- **Policy creation, communication, and distribution**—researching, drafting, disseminating, discussing, and enforcing employment-related policies such as cell phone use and attendance
- **Legal compliance**—maintaining records for employment eligibility, taxes, safety, and licensure
- **Training and development**—providing necessary information or continuing education
- **Health and safety**—reviewing practices, reporting incidents, and posting logs
- **Change management**—planning, communicating, and stabilizing changes within the company

Human Resource Models

Centralized and Decentralized Decision-Making

Whereas both centralization and decentralization guide how the delegation of authority is distributed throughout an organization, they differ greatly in practice and functionality. **Highly centralized firms** are narrow and prefer to control the decision-making process at the top executive levels. **Decentralized firms** are wide, providing more autonomy and responsibility to middle and lower hierarchical-level staff, allowing for more active involvement from an increased number of employees. The amount of authority delegated will vary greatly between highly centralized and highly decentralized organizations. Many companies practice some level of decentralization and might impose internal operating procedures or standards for integration and control.

Centralized human resources is often known as corporate human resources. The function resides at the corporate level, where department members set consistent policies and standards for the entire firm. The main drawback of **centralized human resources** is that it can be too rigid and not account for the nuances of individual company locations. **Decentralized human resources**, on the other hand, is the human resources function being housed at the local level. Because each site will be able to create policies and standards that work best for them, there will be little consistency among locations. This can be problematic for employees who transfer from one part of the firm to another. In addition, having multiple sets of rules and procedures is inefficient for the company as a whole. The main benefit to decentralized human resources is that each site can quickly be responsive to its own needs. Many large organizations use a blend of these two approaches. There is an overarching corporate human resource group that sets some universal standards, and, local human resource departments have some latitude when providing service to their employee groups.

Center of Excellence (COE) Human Resources Model

A **COE HR model** features internal groups of consultants that have expertise in the different human resource functional areas, like payroll and benefits. Their main role is to provide each firm location with best practice-driven guidance and assistance with problem-solving. Generally, business units must utilize this in-house resource before seeking external help.

Shared Services Human Resources Model

Some larger organizations have begun to centralize certain business functions into **shared service centers**, such as finance, information technology, or human resources. Shared services are essentially the merging and streamlining of business operations that are used by multiple units of the same organization. This helps business units retain more control and identifies ways to work more efficiently, improving service quality and the credibility of each function. For example, a human resources shared services center may process all employment-related changes for an entire enterprise within the company's human resource information system (HRIS) at the request of human resources staff at each location.

Human Resource Function Metrics

Human Resource Staff Per Full Time Employee (FTE)

To calculate this ratio: (number of human resource FTEs / number of total FTEs) x 100.

This ratio allows for the comparison of staffing levels among firms. In general, larger organizations employ more human resource professionals to meet the needs of employees and to build a human resource infrastructure that supports business goals while mitigating risk.

Human Resources Customer Satisfaction

The human resource function is one of service. Every day, human resource professionals must assist both job candidates and employees with a variety of issues. To do this effectively, they must internalize a service mind-set, view each person that they interact with as a customer, and ensure that each interaction is respectful and helpful. To determine the satisfaction level of their customers and find areas for improvement, human resources should periodically solicit feedback about the service that they render.

Key Performance Indicators

Key performance indicators (**KPIs**) measure specific human resource activities that contribute to the efficiency and effectiveness of a company. KPIs provide a company with quantitative measurements that can be used to examine qualities and actions that contribute to long-term success. KPIs and human resource metrics are evaluated and interpreted by leading and lagging indicators. **Leading indicators** anticipate, precede, and predict future performance. For example, a leading indicator could be foreseeing the amount of time to fill key role vacancies to ensure a qualified and efficient workforce. **Lagging indicators** measure the result of a process or change and often gain more consideration because they analyze revenues that executives use to measure success. Human resource scorecards and dashboards present metrics and KPIs to executives in a simplified, useful format. Many are designed to reflect four main perspectives: **strategic**, to measure initiative progress or achievement; **operational**, to measure process effectiveness; **financial**, to measure contributions and sustainability; and **stakeholder**, to measure internal and external customers.

Balanced Scorecards

The expectations of all stockholders, customers, and employees must be satisfied for a company to be sustainable and profitable. A **balanced scorecard** reflects the vision and strategy for this success from the financial outlook, customer perspectives, and internal business processes. Understanding how vision and strategy lead to measurable goals and objectives is especially important for startup businesses seeking investment opportunities. If a scorecard reports that one of these stakeholders is not being satisfied, the company must attempt to realign expectations and correct behaviors to bring stakeholders back on board. Human resources should be included in the design of the balanced scorecard and should help choose what metrics are covered. Common human resource metrics on a balanced scorecard pertain to staffing and training. They may include turnover rate, time to fill, training completion percentage, and so on.

Human Resource Staff Roles or Titles

The following are some of the major human resource staff roles or titles and their levels of responsibility. Of course, the scope of each title varies from company to company, usually based on the size of the firm.

- **Human resource specialist/administrator/coordinator**: members of a department in the earlier stages of their careers who specialize in a particular human resource function, such as talent acquisition, compensation, benefits administration, employee relations, or human resource systems.
- **Human resources generalist/manager**: leaders of a department who are experienced, knowledgeable, and required to understand all of the major human resource functions.
- **Human resources business partner/director**: divisional managers who take on a strategic partnership with leadership and corporate officers to align human resource functions with company goals.

Outsourcing

Outsourcing is the process of contracting with outside specialists to perform selected human resource functions. Businesses may **outsource** some or all of their human resource functions, such as payroll, benefits, or recruiting. The specialists who conduct human resource functions in this relationship are not employees of the business but most likely employees of the company providing the outsourcing service. The value of outsourcing is that it allows managers to focus on more core business matters and decisions, whereas the legal reporting and responsibilities often fall to the company performing the tasks. However, outsourcing can be expensive to implement.

Organizational Effectiveness and Development

Application of Behavioral Assessments

Behavioral and personality assessments can be used for employee development or to evaluate the characteristics of candidates that might factor into job performance. There are thousands of **behavioral and personality assessments** available on the market. Vendors should be able to provide documentation that reflects reliability, what the test is designed to measure, what behaviors it is intended to predict, and where supporting data can be found. When being used for employee development or motivation, behavioral and personality assessments can be used to diagnose dominant traits or behaviors and which may be easy or difficult to change.

Intragroup Dynamics

Group Formation Theories

There are a few group formation theories, including **propinquity or proximity theory** (based on geography), **exchange or benefit theory** (based on rewards), **balance theory** (based on similar attitudes or interests), and **activity theory** (based on occupational task). **Formal groups** might come in three main forms: **command groups** (like the departments on an organizational chart), **task groups** (working collaboratively toward a common task), and **functional groups** (created to accomplish specific goals and objectives for an unspecified period of time). Groups are often formed to achieve a particular task or goal. During the group-forming phase of group development, the group learns about group members and the group task. Members may choose to join a group for a sense of stability or to develop self-esteem. Groups can also foster feelings of power, status, or affiliation.

Group Development Stages

The five stages of group development developed by Bruce Tuckman are as follows:

- **Forming**—this entails superficial introductions and determining boundaries of acceptable behavior.
- **Storming**—this is the most difficult stage. The team must work through conflicts related to authority, vision and values, personality, and cultural differences. The amount of work often seems overwhelming at this point, and team members struggle to listen to the opinions and experiences of others. If quality improvement processes are implemented and there is good communication, however, these barriers can become beneficial later on.
- **Norming**—this entails greater cooperation and more cohesion as the team establishes norms for assignment completion, decision-making, and conflict resolution. There are three parts to norming: reducing conflicts as the team becomes more relaxed; developing a routine through scheduled events, such as meetings; and facilitating cooperation through team-building events.
- **Performing**—this involves effective and unified team performance as the team addresses its objectives. Conflicts are mostly resolved, and the team has a clear purpose and structure.
- **Adjourning**—this is the process of ending the group. Group members say goodbye to each other. Good closure is important.

Group Cohesion

Cohesion may be influenced by similar traits or interests, attraction, shared commitment, and ability to trust. **Task cohesion** defines how well a group works together to accomplish goals, whereas **social cohesion** defines the sense of belonging held by members of the group. Establishing an organizational culture that promotes cohesion allows members of the group to work collaboratively and collectively as one while promoting positive feelings about activities. There can be advantages and disadvantages of cohesion. Advantages might include better quality and quantity of work, increased effectiveness, and increased engagement. Disadvantages might include greater likelihood of groupthink, ignoring ideas that deviate from group norms, and the chance of counterproductive ideas spreading.

Intergroup Dynamics

Intergroup conflict refers to a clash between two or more teams, groups, or departments. This occurs when there are expressions of hostility or intentional interfering with an opposing group's activities. Some causes of **intergroup conflict** might include competition for resources, opposing viewpoints, lack of adaptation to environmental change, or task interdependence regarding the coordination of work. Intergroup conflict is often separated into functional or dysfunctional. **Functional conflicts** may produce enhanced organizational performance as a result of alternative solutions. **Dysfunctional conflicts** often have a negative impact on organizational performance. Due to the disruptive nature, management must address and eliminate dysfunctional conflict when reported or observed. Mediation techniques of communicating and channeling energies, expertise, or resources of the conflicting groups may help negotiate solutions and the attainment of organizational goals.

Organizational Design Structures

Customer Organizational Structure

Often seen in health care, this structure is utilized by firms that provide a service. It organizes departments to provide specialized solutions to different customer segments. Although this structure can provide exemplary customer care, it can pose problems for the organization. Each customer division will have its own rules and processes that can lead to duplication of efforts or conflicting systems.

Functional Organizational Structure

This structure organizes firm departments based on their function or what they do for the company. Manufacturing, customer service, and human resources are just a few functional departments that may be in this type of common organizational structure. This vertical structure works best when decision-making power is centralized. This structure promotes the development of experts in their fields, ensures employees work in their areas of expertise, and is easy to understand. However, there is little in the way of cross-department collaboration, and enacting change may be difficult.

Divisional Organizational Structure

This structure organizes the business based on the firm's different product lines, services, brands, or markets. A **divisional organizational structure** is vertical, and like the functional structure, promotes specialization and expertise. However, there is some collaboration within each division, making the structure less siloed. This structure also features faster decision-making as each division has a leadership team. Although there is coordination within divisions, each division stands alone and is concerned chiefly with its own operations. This leads to duplication of efforts across the firm, hoarding of resources by each division, and potential competition for customers among divisions. In addition, because each division orders its own supplies, the firm could miss out on the better pricing other companies may get for purchasing for the whole organization.

Matrix Organizational Structure

Many organizations facing uncertain environments find that **combining functional and product departmentalization** increases coordination and reporting relationships. This dual, two-dimensional organizational structure supports the organization in achieving goals by dividing focus to gain simultaneous advantages. Employees or departments will report to both product and functional managers that are responsible for performance. One manager may be more administrative or focused on a core business unit such as human resources, information technology (IT), or finance, whereas the other is typically involved with product, service, customer, or location. For example, a systems developer might report to a project manager as well as an IT manager, or a payroll integration specialist might report to a project manager and finance manager. The **matrix organizational structure** is best for uncertain environments that deal with constantly changing products and/or a strong focus on the customer experience. Matrix organizations support functional and divisional partnership, focusing on work and minimizing costs. Technical expertise is paired with marketplace responsiveness. However, reporting relationships may cause confusion, resulting in increased stress and lower performance levels. Functional leaders and product leaders must cooperate to determine priorities and standards.

Geographic Organizational Structure

A type of divisional structure, the firm organizes their business functions or departments based on their geographic location.

Contribution of Efficiency and Effectiveness to Organizational Structure

All organizations must be efficient to be effective. **Efficiency** describes inputs and outputs or how well a company creates products or services from materials and energy resources. **Effectiveness** describes the entire cycle of acquiring inputs, transforming them into useful products or services, selling these products or services to the market, and gaining more inputs. Effectiveness includes the efficiency of internal processes or procedures and how well the company interacts with its environment to win public acceptance. Organizational structure addresses two main concerns: differentiation and integration. **Differentiation** describes how work is divided into specialized jobs. **Integration** describes how to coordinate the work that has been divided. Organizational structure can also be influenced by **five designs**: departmentalization, delegation of authority, span of control, division of labor, and coordinating mechanisms.

Workforce Management

Stages of Human Resource Workforce Planning

Human resource planning systems should support an organization's business plans. Businesses must have the precise blend of knowledge, skills, and abilities among employees. **Human resource planning** can be separated into three forecasting periods: short range (less than one year), middle range (two to five years), and long range (five to 10 years). **Short-range planning** involves projecting workforce staffing requirements. **Middle-range planning** involves a mix of both short- and long-term forecasting. **Long-range planning** requires more strategic analysis and environmental scanning. The supreme test of a human resource planning system is whether it provides the right number of qualified employees at the right time.

Long-Term Forecasting Techniques for Planning Employment Needs

Long-term forecasting often covers a time frame of two to 10 years and is reviewed on an annual basis for adjustment. There are many techniques for **long-term forecasting,** such as unit demand, probabilistic models and simulations, or trend projections and regression analysis. One example of the **probabilistic forecasting** is a **Markov analysis**, which tracks the movement of employees among different job classifications to forecast the movement among departments, operating units, salary levels, or from one category to another. **Expert opinions** may also be considered. The **Delphi technique** consists of having experts provide their best estimates of future needs based on questionnaires and interviews. An intermediary will collect results and provide a summary or report to the experts. If an expert feels differently than the findings of the group, he or she is asked to justify his or her views so the intermediary can revise and redistribute reports.

Demographic Forces That Influence the Labor Market

There are a number of demographic forces that influence the labor market; a few of the most notable include birth rates, education, immigration, and participation rates. Since the baby boomers, **birth rates** have stayed relatively low, and many are anticipating a shortage of skilled workers in the United States now that the baby boomers are preparing for retirement. Moreover, **educational disparity** is increasing despite the number of high school students going to college. Dropout rates have increased, limiting job opportunities for a large percentage of the workforce due to increasing technologies. Those who do pursue an education are seeking more advanced professional training and degrees. Additionally, many **immigrants** provide large applicant pools at both ends of the spectrum. Many Hispanic workers from Mexico and Central America flee due to difficult economic and political reasons and provide farmhand or harvesting assistance in much of the Southwest, whereas employers might seek and provide immigration assistance to those highly skilled in areas such as technology, science, and medicine. Finally, the **participation rates** for men and women have changed dramatically in the past century. Male participation rates have declined in every age group, whereas female participation rates have increased in every age group.

Workforce Analysis

A workforce analysis is required in most affirmative action plans. This analysis results in a **workforce profile** that conveys the talent, knowledge, and skills of the current workforce. The first step is conducting an examination of the **demographics** in the current workforce. Then, a **gap and risk analysis** can be performed to determine any vulnerability. Anticipated changes to how work is performed and how advances in technology can have an effect are documented. Finally, future talent needs can be forecasted. Workforce profile data can be obtained voluntarily or through publicly reported statistics and census results. Workforce profiles calculate employee traits such as age, experience level, average education in the field, as well as status changes as active, full time, part time, or temporary. These might be reported per department, salary band, or as a whole.

Analytical Steps for Evaluating Labor Supply and Demand

Human resource practitioners must understand and follow the ever-changing labor market and talent supply, which can be influenced by the state of the economy, competitors, technology, new regulations, and other factors. Strategic workforce planning evaluates the ability to sustain future needs so the organization can function accordingly. There are four analytical steps in **workforce planning**:

1. The **supply model analysis**, which reviews an organization's current labor supply
2. The **demand model analysis**, which estimates future business plans and objectives
3. The **gap analysis**, which compares the variances in the supply and demand models to identify skill surpluses and deficiencies
4. The **solution analysis**, which focuses on how to tackle gaps in current and future staffing needs through recruiting, training and development, contingent staffing, or outsourcing

Approaches to Restructuring

Restructuring During Mergers and Acquisitions

Human resource and change management professionals are often called upon to provide consultation during **mergers and acquisitions**. This involvement should start at the beginning and carry throughout the integration. Human resource experts ordinarily investigate factors like employee benefit plans, compensation programs, employment contracts, and organizational culture. Experience and many studies have shown that issues with people and culture are the most frequent cause of failure in most mergers and acquisitions. Human resource departments must play an active role in these transitions, and there should be a unified purpose and message from each of the previous units. These steps have been established for joining two companies:

1. Develop a workforce integration project plan.
2. Conduct a human resource due diligence review.
3. Compare benefits programs.
4. Compare the compensation structures.
5. Develop a compensation and benefits strategy for integrating the workforce. Any reduction in pay or benefits must be explained and justified relative to the strategy or economic conditions. It's best to minimize changes and act quickly.
6. Determine leadership assignments.
7. Eliminate redundant functions. The best people should be retained, and the remainder should be laid off, with careful consideration given to avoid adverse impact and Worker Adjustment and Retraining Notification (WARN) Act violations.

Restructuring Through Downsizing

Restructuring through downsizing happens when a firm needs to reduce the number of layers of management to increase efficiency or respond to changes in corporate strategy. This downsizing can occur via layoffs or early retirement agreements.

Conducting a Layoff or Reduction in Force

The following are the steps for conducting a layoff or reduction in force:

1. Select employees for layoff using seniority, performance, job classification, location, or skill.
2. Ensure selected employees do not affect a protected class to avoid adverse or disparate impact.
3. Review compliance with federal and state WARN Act regulations, which require employers to provide 60 days' notice to affected employees while specifying whether the reduction in force is permanent or for a specified amount of time.
4. Review compliance with the Older Workers Benefit Protection Act that provides workers over the age of 40 the opportunity to review any severance agreements that require their waiver of discrimination claims. The act allows a consideration period of 21 days if only one older worker is being separated and 45 days when two or more older workers are being separated. They also must receive a revocation period of seven days after signing the agreement. Additionally, they must be informed of the positions and ages of the other employees affected by the layoffs so that they can assess whether or not they feel age discrimination has taken place.
5. Determine if severance packages including salary continuation, vacation pay, employer-paid Consolidated Omnibus Budget Reconciliation Act (COBRA) premiums, outplacement services, or counseling might be available to affected employees.
6. Be empathetic, have tissues, ensure that all required documentation is available to the employee, and review all information in detail when conducting meetings with employees.
7. Inform the current workforce by communicating sustainability concerns, methods used to determine who would be selected for the reduction in force, and commitment to meeting company goals and objectives to maintain morale and productivity.

Risks and Alternatives to a Layoff or Reduction in Force

Most importantly, remember that it could be considered illegal retaliation to consider any past grievances, complaints, claims, or leave requests in the selection process if a reduction in force is necessary. To ensure fairness and avoid risk exposure, **selection criteria** should include measurable data such as seniority, merit or skill set, full- or part-time status, location, job categories, or prior disciplinary actions. Reductions in force are commonly due to financial strains on the organization. Thus, the goal is to reduce human capital costs by a percentage or specified dollar amount. Some measures that can be introduced as an **alternative to a reduction in force** include eliminating overtime, freezing or reducing compensation, introducing reduced work hours, cutting perks, increasing employees' share of benefit costs, and imposing a hiring freeze.

High-Potential Development Programs

High-potential development programs offer targeted training and other enrichment opportunities to the firm's best and brightest employees. These programs should serve as career road maps, cultivating leadership skills and allowing employees to take on meaningful work so that they can see their impact. Some components of this program may include challenging assignments to promote professional growth, opportunities to mentor others, access to on-demand learning modules, and invitations to networking events both in and out of the firm. To ensure the program's success, participating employees must receive regular and detailed feedback about their performance. Done well, a high-potential development program enables firms to get the best ROI from their staff while keeping them engaged and attracting new waves of high-potential employees for the future.

Succession Planning

Succession planning is a method of planning how management and executive vacancies will be filled so a company has highly trained replacements available to fill available vacancies. First, determine what the requirements are for key positions and create profiles that outline responsibilities. The experience, education, career progress, and future career interests of managerial candidates should also be reviewed. Then, the performance of prospective managers should be assessed to determine whether they are promotable or not and identify developmental objectives to prepare for advancement opportunities. Performance should be evaluated based upon traditional goals and standards. Developmental objectives might include seminars, training programs, special projects, or temporary assignments.

Attrition

Attrition, or **restrictive hiring**, is the act of reducing the workforce by not replacing individuals who leave an organization. Only absolutely essential roles that are critical to strategic business success are filled. Typically, attrition is used to avoid layoffs during times of financial burden. A **hiring freeze** is the least painful way to reduce labor costs. A **hard freeze** means that all open positions will remain open indefinitely, whereas a **soft freeze** means that only nonessential roles will remain open.

Employee and Labor Relations

Types and Structures of Organized Labor

Labor unions can be divided into three levels: local unions, national or international unions, and the federation of unions. **Local unions** often represent a group of employees working for a particular employer or in a single geographical area. These unions frequently tend to have a great deal of direct contact with members, and members rely more heavily on the union for economic support, social interaction, and political power. The business representative and union steward are the most important positions within local unions. The **business representative** performs a critical role in contract negotiations, grievance proceedings, and managing union headquarters. The **union steward** represents member interests and relations with a company. **National and international unions** are collections of local unions, frequently in the same industry and having their own constitution and establishing rules. The American Federation of Labor (AFL) organized union workers and later joined with the Congress of Industrial Organizations (CIO) to form the AFL-CIO, a large and powerful **federation of labor unions** that represents millions of workers.

National Labor Relations Board

The National Labor Relations Board (**NLRB**) was founded by Congress as part of the Wagner Act to defend and protect the rights of employees, employers, unions, and the general public. The NLRB has two major functions: resolving unfair labor practices and conducting representation elections. One division of the NLRB consists of a five-member board, appointed by the president to five-year terms, that hears and decides cases that involve unfair labor practices and disputed elections. They review many cases each year, but only few incite the notion of a severe error or involve precedent-making concerns. The other division consists of a general counsel also appointed by the president and approved by Congress that oversees a large staff of employees over many regional offices. Each regional office has a director who supervises labor attorneys and field examiners. The field examiners might investigate unfair labor practices or conduct elections, whereas attorneys can do the same and also appear in court actions.

Similarities and Differences Between the NLRB and the Federal Labor Relations Council

The Federal Labor Relations Council conducts some of the same functions as the NLRB but for **federal employees**. The council establishes the composition of bargaining units, orders and supervises elections, disqualifies elections due to undemocratic or corrupt actions, and decides charges for unfair labor practices. Many of the guidelines created by the NLRB have been adopted by the Federal Labor Relations Council. For example, if a group of federal employees wanted to organize a union, they would need a majority to vote in favor of union representation through confidential ballot elections. Furthermore, the union must represent all employees in the bargaining unit; however, membership cannot be required as a condition of employment.

Employment Rights and Standards

The International Labour Organization (ILO) was founded in 1919 to address global working conditions. A part of the United Nations, the ILO is comprised of 187 member states. Their mission is to promote decent working conditions that include eliminating child labor, ending unlawful discrimination, protecting human rights, and supporting worker rights to organize. They extensively research compensation practices and advocate for a living wage for all. A living wage is pay that can cover a decent standard of living for the worker's household. Going a step further, they also push for a fair wage, which uses the living wage as the foundation but is adjusted for a given country's pay laws (such as overtime), any collective bargaining involved, and the skill and performance of the worker. The ILO has also championed the standard eight-hour workday, recognizing that overworked employees can experience negative health and safety outcomes. Although not every country adopts every ILO standard and practice, research from the ILO sets the tone for the discussion and aims to keep advancing working conditions for the world's employees.

Unfair Labor Practices

The National Labor Relations Act (NLRA) identifies five types of employer practices that should be considered unfair labor practices. First, it establishes that it is unfair for an employer to interfere in the activities of a union or prevent employees from taking any action related to forming or joining a union. Second, it establishes that it is unfair for an employer to take any action that would allow the organization to control a union or offer special attention or preferential treatment to a particular union. Third, it establishes that it is unfair for an employer to discriminate against any employee because he or she is a member of a union or takes part in any lawful union activity. Fourth, it establishes that it is unfair for an employer to discriminate against any employee because he or she has filed charges with the NLRB or has taken part in any investigation. Fifth, it establishes that it is unfair for an employer to refuse to bargain with a union representing the employer's employees.

Filing a Charge with the NLRB

Unfair labor practices are prohibited actions by law or **NLRB** ruling taken by either the union or management. First, charges of unfair labor practices must be filed within six months of the alleged practice and can be submitted in person or via mail. Then, a preliminary NLRB investigation by regional offices will be assigned to a field examiner or attorney, and either a formal complaint may be issued to the general counsel or the case may be disposed of through withdrawal, settlement, or dismissal. The general counsel may dismiss the case or move forward to a formal hearing. After the NLRB issues a decision, dissatisfied parties may appeal; however, this process can be lengthy and take many years.

LMRA

The **Labor Management Relations Act (LMRA)**, also known as the **Taft-Hartley Act**, identifies a number of union practices that should be considered unfair labor practices. First, the LMRA establishes that it is unfair for a union to force an employee to join or take part in a union or force an employee to accept a particular representative. Second, it establishes that it is unfair for a union to refuse to bargain with the representative of an employer or restrict the ability of an employer to negotiate a contract and enforce that contract. Third, it establishes that it is unfair for a union to call for an employer to discriminate against employees that are not part of a particular union or that speak out against a union. Fourth, it establishes that it is unfair for a union to encourage individuals outside the organization to take part in a secondary boycott or encourage employers to enter into a hot cargo agreement. Finally, the LMRA establishes that it is unfair for a union to charge unreasonably high membership fees.

Organization of a Union

If employees wish to **organize a union**, they must follow the procedures established by the NLRB to hold benign and diplomatic **elections**. The first step involves filing and obtaining at least 30 percent of the workers in a company to sign **authorization cards** requesting union representation. Once 30 percent of workers have expressed interest, they can petition the NLRB for a representation election. The NLRB will then investigate on four main conditions: 1) whether the company exceeds a certain revenue and falls under jurisdiction, 2) who should represent the workers, 3) whether there is a minimum of 30 percent support of a union by the workers, and 4) if there are any election bars, such as another petition filed within the past year. The **Excelsior rule** requires that the employer must file an election eligibility list that contains the names and addresses of eligible voters that are within seven days of the regional director's approval of a consent election.

Defensive Tools Used by Employers

There are many defensive tools employers use for anti-union tactics, such as the conspiracy doctrine, court injunctions, yellow-dog contracts, and anti-trust statutes. Although heavily debated in early years, the **conspiracy doctrine** is used when employers charge that labor unions are illegally conspiring in restraint of trade. Court findings have ruled that labor unions may be found guilty of conspiracy if objectives or the methods used to achieve objectives are illegal, but the actions of collectively striking or bargaining to raise wages are not illegal. **Court injunctions** are judge-issued orders against a person or group of people to cease the pursuit of a particular action, often to protect property rights from irreparable damages. Violation of an injunction can result in being found in contempt of court and carry heavy penalties including heavy fines or imprisonment. Court injunctions have been frequently used to enforce **yellow-dog contracts**, which are written statements employers required workers to sign during the application process to confirm that individuals were not members of a union, that they accepted the company as a nonunion employer, and that they would not encourage or join in union-related activities. The **Sherman Antitrust Act of 1890** was established to oppose oppressive business practices associated with monopolies or cartels and made it illegal to form a contract or trust that interfered with free trade.

Bargaining Structures and Processes

Although traditional labor agreements are between a single union and a single employer, labor agreements and **collective bargaining** can take many forms. **Single union-single employer bargaining** is by far the most common. **Multi-employer bargaining** or **coalition bargaining** takes place between multiple employers and a single union; if the agreement includes all employers in an industry, it is referred to as industry-wide bargaining. **Coordinated bargaining** involves multiple unions and a single employer. Finally, national or local bargaining consists of agreements negotiated at the national level on economic issues or local on working conditions or other contractual conflicts. The bargaining process contains **four key stages**: opening presentation of demands, analyzing demands, compromises, and informal settlement or ratification.

Collective Bargaining Agreements

Collective bargaining consists of management and union representatives coming together to reach an agreement that will be acceptable to each respective party. Most labor agreements, or contracts, are negotiated with little fuss or public awareness. Only a few have gained national attention and caused massive economic disruption.

The **Taft-Hartley Act** requires that union and management negotiate on wages, hours, and other terms or conditions of employment. The NLRB and courts have classified **bargaining issues** into three primary groups: illegal items, mandatory items, and voluntary items. Illegal items, such as trying to instate a closed shop, are prohibited by the NLRA. Mandatory items include things like wages, the grievance procedure, and how seniority is handled. Voluntary items, or permissive subjects such as dress code, can be brought up by either the employer or the union representative. Both parties have a right to refuse negotiating on permissive subjects.

Major issues surrounding collective bargaining are who will represent workers, which issues will be negotiated into the contract, what strategies will be used in bargaining, how bargaining impasses will be resolved, and how the contract will be administered. The actual labor agreement can cover many issues or just a few, depending upon the interests of each respective party. However, wording should be carefully considered to avoid any ambiguity or misinterpretation that may cause grievances. Most labor agreements will cover the following:

- Compensation and benefits
- Working conditions
- Seniority and job security
- Individual rights and discipline procedures
- Training and development
- Union security
- Contract duration
- Management freedoms
- How union dues are paid
- Grievance resolution
- Strikes and lockouts

Contract Negotiation

Both the employer and the union representative must negotiate in good faith. This means that they must enter into the negotiation with the goal of reaching consensus. However, that does not mean that either party needs to give in to the other. Bad faith negotiation is prohibited and can be characterized by behaviors such as making radical demands or intentionally delaying the bargaining process.

Negotiation meetings should be held at mutually agreeable times. Human resources needs to be willing to furnish employment-related information to facilitate the discussion. If the two parties cannot agree, they are at what's called a bargaining impasse and may need to use mediation to resolve their differences. Once an agreement is reached, the details must be written down. This document, once voted on by union members, becomes the union contract.

Contract Administration Process

Contract administration is the actual implementation of the labor agreement's provisions. For this process to go smoothly, management and the union steward need to be able to work closely together and collaborate. This will require both parties to communicate effectively and develop a positive professional working relationship.

Work Stoppages

A work stoppage occurs when business operations temporarily cease and may be initiated by either union representation or company management.

Strikes

A **strike** occurs when employees refuse to work to exert influence against a company. A **sit-down strike** occurs when employees report to work without actually working or accomplishing anything. A **wildcat strike** occurs when a group of workers walks off the job in violation of valid labor agreements and usually against orders from the labor union. Although strikes may be protected or unprotected by the NLRA, unions are not allowed to conduct certain types of strikes or boycotts, such as to coerce particular work assignments. **Protected strikes** are either economic in nature over terms or conditions of employment or caused by an unfair labor practice. Economic strikers can be temporarily or permanently replaced, whereas unfair labor practice strikers can be only temporarily replaced.

Handling Strikes

When a strike occurs, human resources should ensure that non-striking employees have safe passage to and from the workplace. If necessary, they should hire temporary replacement workers and temporarily reassign non-striking workers as needed to minimize the disruption to the operation. To be proactive, human resources should have a plan in place to source temporary workers before a strike occurs. If possible, they should also shore up supply chains in advance to withstand any strike activity. Finally, human resources should keep detailed records about the event as these notes may prove critical in negotiations going forward.

Preventing Strikes

Although collective bargaining negotiation breakdowns happen, companies can do several things to reduce the likelihood of a strike before they reach that point. These tactics can also work to prevent nonunion employees from striking.

- Create an employee-centered culture that recognizes worker contributions and prioritizes their needs.
- Promote open communication in the workplace.
- Have (and follow) written grievance handling procedures.
- Give employees some say in company decisions.
- Truly bargain in good faith (if unionized).

Lockouts

A **lockout** occurs when a company refuses to allow employees to work. Lockouts are often used as management's counter weapon against a union's strike because replacement workers can still be used. However, a lockout is not a legal economic weapon if its use is intended to discourage union membership. Lockouts may be used for one of two defensive reasons:

1. A lockout may be instigated to prevent unusual economic hardship created by slowdowns, destructiveness, or uncertainty about a work stoppage.
2. A lockout may occur when employers in a multi-bargaining unit see a union trying to use a successive strikes strategy against members of a multi-employer bargaining unit, often starting with the most profitable.

A primary boycott occurs when disgruntled employees and their supporters decide to not do business with a company. A secondary boycott is a situation in which a union encourages individuals outside the union to stop trading or engaging in business activities with a particular organization. Secondary boycotts are identified as unfair by the LMRA.

Grievances

A grievance is a work-related complaint or formal dispute that is brought to the attention of management. However, in nonunion environments, grievances may encompass any discontent or sense of injustice. **Grievance procedures** provide an orderly and methodical process for hearing and evaluating employee complaints and tend to be more developed in union companies than in nonunion companies as a result of labor agreement specifications. These procedures protect employee rights and eliminate the need for strikes or slowdowns every time there is a disagreement.

Disagreements may be unavoidable in situations where the labor contract is open to interpretation because negotiators cannot anticipate all potential conflicts. **Formal grievance procedures** increase upward communication in organizations and make top management decisions more sensitive to employee emotions. The first step to resolving grievances is for a complaint to be submitted to the supervisor or written and submitted to the union steward.

If these parties cannot find resolution from there, the complaint may be heard by the superintendent or plant manager and the industrial relations manager. If the union is still unsatisfied, the grievance can be appealed to the next step, which may be arbitration if the company is small. Large corporations may have grievance committees, corporate officers, and/or international union representatives who will meet and hear grievances. However, the final step of an unresolved dispute will be **binding arbitration** by an outside third party, where both parties come to an acceptable agreement.

Preventing Retaliation Claims

To prevent retaliation, employees must believe that a) complaints can be easily presented without a lot of hassle, embarrassment, or paperwork; b) complaints will be assessed by a fair and impartial third party; and c) they will not be mistreated or terminated for submitting complaints or pressing for resolution. The final protection is necessary for the success of both union and nonunion **grievance procedures**, although union employees typically have more protections than nonunion employees because their labor agreement is written and enforceable by collective action. However, federal regulations such as the Sarbanes-Oxley Act and Whistleblower Protection Act now include safeguards for employees who have witnessed or stumbled upon illegal or immoral actions and make the information known to the public. Employers can also follow a number of best practices to **avoid retaliation**, such as these:

- Treat all complaints seriously and similarly.
- Allow the employee a chance to be heard, investigate the claim, collect evidence or witness statements, and treat all cases as though they might result in arbitration.
- Review the labor agreement carefully, and follow any required procedures.
- Examine all information prior to making a final determination.
- Avoid any unnecessary delays, and clearly communicate the conclusion.
- Correct the problem if the company is in the wrong.

Ethics

Business ethics is the practice of using a series of appropriate practices, procedures, and behaviors to make sure an organization functions in a socially acceptable fashion. Business ethics ensures that each individual is performing his or her duties in a fair, proper, and morally responsible manner. It is essential for any organization, regardless of type, to maintain a strong sense of what is appropriate and what is unacceptable. A company engaging in questionable, unfair, or illegal practices risks losing its reputation, losing its ability to find and retain customers and suppliers, incurring liability and criminal charges and possibly even its ability to stay in business.

There are a variety of ways a human resource professional can establish and maintain a strong sense of ethics within an organization, but the three most effective ways include: establishing a corporate values statement, establishing a code of conduct, and making sure that each individual follows the ethical codes set by the organization through human resource audits. A corporate values statement is a declaration of the basic behaviors desired of employees, including behaviors such as promoting open communication, being a team player, and treating fellow employees, customers, and other individuals with respect and dignity. A code of conduct is a series of policies, procedures, and practices that expands on the behaviors established by the values statement to define what is considered acceptable behavior and what is considered unacceptable. Finally, human resources audits ensure that members follow the set policies.

There are a variety of policies and procedures a human resources professional might need to establish to support ethical and legal corporate governance practices, including policies to protect employees who report unethical behavior, training programs to educate managers and executives regarding legal and ethical concerns, and checklists and review systems to make sure the organization is documenting and reporting everything appropriately. Policies to protect employees that report unethical behavior might include confidentiality, the acceptance of anonymous reports, and procedures for handling managers that punish employees for reporting unethical behavior. Training programs that educate managers and executives about legal and ethical concerns might include information about sexual harassment, standards for corporate responsibility, ethical requirements for senior financial officers, and the legal concerns associated with fraud. Finally, checklists and review systems might include both scheduled and unscheduled accounting audits.

Alternative Dispute Resolution

Mediation

Mediation involves bringing a third party into negotiations to hear both sides, assess the conflicting issues, clarify differences, suggest compromises, and identify similarities for further negotiations. Mediators usually enter a dispute when either the union or management requests their assistance. Mediation tends to receive less criticism and be more successful if efforts are requested by both parties. It's important to note that mediation is not binding. As such, a resolution may not be reached. There are three main styles:

- **Facilitative mediation**: focuses on helping parties find a solution through a series of inquiries
- **Evaluative mediation**: formal procedure in which mediators are often legal professionals and focused on protecting rights more than the interests of parties
- **Transformative mediation**: attempts to resolve conflicts by validating worth and feelings

Arbitration

Arbitration is the process of resolving a labor dispute with the assistance of an impartial third party that examines information from both sides and renders a judgment. The parties agree beforehand to accept the decision of an impartial judge, called an **arbitrator**, as a binding decision. The decisions of arbitrators are generally more informed and unbiased than the decisions that are made by a jury of peers. Arbitration procedures, issues requiring arbitration, how to select an arbitrator, and limitations on the authority of the arbitrator are often described within the labor agreement. Arbitration is generally used more often for settling **grievances** than settling labor disputes because most employers and labor union leaders will not let an arbitrator bind them to a contract. After an arbitrator has been selected, an arbitration hearing is held, and a submission agreement statement is prepared to outline issues and grant final authority to the arbitrator. Written testimonies, statements, and affidavits are often prepared by parties prior to the hearing, so hearings rarely last more than a single day. The actual hearing may be formal or informal, but the burden of proof will often fall upon whichever party filed the initial complaint. Arbitrators will provide a written review and final award to both parties within 30 days. Arbitration is seen as a useful tool because it can resolve grievances without the expense of going to court and without the operational disruption of a strike. However, because arbitration is binding, both parties will have to live with the outcome and have no rights to appeal.

Employee Discipline Procedures and Approaches

Discipline procedures often consist of several consequences, including training, correction, evaluation, punishment, and termination. The objective of disciplinary action is to remedy a problem, with the goal of helping employees achieve success. **Maintaining order** can be accomplished with an accepted standard of conduct that is appropriate, fair evaluation procedures, and an order of progressively severe consequences for violators. Many organizations have adopted the verbal warning, followed by the written warning, in which future violations may carry penalties up to and including termination. Strong disciplinary systems protect the rights of employees and preserve the interests of the organization. It is important that employees are provided with enough time and opportunities to correct their behavior if they desire but also rigorous enough to discharge previously warned yet unresponsive and problematic employees.

Terminations

Voluntary terminations may be caused by a variety of reasons, such as new job opportunity, relocation, or personal obligations. **Involuntary terminations** most often occur as a result of employment problems, such as poor performance, excessive absenteeism, insubordination, or theft. Employers should have controls that require all terminations to be **reviewed** in advance to avoid the risk of legal or contract violations. The review should determine whether there are valid, job-related reasons for the termination. If the termination is due to a particular incident, the review should conclude that a proper investigation has been documented. Additional documentation should show that the employee was made aware of performance problems and had an opportunity to correct behaviors. Terminations should also be consistent with prior treatment of other employees. Finally, it is imperative to ensure that the employee is not a victim of retaliation of any civil rights.

Employment-at-Will Doctrine

An **employment-at-will doctrine** essentially allows both the employer and the employee the mutual right to end the employment relationship at any time. This philosophy of hiring whomever you want for as long as you want was created to protect workers from wrongful terminations. In more recent years, the voluntary relationship has been challenged by state and case law to protect workers, with the exception of implied contracts, retaliatory discharges, and public policy exceptions. **Implied contracts** may be verbal or written promises by an employer to continue an employment relationship. However, some courts have recognized a promissory estoppel exception when an employer makes a promise that he or she reasonably expects the employee to rely upon, the employee does rely upon it, and the employee suffers financial or personal injury as a result.

Employee Misconduct Investigations

The investigation process usually begins when a complaint is received or if it is determined there is reasonable cause to investigate an employee's conduct. The organization should identify exactly what is being investigated, what sort of evidence is needed to prove or disprove the misconduct, who should be interviewed during the investigation, and which questions need to be asked to gather the necessary evidence. Next, the organization needs to interview the person making the complaint, the individual the complaint is against, and any other employees who have relevant information. Finally, the organization should come to a decision and take the appropriate action.

Weingarten Rights

In *National Labor Relations Board (NLRB) vs. Weingarten*, the Supreme Court established the right of employees to have **union representation** at investigatory interviews in which the employee must defend conduct or behavior. If an employee believes that discipline or other consequences might follow, he or she has the right to request union representation. However, management does not need to inform an employee of their **Weingarten rights**. It is the employee's own responsibility to know and request representation. When requested, management can a) stop questioning until a representative arrives, b) terminate the interview, or c) ask the employee to voluntarily relinquish his or her rights to representation. The company does need to inform the representative of the interview subject, and the representative does have the right to counsel the employee in private and advise him or her what to say.

Handling International Labor Relations

Although **union membership** has declined in the United States, it continues to prosper in other areas like Sweden, Denmark, and Russia. France maintains low union membership; however, their trade unions manage the country's welfare system and fix national agreements on wages and working conditions. Moreover, France has a standard workweek of 35 hours and a standard retirement age of 60 years, and all workers have five weeks of annual holiday. Countries like Japan have **national regulations** for managing their many unions, such as their Labor Standards Act of 1947, which covers employment decisions (hires, transfers, terminations, etc.), working conditions (hours, overtime, and leaves), wages, training, welfare, occupational safety and health, and accident compensation. Additionally, the US **employment-at-will doctrine** is different than other international practices. Many countries provide workers with legal protections against termination, and foreign workers are normally protected by a number of labor laws or union ordinances that hold costly penalties for violations. For example, in Mexico employees are considered permanent after passing a 30-day trial period. The employee may choose to quit, but terminations almost require a criminal conviction. Moreover, the European Union requires that employers notify the Secretary of State if 10 or more employees will be terminated. In the UK and Europe, work councils are common. These councils are groups that fight for the rights of workers and generally function like trade unions.

Technology Management

HRIS

An **HRIS** is a computer system designed to help human resource professionals carry out the day-to-day human resource functions necessary for an organization to continue functioning normally. Most HRISs are designed to collect and store data related to the use of employee benefits, hiring, placement, training and evaluations of employees, payroll, and information about the work performed by the employee during a given period of time. An HRIS is designed to help a human resource professional carry out all primary functions associated with human resource needs, which include benefits administration, payroll, time and labor management, and human resources management. An HRIS not only aids the human resources department; it also helps the entire organization function effectively.

Employee Self-Service

Many HRIS and payroll software now provide employees with an **employee self-service module** that allows employees to create a login and review or edit their personal information. These modules give employees access to pay statements and might provide them with ways to update their addresses, phone numbers, bank information, and tax withholdings; enroll in benefits; or request time off. These systems ease the burden and workload of payroll professionals by reducing the volume of administrative requests and data entry that need to be processed on a regular basis. If the software comes with a welcome portal, this also gives human resource professionals a place to streamline communications, build cultural branding, and post employee handbooks or benefit summaries.

Data and Information Management

Data Integrity

Data integrity involves maintaining and protecting data content to ensure that it is complete, accurate, and reliable. The design, implementation, and usage throughout the **data life cycle** is critical to any system that stores or processes data. Individual users, management, culture, training, controls, and audits can all affect **data integrity**. Poor configuration and inaccurate data entry can corrupt data. Therefore, thorough testing and safeguarding of data is required to avoid spending many hours debugging and reconciling information. Moreover, policies and training on what to do in the event of a breach can help mitigate risk by increasing staff awareness and ability to fight off breaches.

Confidentiality and Disclosures

Confidentiality disclosures should include definitions and exclusions of confidential information while outlining individual responsibilities. **Confidentiality disclosures** are used to keep private or secure information available only to those who are authorized to access it. It is important to ensure that only the proper individuals have access to the information needed to perform their jobs. Moreover, legislation mandates **due diligence** to protect the confidential information of employees and customers. **Technology breaches** in confidentiality could happen via phone, fax, computer, email, and electronic records. For this reason, some businesses might utilize an encryption software, limit the communications that can be sent via email, and include a statement notifying the reader what to do if it is inadvertently sent to the wrong person.

Importance of IT Security

IT security is becoming a more serious topic and rapidly gaining more attention. It is important for human resource practitioners to be conscientious of controls to mitigate organizational exposure and risk. Some companies may have **IT security policies and acknowledgements** in place to reduce liability and identify and document compliance and security controls. Multiple layers of corporate IT security might include the encryption of data files, firewalls, access controls or logins, systems monitoring, detection processes, antivirus software, cyber insurance, and so on. Implementing stronger IT security can provide companies with benefits such as mitigating lost revenue, protecting brand reputation, and supporting mobilization.

Policies and Procedures for Procurement of Technology

Human resources must ensure that management and staff follow the proper policies and procedures for procuring new technology. The IT department and senior leadership should establish policies and procedures that discuss technology upgrade timelines, budgets, potential compatibility issues with existing systems, potential risks for adopting new technologies, and other related topics. The IT department must be consulted prior to downloading new software to ensure that there are no viruses, malware, or other risks associated with it.

Technology Use Policies

Human resources should ensure that employees sign off on technology use policies when they are hired and as the policies change over time. The policies help maintain productivity and minimize risk. At a minimum, they should cover the following:

- The company reserves the right to monitor what employees are doing on the company network or while using IT equipment owned by the company.
- The company network and IT equipment are intended primarily for business use. Minimal personal use is allowable.
- While using the company's network or IT equipment, employees must not access, view, download, send, or create any content that is illegal or vulgar, constitutes discrimination or harassment, or is otherwise inappropriate. Employees must also refrain from spamming others even when the subject matter may be permissible.
- Employees are expected to refrain from excessive personal cell phone use while at work. If they are issued a company phone, they must use it for business reasons, protect it from damage or theft, and be ready to return it when they leave the company or upon request. Using a cell phone while driving on company time is prohibited. Employees must pull over or use a hands-free device.
- Employees may use their own personal devices for work with prior approval from management and the IT department. The IT department will install antivirus and other software designed to keep company information safe. Employees must refrain from backing up company data to the cloud or accessing unsecure websites. Even though the employee owns the device, the company still reserves the right to monitor activity while on the company network.
- Employees should not use any device to record the goings-on of the company unless they have clear permission to do so.
- If employees violate the policy, they may be subject to disciplinary action up to and including termination.

Social Media Policies

Many companies have a technology and social media policy to protect employers from the potential risk and litigation that may arise if an employee accidentally discloses confidential information or says something negative while online. **Employees** who actively use social media at work may fall victim to phishing scams or threaten system security and open the network to potential hackers. **Employers** are at even more risk if an employee solicits or distributes offensive material, uses social media as a platform to write negative remarks about an organization, or even shares proprietary information. However, the **NLRB** has played an influential role in how social media law is being developed and often protects employees who make comments about working conditions. Organizations should include human resources, legal or public affairs, and marketing when developing a social media policy. Moreover, these policies should identify corporate leaders who are responsible for social media communications and explain how improper posts will be handled.

Applicant Tracking Systems

An applicant tracking system (**ATS**) can be particularly useful for organizations that perform high-volume recruiting on a consistent basis, but they can be valuable to businesses of all sizes. Despite the initial cost, most medium to large businesses use an ATS due to the time it can save from reviewing thousands of résumés or automating new hire paperwork. New, cloud-based systems may integrate with social media or popular job boards and receive automatic updates that eliminate the need for pricy servers and on-site specialists. Additionally, an ATS is a positive first impression for applicants because it can make the process easier and save time on their end.

Review Video: Applicant Tracking System
Visit mometrix.com/academy and enter code: 532324

Moreover, an ATS can allow you to do the following:

- Brand your company with a career page.
- Modify or set up standard templates.
- Save forms for compliance or reporting.
- Push employee information to a payroll or human resource module.
- Collect data and metrics for reporting and strategic review.

Human Resources Expertise: Organization Chapter Quiz

1. Which of the following measure specific human resource activities that contribute to the efficiency and effectiveness of a company?

a. Key performance indicators
b. Leading indicators
c. Lagging indicators
d. Sustainability indicators

2. Propinquity theory is based on what?

a. Rewards
b. Geography
c. Occupational task
d. Members

3. Which of the following stages of group development developed by Bruce Tuckman is generally considered the most difficult?

a. Storming
b. Forming
c. Performing
d. Norming

4. All of the following are organizational structures EXCEPT

a. Physical
b. Functional
c. Divisional
d. Matrix

5. Long-term forecasting typically covers a time frame of?

a. 5-10 years
b. 2-10 years
c. 4-8 years
d. 10-20 years

6. Which of the following is used to avoid layoffs during times of financial burden?

a. Succession
b. Subtraction
c. Attrition
d. Diversification

7. Which of the following organizations was founded to address global working conditions?

a. AFL-CIO
b. NLRB
c. ILO
d. LMRA

Human Resources Expertise: Workplace

Human Resources in the Global Context

Stages of International Human Resource Management

Import-export firms embody the initial phase of globalization. At this stage, products are moved across national boundaries. The majority of employees are located only in the home country, with the exception being contract negotiators who study abroad to secure buying and selling agreements. In this phase, human resource policies and procedures follow traditional practices. **Multinational enterprises (MNEs)** have reached the next stage of globalization, in which employees are located in the home country and a number of expatriate managers may be sent to oversee foreign operations. Products may be manufactured in one country then shipped to another country for assembly and further exporting. This phase requires human resource policies and practices to be revised for each country. **Global firms** have reached the final stage of globalization. They may have main strategic corporate units in multiple countries that all interact with headquarters and with each other. Each country could have its own complete operation, or each function of the organization may be located in separate countries. In any case, products and resources are often transferred across borders to meet organizational demands. Global countries strive to implement human resource policies and procedures that meet global needs, with limited adaptations for each cultural location.

Expatriates and Repatriates

Expatriates are individuals who are sent on assignments outside their home country, with the expectation that these employees will return following the completion of the assignment. If an employee is from the same country as the company's headquarters, he or she may be known as either parent-country nationals or headquarters expatriates. **Repatriates** are individuals returning to their home country from an assignment in another country.

First-Country Nationals and Third-Country Nationals

Local nationals, or **first-** or **host-country nationals** are employees who are hired for a job in their own country, when the company is based in another country. These employees may be hired for short- or long-term assignments. For example, a worker based in India takes an assignment for the subsidiary of a company based out of China.

Employees working for an international firm but who are citizens of neither the home country nor host country are **third-country nationals**. These are usually technical or professional employees hired for short-term assignments and are also branded as international freelance employees. These employees will return to their country of origin after the assignment, for example, a manufacturing engineer who is a citizen of the United States but commissioned to work for a Spanish manufacturing company at a satellite office in Rio Grande while plans are established for a new plant.

Best Practices for International Assignments

Many international assignments end in failure. In addition, they can be both costly and difficult to manage. There is a plethora of factors that influence the success of an **international assignment**. Selecting people who fit both the culture and assignment, arranging their transition, preparing them and their families, evaluating performance remotely, and repatriating after the assignment are critical considerations that must be carefully planned to minimize risk. Examine each step of the process, and be diligent to encourage open, inclusive communication throughout the assignment. If the employee's loved ones have a difficult time adjusting, he or she could decide to return early, resulting in an incomplete assignment. Therefore, it is important to also think about spouses or children who may be relocating as well. Organizations that are involved in many international assignments may choose to **outsource** global expertise and administrative responsibilities such as employment law, payroll, or taxes.

Criteria for Selecting Individuals for International Assignments

Careful consideration must be given when selecting individuals for **international assignments**. Frequently used **criteria** for selection might consist of demonstrated performance, professional or technical expertise, specific knowledge, overall perceptiveness, leadership abilities, administrative skills, willingness, reputation, and successful completion of prior international assignments, ability to adapt, and desire to learn a new culture. **Orientation and pre-assignment training** such as language classes are essential for achieving strategic and tactical goals. Moreover, the success of expatriates depends upon the spouse and family's ability to **adjust** to new cultures. Some aspects that may help expedite the family's adjustment overseas include the spouse's ability to work or maintain career advancement, family living accommodations, education for children, and health and dental care.

Expatriate Training and Socialization

Many larger, international enterprise companies have implemented some form of **expatriate training** for managers and their families prior to international assignments. These may address problems with adjustment or cross-cultural training. Foreign assignments, especially those in lesser-industrialized nations tend to be difficult for families to adjust to. They must learn a new language, find acceptance with new friends in new schools, and pursue different careers. To prepare managers for foreign assignments, preparations and training sessions should include language and cultural awareness studies and thorough coverage of local customs and religions. One method involves the use of a **culturegram**, or culture assimilator, which instructs managers of best practices and helps them acquire and practice new cultural practices. Subjects vary from social introductions, time orientations, and standard dress to customary diet and dining etiquette.

Compensation Adjustments Made for Expatriates

An international assignment must be aligned with a **global compensation system** in which respective adjustments are made per assignment. That said, the arrangement must take into consideration cost controls while providing sufficient motivation and rewards for the expat. Multinational organizations must create global compensation plans that are consistent with global mobility and business strategy. Additional consideration should be considered regarding expatriate housing, expenses, and taxes. There are four methods for calculating global compensation adjustments for international assignments:

- The **home-country-based approach**, which is based on the employee's standard of living in his or her home country
- The **host-country-based approach**, which is based upon local national rates
- The **headquarters-based approach**, which is based upon the home country of the organization
- The **balance sheet approach**, which calculates compensation based on home country rates, with all allowances, deductions, and reimbursements before converting into the host country's currency

Health and Safety Considerations for Expatriates

Employers have a responsibility to ensure the health and safety of their employees while they are performing work for the company. To promote expatriate safety, human resources and senior leadership should create an emergency plan in advance of the expatriate's deployment. The emergency plan should include what to do in the case of accident, injury, illness, disease outbreak, extreme political unrest, and other situations that could endanger the expatriate and his or her family. An evacuation strategy is also a critical component of the emergency plan and should detail how the expatriate and his or her family can get to a safe region quickly. To promote good health, the expatriate and his or her family need access to high-quality medical care. Human resources should ensure that medical insurance provided is region specific as each country has a different infrastructure for care. Some nations provide care to anyone living there, whereas others require private insurance to be treated. Human resources should also make sure that the insurance is provided by a licensed carrier and that it offers a solid network of quality providers.

Employee Repatriation

Employee repatriation is taking care of employees after an international assignment when they have returned to their home country. It is important to **plan for the employee's return** well in advance, before the assignment has even begun and have career development discussions to identify suitable positions that utilize global skills. Research reveals that approximately 30 percent of expats leave employers upon return, often citing external competitiveness or saying that an appropriate job for them was not available. **Communication** is also a key element. Staying connected through email, newsletters, a mentor or buddy system, and home visits can ensure the employee remains in the loop. Recognize the employee's return with a reception and maybe ask him or her to provide a speech or presentation of the international operations. Additional services might include retraining courses, reverse culture shock counseling, and outplacement services for the employee's spouse.

Requirements for Moving Work

Off-Shoring

Off-shoring is the act of getting work done in another country by local employees abroad that was previously done in-house by domestic employees. Although benefits are usually lower costs, better availability of certain skills, and getting work done through faster channels, **off-shoring** frequently receives criticism for transferring jobs, language and cultural barriers, and intellectual property or geopolitical risks. However, sometimes the business reasons for off-shoring are strategic: to reach new markets or talent pools not available domestically. Some countries that receive allocated work from the Americas include India, China, Russia, Mexico, Philippines, Brazil, and Hungary due to the allegedly lower cost of labor in these areas. The rush of outsourcing information technology, human resources, and other white-collar jobs may continue, but companies will need to consider pros and cons, training and knowledge transfer, as well as cultural traditions to make operations successful. Otherwise, the quality of products and services may decline, cultural challenges may arise, and consumer backlash could affect company image.

- **Near-shoring**: A form of off-shoring, near-shoring is the process of moving business operations to a nearby or bordering nation whereby the company can benefit from both reasonable proximity and lower labor costs.
- **On-shoring**: The opposite of off-shoring, on-shoring entails a business moving to its home country to reduce costs.
- **Co-sourcing**: Co-sourcing occurs when a firm uses a blend of company employees and external resources to render services to customers.

Diversity and Inclusion

Approaches to an Inclusive Workplace

First, identify any areas of concern. An internal workforce should reflect the available labor market. Examine the corporate culture and communications to ensure that they advocate for a diverse and inclusive workplace. Review or amend policies and practices to support an inclusive culture. Focus on the behavioral aspects, how people communicate, and how people work together. Are all perspectives respected and input from all positions valued? Address any areas that might not welcome protected classes or disabilities. Then brainstorm approaches and ideas for an **inclusive workplace**. Once a **diverse culture** is established, target recruiting efforts to reach a broad audience. Some ideas may include college recruiting, training centers, career fairs, veteran's offices, and state unemployment offices or career centers. Set business objectives for areas that can be improved upon, document what changes will be implemented, and review progress.

Diversity Training

Although we most often think of diversity as the inclusiveness of minorities, diversity may also embrace a robust variety of traits such as generation, gender, sexual orientation, race, ethnicity, language, religious background, education, or life experiences. Diversity is the ability to consider and value the perspectives of all people. It is important for human resource practitioners to recognize that everyone has both conscious and unconscious biases. **Diversity and inclusion training** supports establishing a nonjudgmental and collaborative workforce that is respectful and sensitive to differences among peers. Additionally, it can teach humility and self-awareness. Training program methods may be extensive or address specific gaps. Moreover, diversity and inclusion training may introduce new perspectives to the workforce, promoting creativity and innovation.

Managing a Multigenerational Workforce

Human resource practitioners must learn how to manage a **multigenerational workforce**. We currently have baby boomers nearing retirement, Generation X gaining experience, and millennials becoming leaders in the workforce. Soon, Generation Z will join in the workforce. How can employers address the management needs of this multigenerational workforce and their diverse sets of values? The most obvious change in values is the **loyalty factor** of each generation. Baby boomers began their careers believing they might have only a few employers over the course of their working years, whereas Generation X workers are more likely to change employers frequently to gain experience and better salaries. Millennial and Generation Z workers show the least amount of loyalty to their employers. Instead, they want to define their own careers and work their way. Millennial workers are more **entrepreneurial**, and Generation Z workers are anticipated to flood the **freelance markets**. Work/life balance and the chance to make a difference are valued more in the younger workforce. In return, they bring more tech savvy, social media branding, and adaptability. Millennial workers desire constant **feedback**; annual reviews will not do. Weekly or even daily one-on-one meetings will help motivate millennial workers and provide them with favored inspiration and direction. Millennials want plenty of learning opportunities and a manager who is concerned with their **career growth**. Coaching, mentoring, and on-the-job training are attractive qualities for this generation. Millennials flourish when they have freedom for creative expression and clear areas of responsibility.

Demographic Barriers Encountered in Today's Workplace

The Civil Rights Act prohibits **sex or religious discrimination** regarding any employment condition, including hiring, firing, promotional advancements, transfers, compensation, or admissions into training programs. The condition in which many women experience subtle forms of discrimination that limit their career advancement is referred to as the **glass ceiling**. It encompasses a host of attitudinal and organizational barriers that prevent women from receiving information, training, encouragement, and other opportunities to assist in advancement. The Civil Rights Act does not protect sexual orientation, but other legal actions at the federal level have come to protect those attracted to or married to the same sex in recent years. The EEOC has ruled that **gender identity discrimination** can be asserted as claims of sex discrimination under existing law. Preferential treatment for any particular gender or religious quality is strictly prohibited unless there is a bona fide occupational qualification. Customer preference is not a defense against discrimination to appearances that deviate from the norm, such as a Muslim woman wearing a hijab (headscarf), Rastafarian dreadlocks, Jewish sidelocks, or a Sikh's turban and uncut hair.

Supporting a LGBTQ Workforce

There has been increasing attention on the rights of the **lesbian, gay, bisexual, transgender, and queer (LGBTQ) community** in the past few years. Many states have expanded civil rights to include **LGBTQ discrimination protection** for sexual orientation of employees and applicants. In most cases, gender identity is also protected. Presidents Obama and Trump have both enforced **workplace regulations** for the LGBTQ community; ensuring a work environment free from harassment and oppression has never been more important. There are a few states that have not joined in the fight for LGBTQ equality. However, employers should remain vigilant in adhering to local regulations and accommodating LGBTQ needs, which may require the availability of benefits for domestic partners or a unisex restroom for transgender workers.

Workplace Accommodations

Accommodations for Disabilities

If a job candidate or employee is disabled, but otherwise qualified, the employer must make reasonable workplace accommodations. For the accommodation to be reasonable, it must not cause the employer undue hardship. Some examples of disability accommodation are making the building more accessible (via ramps, elevators, redesigned restrooms, etc.); altering work duties, location, or schedule; ordering assistive equipment (like a screen magnifier or standing desk); modifying policies, performance assessment tools, or training materials, and more. Human resources should create a policy detailing how accommodation requests should be made, how they will be evaluated, and what appeals process exists if the request is denied.

Accommodations for Religion

Employers must accommodate job candidate or employee sincerely held religious beliefs so long as doing so doesn't cause the company undue hardship. Possible religious accommodations include allowing time off for religious holidays and having different dress and grooming rules. Human resources should create a policy detailing how accommodation requests should be made, how they will be evaluated, and what appeals process exists if the request is denied.

Accommodations for Veterans and Active Military

Employers must accommodate disabled veterans in the same manner as they would any other job candidate or employee. There are two main laws, Family and Medical Leave Act (FMLA) and Uniformed Services Employment and Reemployment Rights Act (USERRA, fully discussed in an upcoming section), that protect the employment of veterans and active duty military. Employers may choose, however, to provide additional accommodation to service members. While the employee is away serving, the firm could decide to continue paying for medical coverage and make up the difference in compensation between the salary and military pay. Human resources should create a policy detailing how accommodation requests should be made, how they will be evaluated, and what appeals process exists if the request is denied.

AFFIRMATIVE ACTION PLANS

Affirmative action plans (**AAPs**) require employers to implement timelines that correlate with measurable goals to prevent discrimination and enforce **Executive Order 11246**, commonly known as **Order Number 4**. This order prohibits employment discrimination by federal contractors and subcontractors whose contracts exceed $10,000 per year or first-tier subcontractors whose contracts exceed $50,000 and have 50 or more employees. **Executive Order 11478** extended the same anti-discrimination provisions to employees of the federal government. **Executive Order 11246** also established the **Office of Federal Contract Compliance Programs (OFCCP)** to monitor AAPs. The OFCCP uses many tool and analysis techniques to investigate possible discrimination. Coverage was again extended in 2013 to include individuals with disabilities. It is important to note that the statute of limitations to file a complaint with the OFCCP is 180 days.

DISPARATE TREATMENT

Disparate treatment is the act of treating a person differently due to race, religion, sex, or natural origin. A claim of **disparate treatment** requires proof of **discriminatory motive**, such as blatant statements that pose direct evidence of discrimination. Disparate treatment may also be exposed through factual differences in treatment, proven by a cohort analysis comparison of the treatment in similar individuals. For example, a business that required female employees to follow a strict dress code while the male employees of the business could wear whatever they liked would be guilty of disparate treatment because of treating employees differently based on gender. This type of discrimination was first identified by Title VII of the Civil Rights Act.

DISPARATE IMPACT

Disparate impact describes more unintentional discrimination. It's the type of discrimination in which an employer institutes a policy that appears to be reasonable but prevents individuals of a certain color, with certain disabilities, with a certain military status, of a certain national origin, of a certain race, of a certain religion, or of a particular sex from receiving employment or any of the benefits associated with employment (such as promotions or pay). For example, certain preemployment tests have been proven to discriminate against certain protected classes, although they may not appear as such. Disparate impact does not require the proof of discriminatory motive, and remedies do not include punitive damages.

FOUR-FIFTHS RULE AND ADVERSE IMPACT ANALYSIS

The EEOC defines **adverse impact** by the **four-fifths rule** as follows: "A selection rate for any race, sex, or ethnic group which is less than four-fifths (4/5 or 80 percent) of the rate for the group with the highest rate will generally be regarded by the federal enforcement agencies as evidence of adverse impact."

Let's say that Alpha Company requires a previously outlined exam for specified positions. Two hundred applicants took this exam, including 124 Caucasian males and 57 Latino males, and only 108 passed. Of the 108 who passed the exam, there were 72 Caucasian males and 28 Latino males. The four-fifths rule may now be used to determine if the exam used by Alpha Company has an adverse impact. Caucasian males had the highest pass rate at 58.06 percent, and four-fifths of that rate is 46.45 percent. Latino males had a 49.12 percent pass rate, which is greater than 46.45 percent. Thus, we can conclude that the exam presented by Alpha Company does not have an adverse impact. However, if the four-fifths rule had determined adverse impact, the burden of proof would fall upon Alpha Company to convince the courts that the exam was a) job related for the specified positions and b) consistent with business necessity.

Risk Management

Risk management refers to the process of identifying, analyzing, and prioritizing **risks or potential uncertainties** while developing strategies to protect the financial interests of a company. Risks or potential uncertainties may include workplace safety, workers' compensation, unemployment insurance, security, loss prevention, health and wellness, data management, privacy protection, project failures, and contingency planning. Depending upon the size of the company or severity of the threat, some or all of these areas might be assigned to human resources. The underlying goal of risk management is to mitigate the costs of these uncertainties as much as possible.

Risk Types

- Hazard risk involves potential liability or loss of property and is generally mitigated by insurance. Workplace accidents, fires, and natural disasters are examples of risk that fall into this category.
- Financial risk involves potential negative impacts to a firm's cash flow. A major customer not paying invoices on time is an example of this type of risk.
- Operational risk involves the impact to a firm's ability to function effectively and may include technology failures, process breakdowns, and human error.
- Strategic risk involves a firm's plans becoming outdated due to shifts in the economy, politics, customer demographics, or the overall competitive landscape.

Risk Assessments

Risk assessments are a critical element of risk management. A **quantitative risk assessment** will allow the business to assign actual dollar amounts to each risk based on value, exposure, single loss expectancy, annualized rate of occurrence, and annualized loss expectancy. **Single loss expectancy** is measured when a value is placed on each asset, and the percentage of loss is determined for each acknowledged threat. The **annualized loss expectancy** can be calculated by multiplying the single loss occurrence and the annualized rate of occurrence. In these calculations, potential loss amounts are used to consider if implementing a security measure is necessary. Qualitative risk assessment, on the other hand, does not assign a defined monetary value to the risk. It uses descriptive statements to describe the potential impact of a risk, which can include a general reference to financial loss. For example, a major system breach would result in customer data being compromised, severe damage to the firm's reputation, and a significant financial blow to the organization due to handling the crisis, shoring up the system to prevent further issues, and responding to possible lawsuits by those affected.

Handling Risks

The business has several options when a risk has been identified: accept the risk, retain the risk, avoid the risk, diminish or mitigate the risk, or transfer the risk. If the risk could be easily handled and doesn't pose a large threat to the organization, it may be wise to accept it. Preparing for it in advance could be a waste of time and resources. In addition, a firm might choose risk retention, or keeping the risk in-house, if doing so is financially prudent. Although not all situations allow for this, it may be wise to try and avoid larger risks. For example, if a firm believes a feature on its product isn't going to be functional for the product launch, it could decide to introduce it as an upgrade later or omit it entirely. If accepting the risk or avoiding it isn't possible, the company could decide to mitigate or diminish it. For example, if human resources think that workers will miss important changes to their benefits during open enrollment, they could offer training sessions and extra office hours to help employees understand their options. Finally, firms may be able to transfer, or share, some risks. When a business purchases an insurance policy of any kind, it is transferring risk to the insurer. A company could also transfer risk to suppliers with specific contract clauses.

Security Concerns and Prevention

Workplace Violence

Due to the growing number of workplace assaults and homicides, it is suggested that human resource managers be prepared and implement policies such as the following:

- **Zero tolerance**—prohibiting any act of violence in the workplace, including verbal threats
- **Prevention**—presenting strategies and training to help managers recognize danger signs
- **Crisis management**—plans for responding to threats or acts of violence
- **Recovery**—providing support and counseling for victims and survivors that may suffer trauma

To reduce the likelihood that a troubled employee might become violent, managers should be encouraged to practice the following:

- Disciplining employees should be done one-on-one as a private matter as opposed to in public.
- Employees should have an opportunity to explain or tell their side of the story.
- Managers should refrain from disciplining employees when the manager is angry. Even if the employee's behavior may warrant immediate action, the employee should be removed from the scene, and disciplinary action should be discussed and decided at a later meeting.
- Try to calm angry workers or have a friend accompany them when leaving.

Fraud and Theft

A serious concern for all companies is illegal or dishonest behavior, such as theft, embezzlement, falsifying records, or misuse of company property. Committing **fraud** often involves at least one of three main forces: situational pressure, opportunity to commit fraud, or personal integrity. When employees are suspected of stealing, companies must decide whether to conduct an investigation or prosecute. Investigations and prosecutions can be costly; however, most cases are investigated, and some will result in termination, whereas others may result in prosecution. Organizations may also adopt **anti-fraud programs** to increase early detection and decrease opportunities. These programs often contain these elements: reporting, oversight, prudence, communication, compliance, enforcement, prevention, and advocating personal integrity. Companies prone to theft and dishonest behavior, such as retail corporations, often have **loss prevention departments** dedicated to protecting assets and cash while minimizing and detecting inventory shrinkage.

Corporate Espionage

When employees give corporate trade secrets to another organization, they are committing **corporate espionage**. They are giving the receiving firm a competitive advantage and may cause the other company to lose customers, sales, human capital, market share, or all of the above. Firms can protect themselves by requiring employees to sign nondisclosure or noncompete agreements. These outline what information is protected and what happens when an employee (or former employee) violates the agreement. Companies should also restrict their most important classified information to a small group of personnel that need it to do their jobs.

Sabotage

Sabotage in the workplace is the act of destroying or disrupting business operations. It can be overt through behaviors such as erasing important files, intentionally failing to complete certain key tasks, or spreading rumors. It can also be much more subtle and occur through behaviors such as taking a meeting off topic, practicing perfectionism, or being totally unwilling to bend the rules for overall gain or greater good. To combat deliberate sabotage efforts, firms should have a code of conduct in place that forbids such behavior and spells out what happens when an employee violates the code. To address the less direct forms of sabotage, leaders should be trained to detect that it's happening and firmly take charge to nip those behaviors in the bud.

Kidnapping and Ransom

When employees are kidnapped and ransomed, it's a terrifying ordeal for them, their families, and the organization. However, the firm can take several steps to both prevent a kidnapping from occurring and handle it effectively should it happen. First and foremost, the company should address the threat of kidnapping in a given area. It should also create a clear plan for how it would negotiate in a hostage situation. If an area is high risk, the firm should consider if it's worth having personnel there. If employees are sent or located in that area, firms should teach them how to detect threats and be mindful of their surroundings. They should also be trained how to act if they are kidnapped. Best practices include speaking about their personal lives and families so that kidnappers see them as humans and not as a commodity for sale. Those who are kidnapped should avoid speaking about hot button issues like politics or religion. Companies should also inform employees what to do when they're rescued. For example, employees shouldn't run toward the rescue team because they might be mistaken as being a part of the enemy group. As the situation is happening, the company should provide support to the hostage employee's family and keep a low media profile. The media can make things worse depending on what information gets released and is seen by the kidnappers. Finally, companies should consider purchasing kidnap and ransom insurance, which will help cover the cost of the ransom should a kidnapping occur.

Approaches to a Drug Free Workplace

Shows like A&E's *Intervention* and recent news of the opiate epidemic address some of the many personal struggles for employees involved in or suffering from **alcoholism and drug abuse**. Moreover, these problems are not temporary, and many need help correcting these behaviors. Alcoholism is now a **protected disability** under the American with Disabilities Act (ADA). The act does not protect employees who report to work under the influence, nor does it protect them from the consequences of their actions or blatant misconduct. Problems caused by drug abuse are similar to those caused by alcoholism. However, additional problems associated with drug abuse are the likelihood of stealing, due to the expensive cost of the employee's habit, and its illegal nature. The ADA does not protect current drug use as a protected disability.

Drug-Free Workplace Act

The Drug-Free Workplace Act of 1988 requires that government contractors make a good faith effort to ensure a drug-free workplace. Employers must prohibit illegal substances in the workplace and must create drug awareness trainings for employees. Any federal contractor with contracts of $100,000 or more must adhere to a set of mandates to show they maintain a drug-free work environment.

- Employers must develop a **written policy** prohibiting the production, distribution, use, or possession of any controlled substance by an employee while in the workplace.
- Employers are required to develop **standards of enforcement**, and all employees must receive a copy of the policy and understand the consequences of a violation.
- Employers need to implement **drug awareness trainings** to help employees understand the hazards and health risks of drug use.

Although drug testing is not required, it is intended that employers have some type of **screening** in place.

Cautionary Measures When Designing Drug Testing Programs

Many employers utilize drug testing to screen applicants and, in some cases, current employees. Generally speaking, employers can legally require applicants to pass a **drug test** as a condition of employment or adopt programs that test active employees as long as the programs are not discriminatory. Due to the controversial nature, employers must be meticulously cautious when designing these programs to ensure practices will be upheld if brought to court. *Wilkinson vs. Times Mirror Corporation* established the following elements for testing programs:

1. Samples are collected at a medical facility by persons unrelated to the employer.
2. Applicants are unobserved by others when they furnish samples.
3. Results are kept confidential.
4. Employers are notified only if the applicant was passed or failed by a medical lab.
5. Applicants are notified of the portion they failed by the medical lab—some instances will provide applicants an opportunity to present medical documentation prior to the employer receiving results.
6. There is a defined method for applicants to question or challenge test results.
7. Applicants must be eligible to reapply after a reasonable time.

Preparing for Emergencies and Natural Disasters

Because it is an employer's obligation to provide a safe and healthy work environment, many companies have begun to create **emergency and disaster plans** for handling situations such as fires, explosions, earthquakes, chemical spills, communicable disease outbreaks, and acts of terrorism. These plans should include the following steps:

1. Clarify the **chain of command**, and inform staff who to contact and who has authority.
2. Someone should be responsible for **accounting** for all employees when an emergency strikes.
3. A **command center** should be set up to coordinate communications.
4. Employees should be **trained annually** on what to do if an emergency strikes.
5. Businesses should have **first-aid kits and basic medical supplies** available. This includes water fountains and eye wash stations in areas where spills may occur.
6. An **emergency team of employees** should be named and trained for the following:
   a. Organizing evacuation procedures
   b. Initiating shutdown procedures
   c. Using fire extinguishers
   d. Using oxygen and respirators
   e. Searching for disabled or missing employees
   f. Assessing when it is safe to reenter the building

Safety and Health Management Plans

According to Occupational Safety and Health Administration (OSHA), there are four characteristics a safety and health management plan should have to be considered effective. First, an effective plan should establish a specific system that an organization can use to identify hazards in the workplace. Second, the plan should establish a training program that teaches employees to avoid hazards and to perform tasks in the safest way possible. Third, an effective safety and health management plan should include specific procedures and programs designed to eliminate hazards that the organization identified or at least minimize the risk that a hazard will injure or kill an employee or cause an employee to become ill. Finally, it should allow employees at all levels of the organization to be involved in the identification, prevention, and elimination of hazards in the workplace.

Emergency Action Plans

There is certain information that should be included in every organization's emergency action plan. All emergency action plans should explain the alarm system that will be used to inform employees and other individuals at the worksite that they need to evacuate, should include in-depth exit route plans that describe which routes employees should take to escape the building, and should include in-depth plans that describe what actions employees should take before evacuating, such as shutting down equipment, closing doors, and so on. All emergency action plans should also include detailed systems for handling different types of emergencies and a system that can be used to verify that all employees have escaped the worksite.

Fire Prevention Plans

There is a variety of different information that should be included in a fire prevention plan, and the specific information included in a fire prevention plan will vary from organization to organization. However, certain information should be included in every organization's fire prevention plan. All fire prevention plans should provide detailed descriptions of the specific areas where employees can find fire extinguishers and other fire prevention equipment, detailed descriptions of the types of fire hazards present in the workplace, and detailed descriptions of the appropriate procedures that should be followed to avoid these fire hazards. Fire prevention plans should also provide detailed descriptions of any hazardous waste that may be a fire hazard and the appropriate way to dispose of or store hazardous waste to avoid a fire.

Emergency Response Plan

All emergency response plans should identify the records and resources essential to the organization, identify the individuals responsible for protecting those records and resources, and describe the procedures that individuals should follow to safeguard the records and resources essential for the organization to continue functioning. Emergency response plans must also establish a system the organization can use to continue communicating with vendors and the public during and after an emergency.

Disaster Recovery Plans

Certain information should be included in every organization's disaster recovery plan. Equipment and locations that can be utilized temporarily in the event of an emergency should be identified. Also, agencies and personnel that may be able to help the organization continue functioning immediately after an emergency should be identified. It is also wise to establish a set of procedures the organization can use to bring the personnel and equipment together after an emergency. Disaster recovery plans should also identify alternative sources the organization can use to receive supplies or products if the emergency disables the organization's normal supply chain.

Business Continuity Planning and Recovery

Business continuity planning is a process in which an organization attempts to ensure the organization will be able to continue functioning even after an emergency. This type of planning is important because there are a large number of emergencies that an organization can face, and each one may affect the ability of the organization to continue functioning normally. As a result, business continuity planning is a process that organizations use to create a plan or group of plans that will help the organization return to normal after a natural disaster or similar emergency occurs. The process of business continuity planning usually begins with an organization conducting a threat assessment such as a SWOT analysis. Once the organization has identified the threats that exist, the organization can rank those threats based on the risk associated with each threat. Finally, the organization can create a plan or set of plans that establish a system the organization can use to recover from emergencies, which the organization can continually update as threats to the organization change.

Review Video: Emergency Response, Business Continuity, and Disaster Planning
Visit mometrix.com/academy and enter code: 678024

Workplace Illness, Injury Prevention, Investigation, Reporting, and Accommodation

The **Occupational Safety and Health Act of 1970** mandates that it is the employer's responsibility to provide an environment that is free from known hazards that are causing or may cause serious harm or death to employees. The only workers who are not protected by this act are those who are self-employed, family farms where only family members work, and workplaces that are covered by other federal statutes or state and local government. This act is monitored and enforced by **OSHA**. OSHA ensures employees have a safe workplace free from recognized hazards. It also requires all employers and each employee to comply with occupational safety and health standards, rules, and regulations. Employers may be found in violation if they are aware or should have been aware of potential hazards that could cause injury or death.

Occupational Injuries to be Reported

OSHA requires that any occupational injury or illness be **recorded** if it results in medical treatment that goes beyond first aid, restricted work activity or job transfer, time away from work, loss of consciousness, or death. An incident that results in an inpatient hospitalization must be reported within 24 hours, and any incident resulting in an employee's death must be reported to the nearest OSHA office within eight hours. For each recordable injury or illness, an **OSHA Form 301 Injury and Illness Incident Report** must be completed within seven calendar days. Employers are obligated to keep a log of all incidents on **OSHA Form 300 Log of Work-Related Injuries and Illnesses**, and a concise report of annual incidents should be reported on **OSHA Form 300A Summary of Work-Related Injuries and Illnesses** at the end of each year. Forms 300 and 300A should be posted no later than February 1 through April 30, and all documentation should be kept for five years so it is available on request for examination. Any procedure or doctor's visit that can be labeled as first aid does not need to be recorded. However, any needle-stick injury, cut from a sharp object contaminated with another person's blood, or incision that requires stitches should be reported.

Illness and Injury Prevention

Preventing workplace illness and injury includes training employees, following OSHA standards, and being mindful of and preparing for the potential hazards typically seen in the line of duty.

Safety Training Programs

Most organizations can follow a series of basic steps to create an effective safety training program. First, a safety risk assessment is conducted to determine the safety hazards present in the workplace. Then each hazard is investigated to determine if training will help eliminate the dangers associated with the hazard. If so, information can be identified that each member needs to know about the hazard, and a series of training goals and objectives based on these needs can be established. Once training goals have been established, a training program can be created and implemented, and then the results can be evaluated.

Workplace Injury or Illness Investigation

When an employee is injured on the job or becomes ill as a result of completing work duties, the employer must investigate the incident to understand why it happened. This investigation should identify ways to prevent similar incidents from occurring in the future. An employer's internal investigation should entail interviewing the sick or injured employee, assessing that employee's immediate work environment, and interviewing other employees who may have witnessed the incident or worked under the same conditions. The OSHA Form 301 Injury and Illness Incident Report should be completed for all recordable incidents. However, employers may want to document the incident further for internal purposes. If that's the case, they should create a standardized form for collecting the details to ensure that each investigation is conducted in a similar fashion and that no important information gets overlooked. Sometimes, OSHA will investigate an employer. These investigations may occur either on- or off-site.

On-Site Investigations

In certain situations, OSHA may decide it is necessary to conduct an on-site investigation into the working conditions of a particular worksite. These investigations are usually unannounced, but each investigation will follow a set of specific procedures established by OSHA, which an employer or human resource professional should keep in mind. First, a trained investigator from OSHA known as a compliance safety and health officer (CSHO) will travel to the worksite and inform the employer or a member of the employer's staff that he or she has come to perform an investigation of the worksite. Once the employer has verified that the CSHO's credentials are in order, at an opening conference, the CSHO will inform the organization's management of exactly what is being investigated at the worksite and why the investigation is taking place. The CSHO will then tour the facilities with a member of management and usually with an employee. Once the CSHO has completed his or her tour, the CSHO will then inform the employer of any violations at a closing conference.

The number of investigations OSHA can conduct at any one time is relatively low as the agency has a limited number of CSHOs available at any given time. As a result, OSHA uses a priority system to identify which worksites should be investigated first based on the level of danger associated with the worksite. This priority system includes five levels, and each priority level represents a certain amount of danger associated with the worksite. The five levels of the priority system from lowest to highest priority are follow-up inspections, planned or programmed high-hazard inspections, inspections resulting from employee complaints, inspections resulting from catastrophes or fatal accidents, and inspections resulting from imminent danger.

Follow-up investigations are any investigation conducted by a CSHO to verify that an employer has taken action to eliminate any health or safety violations the CSHO previously identified. Follow-up investigations are considered to be the fifth priority level, which is the lowest priority assigned by OSHA. A planned or programmed high-hazard inspection is an investigation scheduled for a particular worksite because the worksite is involved in an industry identified as extremely dangerous. These investigations are considered to be the fourth priority level, which is the second-lowest priority assigned by OSHA. Investigations resulting from an employee complaint include any situation in which OSHA has received a specific complaint from an employee about unsafe or unhealthy working conditions and that employee has requested an investigation. These investigations are considered to be the third priority level, which is the mid-level priority.

The OSHA investigation priority system consists of five levels, and the two highest priority levels are the catastrophes and fatal accidents level and the imminent danger level. Investigations resulting from catastrophes and fatal accidents refer to any investigation required because at least three employees have been hospitalized due to an accident at a worksite or at least one employee has died from an accident at a worksite. These investigations are considered to be the second priority level and are therefore given the second-highest priority. Investigations resulting from imminent danger refer to any investigation required because it is likely an individual will die or be seriously injured in the near future due to the working conditions of a particular worksite. Investigations at the imminent danger level are assigned the highest priority by OSHA and are usually investigated first.

Off-Site Investigations

In certain situations, OSHA may decide it is necessary to conduct an off-site investigation into the working conditions of a particular worksite. OSHA may conduct an off-site investigation if the employees at a worksite do not appear to be in imminent danger of harm due to the health and safety violations that may be occurring at a worksite, the worksite is not related to an industry identified as high risk or already scheduled for an investigation, the employer does not have a history of any serious violations, and the employer has complied with any OSHA requests made prior to the complaint or report. If OSHA determines an off-site investigation is necessary, but an on-site investigation is not, it will contact the employer by phone and identify the specific violation(s) that have been reported. Once the employer has been contacted, the company has five days to mail or fax a written description of any health and safety issues identified and a plan for addressing those issues.

Workplace Illness or Injury Accommodations

Workers' Compensation

Workers' compensation provides reimbursement of accident expenses and income continuation for employees who sustain a work-related injury. To be covered and eligible for benefits, a worker must be performing a covered job as an employee of a covered employer. There are **three types of benefits** available: medical expenses, income continuation, and death benefits. Funds are available through an insurance program, and premiums are paid by the employer while being administered by each state per local law or the federal government for federal workers. There is usually a certain waiting period before wage replacement payments are available, and they typically amount to 50 to 70 percent of a worker's average weekly wages.

Mental Health

Although mental health is not covered by OSHA, it is integral to a healthy and successful workforce, and employees could receive workers' compensation for physical or mental breakdowns that are caused by the cumulative trauma of a highly stressful occupation. Four of the main challenges to **mental health** are burnout, anxiety, depression, and boredom. Additionally, individuals respond to environmental stressors with three phases: the **alarm reaction** (the adrenaline rush in which the endocrine system triggers the body into fight-or-flight mode); the **resistance stage** (in which the body tries to regain balance); and the **exhaustion phase** (at which point the body has endured severe weakening and can no longer adapt). There are a few common **coping strategies**: eliminate the stressor, often through the avoidance of exposure or additional responsibilities; relaxation techniques, such as massage, yoga, breathing exercises, or biofeedback; social support, frequently through a network of family, friends, or community membership; and physical exercise programs that remove tension caused by stress.

Light or Modified Duty

Whenever employees are on worker's compensation leave, the goal should be to get them back to work as soon as safely possible. While employees are out, human resources should keep in regular contact with them regarding their recovery and anticipated return to work timeline. Depending on their condition, skills, and available work within the organization, employees may be able to come back to work early, serving in a modified or light-duty capacity. For example, an employee with a leg injury may be unable to stand for prolonged periods of time, making work on a production line medically inadvisable. However, this employee is also qualified to perform data entry and other clerical tasks that can be completed sitting down. If such work is available, the employer should offer it to the employee. If the employee is covered by the FMLA, he or she may refuse the modified duty. The employer cannot retaliate against the employee for this decision. The company can, however, discontinue workers' compensation or disability payments if the employee refuses work that's allowed under a doctor's advisement. Light or modified duty benefits both the employee and the employer. It gets the employee back into the organization and earning a full paycheck sooner. It also reduces the employer's workers' compensation costs and increases firm productivity and employee morale.

Measuring Quality Assurance

Quality assurance can be tracked and measured utilizing total quality management to reduce errors and improve service. Many **total quality management programs** share common elements, such as customer focus, strategic planning, or continuous improvement. Moreover, most of these programs include the following steps:

1. Performance planning—identifying goals and desired behaviors
2. Customer-centric products and services—setting and communicating performance standards
3. Statistical control methods for measuring results and providing feedback
4. Implementing performance improvement strategies
5. Evaluating results and benchmarking

Total quality management is a strategy to maintain the highest level of quality possible for the output produced by each specific task carried out by the organization. In most organizations, total quality management is implemented by using a series of procedures that are designed to establish a quality-oriented organizational culture and a system for monitoring and controlling the quality of each task performed.

Harassment and Discrimination Prevention

Companies should complete regular **harassment training** because employers must exercise reasonable care to avoid and prevent harassment. Otherwise, employers may be found liable for the harassing behaviors of vendors, clients, coworkers, and supervisors. Harassment is defined as any demeaning or degrading comments, jokes, name-calling, actions, graffiti, or other belittling conduct that may be found offensive. Any form of **derogatory speech** can be considered harassment, including neutral words that may be perceived in a vulgar or intimidating way. Furthermore, the Civil Rights Act of 1964 protects individuals from harassment on the basis of race, color, religion, sex, or national origin. More importantly, damages awarded under Title VII can total anywhere from $50,000 to $300,000, depending upon the size of the employer.

Corporate Social Responsibility

Influence of Organizational Philosophy on Culture

Organizational philosophy is a key element of culture and creates the foundational culture, values, beliefs, and guidelines for doing business. This philosophy cultivates the relationships among the organization, employees, customers, and shareholders. An organization's philosophy is derived from the **mission statement** and describes the set of values, beliefs, and norms of doing business. The organizational philosophy may provide a basis for establishing **departmental philosophies** as well. Moreover, employees and managers need to clearly understand the organizational philosophies, cultures, policies, and procedures so they can all act in alignment with organizational goals and strategies.

Creating Shared Values

Organizational culture is often based upon a set of **shared values**. Shared values are the principles, traditions, attitudes, and beliefs that influence the members of an organization. Ideally, these values support the vision and mission of the organization. For example, highly competitive industries such as national sports leagues might list assertiveness and emphasizing outcomes as values. Inclusive industries in human services might list traits like fairness, tolerance, respect, and team orientation as values. Many startup and lean environments will list innovation, precision, successful experimentation, and strong task analysis as key values. Regardless of which shared values an organization chooses, a set of these values should be clearly communicated to applicants, employees, and shareholders so that all parties are in alignment for sustainability and success.

Principles of Corporate Citizenship and Governance

To have an effective corporate citizenship and governance system in place, human resources should engage in the following:

- Create a code of corporate conduct and ethics so that all members of the firm know what behaviors are expected of them.
- Create a policy detailing how leaders and employees will be trained on the code, how any code violations should be reported, how whistle-blowers will be protected, how issues will be investigated, what consequences violators will face, and how reports will be tracked and documented.
- Ensure that leaders and board members uphold their fiduciary responsibility and always act with the best interests of the company in mind.
- Help spearhead or support environmental initiatives like reducing consumption and waste or using more eco-friendly supplies.
- Help spearhead or support activities that attempt to solve societal problems like poverty or a lack of access to clean water.

Community Engagement

Community engagement involves creating partnerships through dedication and community involvement. Both the internal organization and external community are strengthened through an exchange of responsibility, knowledge, and services. The millennial generation entering the workforce is changing the way businesses strategize ways to attract and retain younger workers. This group in particular is drawn to organizations that are active in philanthropy and community engagement. Whereas **community engagement programs** are designed to help the populations they serve, they may also be used to teach staff sensitivity, greater understanding, and leadership skills through employee volunteerism. Advocates of corporate community engagement programs also find that it achieves triple returns, providing benefits to the charity or nonprofit organization in the form of free services, to the employees in the form of useful experience, and to the employer in the form of a more cognizant workforce. Community engagement can also provide advantages in recruitment, teamwork, morale, retention, corporate brand, reputation, and sales.

Corporate Philanthropy and Charitable Giving

The elements of **corporate social responsibility** differ greatly; some may emphasize philanthropy, donating a percentage of profits to charity, or volunteering activities. Organizations often find philanthropy and charitable work financially rewarding, especially when synchronizing business strategies to cause agendas. Not only can **corporate philanthropy** increase revenues, but it has also been known to boost morale and employee engagement. The corporate culture surrounding philanthropy and charitable giving should be covered during new hire orientations. Employees should feel empowered to see opportunities and explore creative ways to solve challenges efficiently. Human resource practitioners can support corporate philanthropy to demonstrate good values, build image, and foster a sense of efficiency. Volunteers serve as **philanthropic representatives of the company** in the community and can have a strong impact on the public. However, every company will need to determine the best approach for corporate philanthropy that aligns with organizational goals and values. Employers can set up payroll deductions so that employees can easily donate to causes that they support. The employer may also elect to match the employee's contributions.

Employee Volunteer Programs

There are many companies that have implemented **volunteer programs** to encourage their employees to participate in charitable activities; some provide employees with supplemental time off during work hours. Employers may also set up community service days when the business closes or runs with a reduced crew and donates time to help the community. This could look like stocking shelves in a food pantry, cleaning up a local park, or visiting sick children in the hospital. Leadership may also decide to get on the board of directors for community organizations that matter to them. Whereas many companies will create **guidelines** of acceptable activities or reject things like hours spent participating on political campaigns, others might attempt to diversify local, national, and global support. The bottom line is that the firm must decide which causes and organizations to support. Some employers will also impose **exclusions**, such as limiting eligibility to employees with satisfactory performance, or require manager approval to ensure that time off will not conflict with scheduling or productivity. These programs are intended to help the communities they serve, but they also help employees develop **soft skills**. Understanding, sensitivity, empathy, collaboration, communication, and leadership are some desirable workplace traits that are cultivated by volunteering activities. Moreover, organizations that are able to make a connection between volunteering programs and diversity will provide opportunities to build an inclusive workplace, cultural competence, and an ability to get along with individuals from diverse backgrounds. Volunteer programs should be well communicated, including how to sign up, and rules for scheduling time to participate in advance. Although participation can be encouraged, human resources and leadership must keep these programs strictly voluntary and not pressure staff into taking part. The benefits of donating time or money are that it feels good to do it, it puts the firm in a favorable light, and it helps others. Additionally, offering ways to give back can be a morale booster and a means to recruit and retain talent.

U.S. Employment Law and Regulations

Compensation

FLSA

The **FLSA of 1938,** also known as the Wagner-Connery Wages and Hours Act, or the Wage Hour Bill, sets minimum wage standards, overtime pay standards, and child labor restrictions. The act is administered by the Wage and Hour Division of the Department of Labor. FLSA carefully separates employees as exempt or nonexempt from provisions, requires that employers calculate **overtime** for covered employees at one and one-half times the regular rate of pay for all hours worked in excess of 40 hours during a week, and defines how a workweek should be measured. The purpose of **minimum wage standards** is to ensure a living wage and to reduce poverty for low-income families, minority workers, and women. The **child labor provisions** protect minors from positions that may be harmful or detrimental to their health or well-being and regulates the hours minors can legally work. The act also outlines requirements for employers to keep records of hours, wages, and related payroll items.

Equal Pay Act

The **Equal Pay Act**, which was passed in 1963, prevents wage discrimination based on gender. It requires an employer to provide equal pay to both men and women performing similar tasks unless the employer can prove that there is an acceptable reason for the difference in pay, such as merit, seniority, quantity or quality of work performed. This act also establishes the criteria that must be considered to determine whether a particular position is similar. This includes the effort necessary for the tasks related to the position, the level of responsibility associated with the position, the skills required to perform the position, and the working conditions associated with the position.

Lilly Ledbetter Fair Pay Act of 2009

This law overturns the 2007 Supreme Court decision in the *Ledbetter v. Good Year Tire & Rubber Co.* case, which ruled that the statute of limitations to make a discriminatory pay claim was 180 days from the first discriminatory paycheck. The Lilly Ledbetter Fair Pay Act of 2009 results in the statute of limitations restarting with each discriminatory paycheck. The act applies to all protected classes and covers both wages and pensions. Due to the scope of the act, employers could face claims years after an employee has left the company. This act was designed to make employers more proactive in resolving pay inequities.

ERISA

ERISA was passed in 1974 to protect employees who are covered under private pensions and employee welfare benefit plans. ERISA ensures that employees receive promised benefits and are protected against early termination, mismanaged funds, or fraudulent activities. ERISA mandates that employers adhere to eligibility requirements, vesting requirements, portability practices, funding requirements, fiduciary responsibilities, reporting and disclosure requirements, as well as compliance testing. Most employees who have at least 1,000 hours of work in 12 months for two consecutive years are eligible to participate in **private pension plans**. Employees have the right to receive some portion of employer contributions when their employment ends. Employees must be allowed to transfer pension funds from one retirement account to another. Sufficient funds must be available from the employer to cover future payments. Employers must appoint an individual to be responsible for seeking ideal portfolio options and administering pension funds. Employers must adhere to extensive reporting requirements, provide summary plan documents, and notify participants of any changes. Employers are required to complete annual minimum coverage, actual deferral percentage, actual contribution percentage, and top-heavy testing to prevent discrimination in favor of highly compensated employees.

Federal Wage Garnishment Law

The **Federal Wage Garnishment Law of 1968** imposes limitations on the amount of disposable earnings that may be withheld from an employee's income in a given pay period to satisfy a **wage garnishment order** for failure to pay a debt. The law restricts the amount that can be withheld to 25 percent of an employee's disposable weekly earnings or an amount that is 30 times the FLSA minimum wage, whichever is less. However, overdue payments to the IRS, child support in arrears, and alimony payments are a few exceptions that allow for more significant amounts to be withheld. Employers must immediately begin income withholdings upon receipt of a garnishment order, and funds must be sent to the respective agency within seven days. Failure to do so could impose hefty fines and penalties for the employer. There are certain protections for employees, whereby employers may not take disciplinary action or discriminate due to the receipt or obligation to comply with wage garnishment orders.

Employee and Labor Relations

NLRA

The **NLRA** was passed by Congress in 1935 after a long period of conflict in labor relations. Also known as the **Wagner Act**, after the New York Senator Robert Wagner, it was intended to be an economic stabilizer and establish collective bargaining in industrial relations. Section 7 of the NLRA provides employees with the right to form, join, or assist **labor organizations** as well as the right to engage in **concerted activities** such as collective bargaining through representatives or other mutual aid. Section 8 of the NLRA also identifies five **unfair labor practices**:

1. Employers shall not interfere with or coerce employees from the rights outlined in Section 7.
2. Employers shall not dominate or disrupt the formation of a labor union.
3. Employers shall not allow union membership or activity to influence hiring, firing, promotion, or related employment decisions.
4. Employers shall not discriminate against or discharge an employee who has given testimony or filed a charge with the NLRA.
5. Employers cannot refuse bargaining in good faith with employee representatives.

Taft-Hartley Act

Because many employers felt that the NLRA gave too much power to unions, Congress passed the **Labor Management Relations Act** in 1947. Also known as the **Taft-Hartley Act**, the act sought to avoid unnecessary strikes and impose certain restrictions over union activities. The act addresses **four basic issues**: unfair labor practices by unions, the rights of employees, the rights of employers, and national emergency strikes. Moreover, the act prohibits unions from the following:

- Restraining or coercing employees from their right to not engage in union activities
- Forcing an employer to discriminate in any way against an employee to encourage or discourage union membership
- Forcing an employer to pay for work or services that are not needed or not performed
- Conducting certain types of strikes or boycotts
- Charging excessive initiation fees or membership dues when employees are required to join a union shop

Landrum-Griffin Act

The government exercised further control over union activities in 1959 by the passage of the **Labor Management Reporting and Disclosure Act**. Commonly known as the **Landrum-Griffin Act**, this law regulates the **internal conduct of labor unions** to reduce the likelihood of fraud and improper actions. The act imposes controls on five major areas: reports to the secretary of labor, a bill of rights for union members, union trusteeships, conduct of union elections, and financial safeguards. Some key provisions include the following:

- Granting equal rights to every union member with regard to nominations, attending meetings, and voting
- Requiring unions to submit and make available to the public a copy of its constitution, bylaws, and annual financial reports
- Requiring unions to hold regular elections every five years for national and every three years for local organizations
- Monitoring the management and investment of union funds, making embezzlement a federal crime

Review Video: US Employment Law: Employee and Labor Relations (NLRA)
Visit mometrix.com/academy and enter code: 972790

NLRB vs. Weingarten (1975)

This case resulted in union employees being able to request coworker presence at investigatory meetings that may involve disciplinary action. In 2000, the NLRB expanded this protection to nonunion employees. These are known as **Weingarten rights**.

Lechmere, Inc. vs. NLRB (1992)

This case determined that nonemployee union organizers may solicit employees on private company property if no other reasonable alternative to contact employees exists. This preserves the employees' right to organize.

Equal Employment Opportunity

EEOC

The EEOC was created to enforce Title VII and the ADA. The EEOC holds jurisdiction over any charges under those titles and has the power to authorize or bring suit in federal court on behalf of an employee. The EEOC may help an aggrieved party prosecute or issue a right to sue notice, giving permission for the person to pursue the case independently. The primary responsibility of the EEOC is to **prevent discrimination** based on race, color, religion, sex, origin, disability, or age. Employers are obligated to furnish any information the EEOC requests, including annual reporting for employers with 50 or more employees. There are **five steps** the EEOC follows when handling discrimination cases: 1) a charge filed within 180 days, 2) an attempt at a no-fault settlement, 3) an EEOC investigation, 4) an attempt to resolve through conciliation, and 5) a recommendation for or against litigation. Drastic remedies may be decreed upon an employer found guilty of discrimination, not limited to reinstatement of the employee, back pay, elimination of testing, hiring quotas, and new training programs.

Civil Rights Acts

The **13th and 14th Amendments** address equal protection in employment rights by state and local governments for all citizens. Moreover, major prohibitions against racial discrimination in hiring, placement, and continuation of employment contracts by private employers, unions, and employment agencies date back to the early **Civil Rights Acts of 1866 and 1870**. Furthermore, the **National Labor Relations Act of 1935** indirectly prohibits racial discrimination in labor unions by requiring fair representation for all. However, New York was the first state to pass additional regulations to eliminate discrimination in state employment due to race, creed, color, or national origin with their **Fair Employment Practices Act of 1945**. This was well before **Title VII of the Civil Rights Act of 1964** prohibited employment discrimination based on race, color, religion, sex, or national origin to all employers with 15 or more employees. Title VII was amended by the **Equal Employment Opportunity Act of 1972**, which strengthened the enforcement and expanded coverage so that one person could file suit on behalf of many affected individuals for equal damages. The act was last revised in 1991 to more clearly define which actions are discriminatory and outline prosecution procedures for jury trials and monetary damages.

The Civil Rights Act Section 703(e) states that it is **legal to discriminate** on the basis of sex, religion, or national origin in special occasions where the specified characteristic is a "'bona fide occupational qualification (**BFOQ**) and reasonably necessary to normal operations and the survival of that particular business or enterprise." It is the employer's responsibility to prove and corroborate a BFOQ and its necessity to business operations and that no other options are available that would have less discriminatory impact. The Supreme Court does not obligate employers to make religious accommodations that could impose upon the rights of other workers, decrease production efficiencies, accommodate unfair perks that would not benefit others, provide undue hardship, or breach a collective bargaining agreement. Moreover, the courts have rejected client preference or traditional BFOQs, and only a select amount of cases have upheld race or gender as legitimate BFOQs. Examples of sex being upheld as BFOQs by the courts are 1) when social modesty morals and privacy conflicts are the main concern for clients; 2) when a position requires a defined aesthetic authenticity; or 2) when one sex is biologically unable to perform job duties. **EEOC guidelines** encourage employers to prepare written job descriptions listing the essential functions of a job.

ADA

The ADA was established in 1990 to protect individuals with physical or mental impairments from job discrimination. The law requires that all employers with 15 or more employees make reasonable accommodations to employ disabled people who are otherwise qualified. Individuals are considered otherwise qualified if they can perform the essential functions of the job with reasonable accommodations. There may be occasions in which the act does not cover people who have disabilities that might pose a direct threat to themselves or the general public because reasonable accommodations cannot eliminate the potential threat. In addition, if an employer would face undue hardship (generally high cost relative to company size), accommodations can be refused. Employers should engage in an interactive dialog with the employee (or job candidate) to come up with a reasonable accommodation whenever possible.

Amendments to the act broaden the definition of disability to include anything that severely limits a major life activity or bodily function. Major life activities include but are not limited to seeing, thinking, reading, or working. Further, EEOC has noted that the following **impairments** will easily be concluded to meet the definitions of a disability: deafness, blindness, intellectual disabilities, partially or completely missing limbs, mobility impairments that require the use of a wheelchair, cerebral palsy, diabetes, autism, epilepsy, HIV/AIDs, cancer, multiple sclerosis, muscular dystrophy, major depression, bipolar disorder, posttraumatic stress disorder, obsessive compulsive disorder, and schizophrenia. Additionally, changes to the act prohibit reverse discrimination claims from non-disabled workers.

ADEA

The **Age Discrimination in Employment Act** (ADEA) was first passed in 1967 to protect job applicants and employees between 40 and 60 years of age. The ADEA applies to all private employers with 20 or more employees, government agencies, and labor unions with 25 or more members. The act also prohibits these parties from **discriminating against older workers** in benefit plan designs. Although the upper age limit was raised to 65 and 75 in subsequent years, the Consolidated Omnibus Budget Reconciliation Act eliminated an upper limit to cover almost everyone at least 40 years of age, the exception to this coverage being that certain executives may be forced into retirement at age 65.

Pregnancy Discrimination in Employment Act of 1978

There are two main clauses of the Pregnancy Discrimination in Employment Act of 1978. The first clause applies to Title VII's **prohibition against sex discrimination**, which also directly applies to prejudice on the basis of childbirth, pregnancy, or related medical conditions. The second clause requires that employers treat women affected by pregnancy the **same as others** for all employment-related reasons and similarly in their ability or inability to work. In short, the Pregnancy Discrimination in Employment Act makes it illegal to fire or refuse to hire or promote a woman because she is pregnant, force a pregnancy leave on women who are willing and able to perform the job, and stop accruing seniority for a woman because she is out of work to give birth.

Vocational Rehabilitation Act

The Vocational Rehabilitation Act was intended to increase occupational opportunities for disabled individuals and to prohibit discrimination against "handicapped" persons. The **Rehabilitation Act** applies to federal government contractors and subcontractors holding contracts or subcontracts of $10,000 or more. Contractors and subcontractors with greater than $50,000 in contracts and more than 50 employees must develop written affirmative action plans that address hiring and promoting persons with disabilities. Although there are regulations that protect those engaged in addiction treatment, this act does not protect against individuals who currently suffer with substance abuse that prevents them from performing the duties of the job or whose employment would constitute a direct threat to the safety and property of others.

UGESP

The Uniform Guidelines on Employee Selection Procedures (UGESP), which were passed in 1978, are actually a collection of principles, techniques, and procedures designed to help employers comply with federal anti-discrimination laws. The primary purpose of these guidelines is to define the specific types of procedures that may cause disparate impact and are considered illegal. The UGESP relates to unfair procedures that make it much less likely that an individual belonging to a protected class would be able to receive a particular position.

Griggs v. Duke Power Co. (1971)

Prior to the 1964 Civil Rights Act, Duke Power Co. segregated employees by race. Once the act passed, the company started requiring a high school diploma and a certain score on an IQ test to qualify for any positions above manual labor. As a result, many African Americans could not obtain the higher-paying jobs. This 1971 case determined that employers must be able to demonstrate that position requirements are actually linked to being able to perform the work. It also determined that employers may be charged with discrimination, even if they did not intend to discriminate. This is known as disparate impact.

Phillips v. Martin Marietta Corp. (1971)

Linked to the 1964 Civil Rights Act, this case ruled that a company cannot refuse to employ women with young children if they employ men with young children unless there is a legitimate business necessity.

Job Safety and Health

Sexual Harassment

The Civil Rights Act of 1964 bans **sexual harassment** and makes it an employer's responsibility to prevent it. Sexual harassment can be defined as unsolicited sexual advances, requests for sexual favors, and any other conduct of a sexual nature that meets any of the following conditions:

1. Obedience to such conduct is construed as a condition of employment either explicitly or implicitly.
2. Obedience to or rejection of such conduct is used as the basis for employment decisions affecting an individual.
3. Such conduct produces an intimidating, hostile, or offensive working environment or otherwise has the effect of interfering with an individual's work performance.

Sexual harassment is separated into two types: **quid pro quo (this for that) cases** and **hostile environment cases**. Victims do not need to suffer loss, but the harassment needs to be pervasive or severe. Employees may be offended by any sexual conduct in the workplace, such as lewd comments, jokes, pornographic pictures, or touching. Employees who voice discomfort may request that the environment be changed. If an employer fails to correct the offensive environment, employees may press charges without needing to demonstrate physical or psychological damage.

Leave and Benefits

FMLA

The FMLA of 1993 is a federal regulation that provides employees the right to a maximum limit of 12 weeks of **unpaid leave** each 12-month period for the specified care of medical conditions that affect themselves or immediate family members. To be eligible for FMLA leave, an employee must have worked for a covered employer for the preceding 12 months and for a minimum of 1,250 hours during that time. All private employers, public or government agencies, and local schools with 50 or more employees within a 75-mile radius must adhere to the regulations. Qualifying events covered under FMLA include the following:

- The birth or adoption of a new child within one year of birth or placement.
- The employee's own serious health condition that involves a period of incapacity.
- An ill or injured spouse, child, or parent who requires the employee's care.
- Any qualifying exigency (such as arranging childcare, tending to legal matters, and attending military ceremonies) due to the employee's spouse, child's, or parent's active-duty foreign deployment.
- The care of an ill or injured covered service member as long as the employee is a spouse, child, parent, or next of kin. In addition, time to care for military personnel or recent veterans has been expanded to 26 weeks in a 12-month period.

The FMLA has undergone some significant amendments, and human resource practitioners should be aware of the following:

- If a company fails to denote an employee's leave as FMLA leave, the employee may be eligible to receive compensation for any losses incurred.
- Prior to 2008, all FMLA disputes required Department of Labor or legal intervention. Now, employees and employers are encouraged to work any issues out in-house to avoid the cost of litigation.
- Light duty does not count toward FMLA taken.
- FMLA covers medical issues arising from preexisting conditions.
- Due to their unique scheduling, airline employees are eligible for FMLA after 504 or more hours worked during the preceding 12 months.

COBRA

The **Consolidated Omnibus Budget Reconciliation Act (COBRA) of 1986** requires that all employers with 20 or more employees continue the availability of **healthcare benefits coverage** and protects employees from the potential economic hardship of losing these benefits when they are terminated, working reduced hours, or quit. COBRA also provides coverage to the employee's spouse and dependents as qualified beneficiaries. Events that qualify for this continuation of coverage include the following:

- Voluntary or involuntary termination for any other reason than gross misconduct
- Reduction in hours that would otherwise result in loss of coverage
- Divorce or legal separation from the employee
- Death of the employee
- The employee becoming disabled and entitled to Medicare
- The dependent no longer being a dependent child under plan rules (older than 26)

Typically, the employee and qualified beneficiaries are entitled to 18 months of continued coverage. There are some instances that will extend coverage for up to an additional 18 months. Coverage will be lost if the employer terminates group coverage, premium payments are not received, or new coverage becomes available.

HIPAA

The **Health Insurance Portability and Accountability Act** (HIPAA) was passed in 1996 to provide greater protections and portability in healthcare coverage. Some individuals felt locked into current employer plans and feared that they would not be able to obtain coverage from a new employer plan due to preexisting conditions. Some of the **key HIPAA provisions** are preexisting condition exclusions, pregnancy, newborn and adopted children, credible coverage, renewal of coverage, medical savings accounts, tax benefits, and privacy provisions. Employees who have had another policy for the preceding 12 months cannot be excluded from coverage due to a preexisting condition or pregnancy or applied to newborn or adopted children who are covered by credible coverage within 30 days of the event. **Credible coverage** involves being covered under typical group health plans, and this coverage must be renewable to most groups and individuals as long as premiums are paid. **Medical savings accounts** were created by Congress for those who are self-employed or otherwise not eligible for credible coverage. Individuals who are self-employed are also allowed to take 80 percent of health-related expenses as a deduction. Finally, HIPAA introduced a series of several regulations that impose **civil and criminal penalties** on employers who disclose personal health information without consent.

PPACA

The **Patient Protection and Affordable Care Act** (PPACA) is a comprehensive healthcare law that was passed in 2010 to establish regulations on medical services, insurance coverage, preventative services, whistle-blowing, and similar practices. A few key provisions of PPACA include the following:

- **Individual mandate**—required all individuals to maintain health insurance or pay a penalty; however, it was removed from the statute effective tax year 2019
- **State healthcare exchanges**—provides individuals and families a portal in which they can shop through a variety of plans and purchase healthcare coverage
- **Employer shared responsibility**—requires that employers with more than 50 employees provide affordable coverage to all employees that work 30 or more hours per week or pay a penalty
- **Affordable coverage**—does not allow employers to shift the burden of healthcare costs to employees and imposes a penalty for employees who obtain government subsidies for coverage
- **Flexible spending accounts (FSAs)**—imposes a cap on pretax contributions to flexible spending accounts, health reimbursement arrangements (HRAs), and HSAs
- **Wellness incentives**—allows employers to provide premium discounts for employees who meet wellness requirements
- **Excise tax on "Cadillac" plans**—will impose excise tax on employers that provide expensive coverage beginning in 2022
- **W-2 reporting requirements**—requires employers to report the cost of coverage under employer-sponsored group health plans on each employee's W-2 form
- **Summary of benefits coverage**—requires insurance companies and employers to provide individuals with a summary of benefits coverage (SBC) using a standard form
- **Whistle-blower protections**—amends the FLSA to prohibit employers from retaliating against an employee who applies for health benefit subsidies or tax credits

National Federation of Independent Business v. Sebelius (2012)

Opponents of the PPACA argued that certain provisions of the law, such as the individual mandate, were unconstitutional. The court ultimately ruled that PPACA was constitutional, and it remained intact until President Trump reversed the individual mandate effective 2019. Other elements of the PPACA legislation are still currently in place.

Miscellaneous Protection Laws

GINA

Genetic Information Nondiscrimination Act (GINA) is a federal law for all employers passed in 2008 that makes it illegal for genetic information about a person or a family member to be used to **deny enrollment** in an insured or self-insured health care plan or to change the individual's premiums or contribution rates. The Department of Labor has defined genetic information as a disease or disorder in an individual's family medical history, the results of an individual's or family member's genetic tests, the fact that an individual or family member has sought or received genetic services, and genetic information of a fetus held by an individual or an individual's family member or an embryo lawfully carried by an individual or family member that receives assistive reproductive services. GINA also forbids an employer from requesting or otherwise collecting a person's genetic information unless the information is used in certain wellness programs, inadvertently obtained, needed to comply with certification requirements or regulations, or when observing biological effects of toxins in the workplace. The information an employer might obtain when requesting medical documentation for extended absences, requested leave, or accommodations is commonly accepted. Court remedies for GINA are similar to those existing for sex and racial discrimination.

Employee Polygraph Protection Act of 1988

The **Employee Polygraph Protection Act of 1988** was designed to protect individuals seeking employment from being required to submit to polygraph tests. This act specifically forbids private employers from basing hiring decisions on polygraph tests unless the individual is seeking a position involving pharmaceuticals, working in an armored car, or serving as a security officer. This act does not apply to any government agency or federal contractor or subcontractor with the Federal Bureau of Investigation, national defense, or national security contracts. If an employer requires a polygraph test and the position is not related to one of these areas, the company can be fined up to $10,000.

IRCA

The **Immigration Reform and Control Act** (IRCA) was passed in 1986 by Congress to reduce the volume of illegal immigrants coming into the United States for employment opportunities. The IRCA prohibits any employer from hiring **illegal immigrants**. Denying employment was considered necessary because border patrols could not handle the flow of unauthorized immigration. The act also prohibits employers with four or more employees from discriminating against applicants based upon citizenship or natural origin. The **Homeland Security Act of 2002** transferred control of immigration from the Department of Justice to the Department of Homeland Security's two bureaus: the Immigration and Customs Enforcement (ICE) and the U.S. Customs and Immigration Services (USCIS). New employees of all U.S. employers are required to complete and sign an **I-9 verification form** designed by the USCIS to certify that they are eligible for employment. The form requires two types of **verification**: 1) proof of identity and 2) evidence of employment authorization. The I-9 form must be completely executed by both the employee and employer within three days of hire. Employers must retain these forms for three years or for one year past the date of termination, whichever is longer. Employers need to take proactive steps to make certain their workforce is lawful. At the least, employers should verify information against the Social Security Administration.

USERRA

The **Uniformed Services Employment and Re-Employment Rights Act (USERRA) of 1994** is applicable to all employers. USERRA forbids employers from denying employment, reemployment, retention, promotion, or employment benefits due to service in the uniformed services. Employees absent in services for less than 31 days must report to the employer within eight hours after arriving safely home. Those who are absent between 31 and 180 days must submit an application for reemployment within 14 days. Those who are absent 181 days or more have 90 days to submit an applicant for reemployment. Employees are entitled to the positions that they would have held if they had remained continuously employed. If they are no longer qualified or able to perform the job requirements because of a service-related disability, they are to be provided with a position of equal seniority, status, and pay. Moreover, the **escalator principle** further entitles returning employees to all of the seniority-based benefits they had when their service began plus any additional benefits they would have accrued with reasonable certainty if they had remained continuously employed. Likewise, employees cannot be required to use accrued vacation or PTO during absences. USERRA requires all healthcare plans to provide **COBRA coverage** for up to 18 months of absence and entitles employees to restoration of coverage upon return. Pension plans must remain undisturbed by absences as well. However, those separated from the service for less-than-honorable circumstances are not protected by USERRA.

WARN Act

The **WARN Act** applies to employers with more than 100 full-time workers or more than 100 full- and part-time workers totaling at least 4,000 hours per week. The WARN Act requires that employers provide a minimum of 60 days' notice to local government and affected workers in the event of a plant closing that will result in job loss for 50 or more employees during a 30-day period and mass layoffs that will result in job loss for greater than 33 percent of workers or more than 500 employees during a 30-day period. There are few situational exceptions to the WARN Act, including natural disasters and unforeseeable business circumstances.

Privacy Protection Act

The Privacy Protection Act of 1974 was passed to protect the privacy of individuals employed by government agencies or by government contractors. Although this act prohibits government agencies from disclosing individual personnel records, the **Freedom of Information Act** requires these agencies to release certain information, like what the organization does or how it is organized. However, requests for information that could constitute a disclosure of personal privacy are exempt and remain protected. The Privacy Act also established the **Privacy Protection Study Commission**, which has outlined three main policy goals:

- minimize intrusiveness
- maximize fairness
- create legitimate expectations of confidentiality

The Privacy Commission also advocates five basic employee rights regarding procedures:

- notice
- authorization
- access
- correction
- confidentiality

Human Resources Expertise: Workplace Chapter Quiz

1. How many methods are there for calculating global compensation adjustments for international assignments?

a. Three
b. Four
c. Five
d. Six

2. Which of the following refers to a business moving to its home country to reduce costs?

a. Offshoring
b. Near-shoring
c. Co-sourcing
d. Onshoring

3. Which two main laws protect the employment of veterans and active-duty military?

a. FMLA and USERRA
b. USERRA and FLSA
c. FMLA and USVRRA
d. USLA and FMERRA

4. The four-fifths rule is used by the Equal Employment Opportunity Commission (EEOC) to determine what?

a. Affirmative action plans
b. Adverse impact
c. Disparate treatment
d. Disparate impact

5. None of the following are protected by the Occupational Safety and Health Act of 1970 EXCEPT?

a. Those who are self-employed
b. Family farms where only family members work
c. Those who work in extremely safe workplaces like libraries and bakeries
d. Workplaces that are covered by other federal statutes or by state and local government

6. Which of the following forms is a concise report of annual incidents that should be reported at the end of each year?

a. Form 301
b. Form 300
c. Form 301A
d. Form 300A

7. Which of the following is NOT one of the main challenges to mental health?

a. Burnout
b. Complacency
c. Anxiety
d. Depression

Chapter Quiz Answer Key

Behavioral Competencies: Leadership

1. D: Inclusive leadership is promoting an atmosphere of respect in which all employees have equal ability to share and utilize the skills they bring to the organization.

2. D: Douglas McGregor said that there are two ways for leaders to view employees: either through Theory X or Theory Y. When a leader subscribes to Theory X, he or she sees employees as lazy and only motivated by disciplinary action.

3. B: People management can be separated into four phases: directing, coaching, supporting, and delegating.

4. B: Herzberg concluded that an employee's motivation is affected by both hygiene factors and motivators. Hygiene factors are extrinsic and include salary, benefits, and work environment. Motivators are intrinsic and include growth and recognition.

5. A: Victor Vroom's expectancy theory assumes that rationality will drive employees toward the option that provides maximum pleasure and minimal pain.

6. B: Self-determination theory identifies three core intrinsic motivators: autonomy, competence, and relatedness.

7. B: Task identity is when employees can see how their roles affect the entire organization so that they no longer feel like they operate in isolation.

Behavioral Competencies: Interpersonal

1. D: All of these are intergroup interventions except static membership. Rotating membership, often useful in international relations, is a strategy involving moving members from one group to the other group. Group attitudes are strongly influenced by the group's members, so transferring people between groups may help build awareness and perspective.

2. C: With the cooperation style, preserving relationships is viewed as more important than being right.

3. A: When accommodation is employed, one party decides to give in to the other. Once the other party has what it wants, the conflict should be over. This technique can be useful when the accommodating party wants to preserve the relationship, end the conflict, or isn't that personally invested in the outcome of the situation.

4. B: A few key elements to relationship building include: connecting with others to find shared interests or goals, fostering a sense of community, and supporting others to solve problems or achieve goals.

5. C: Some essential principles of networking include the following:

- Create an engaging elevator speech about yourself
- Smile and be positive
- Differentiate yourself
- Set goals and achievement plans
- Strive to share information and facilitate opportunities for others
- Build up your personal reputation and credibility
- Follow up on all meetings and referrals

6. C: Cultural intelligence is a measure of one's capability to interact suitably with people from other cultures and to behave appropriately in multicultural situations. It involves the following:

- Motivational drives: personal interests and confidence in multicultural situations
- Knowledge and attitudes: learning and accepting how cultures are similar or different
- Cognitive or strategic thinking: awareness and ability to plan for multicultural interactions
- Behavioral actions: talent for relating and working with others of differing backgrounds

7. D: Edgar Schein developed his well-known model of organizational culture in the 1980s. Many of Schein's studies indicate that culture is rooted with the CEO and developed over time. The model separates culture into three core layers: artifacts, values and beliefs, and underlying assumptions.

Behavioral Competencies: Business

1. A: An asset is any resource possessed by the company as a result of previous actions and from which future gains are expected.

2. A: In a business case, current status describes how the solution will affect current operations.

3. A: OLAP, also known as online analytical processing, is on demand and facilitates decision-making.

4. C: Liquidity ratios measure the business's available cash or ability to pay off short-term debts.

5. B: Three of the most common sales and marketing business metrics are the number of customers or orders for the period, the average amount received for each order, and the gross profit margin.

6. A: Three of the most common information technology metrics an organization might use are the number of online orders, the availability of information resources, and the number of views per page or listing.

7. B: One popular method of business analysis is the SWOT analysis, which looks at the strengths, weaknesses, opportunities, and threats of the enterprise. Business analysis may be used to investigate business processes, management styles, team collaboration, employee engagement, information systems, or organizational communication and culture, among other things.

Human Resources Expertise: People

1. D: Most often used in manufacturing, Lean Six Sigma streamlines processes and eliminates activities identified as waste. There are eight types of waste: defects, overproduction, waiting, non-utilized talent, transportation, inventory, motion, and extra processing.

2. A: Critical chain is a form of project management that reduces the likelihood of the project's completion being delayed. The project is scheduled backward from the date the deliverables are due, and time buffers are added to protect the tasks that ultimately drive the duration of the project.

3. D: Gantt charts have dates listed along the top and tasks listed along the left side. The anticipated time for completing each task or subtask is reflected as a bar, and shading conveys progress. The end result looks almost like a staircase. Milestones are frequently represented as diamonds, and small arrows indicate dependencies.

4. D: A work breakdown structure (WBS) is a method for breaking a project down into a series of separate, smaller tasks. It's based on the 100 percent rule, which states that the smaller tasks must total 100 percent of the work necessary to complete the project.

5. C: The five forces model suggests that profit potential is a function of the interactions among suppliers, buyers, rival firms, substitute products, and potential entrants. Organizations can analyze these factors to determine profit potential and create a secure, competitive position.

6. A: The PESTLE analysis is an extension of the SWOT analysis and looks at how the following factors impact a business:

- P—political: Changes made by the government can affect a business in the form of tariffs, tax policy, and fiscal policy.
- E—economic: Changes to inflation, interest rates, and foreign exchange rates can affect the firm's finances and operations.
- S—social: Cultural trends affect consumer purchases, which affect an organization's revenue and profit.
- T—technological: Technology used in a business can enhance or detract from a company's innovation level and competitive advantage.
- L—legal: External laws and internal policies affect a firm's day-to-day operations.
- E—environmental: Climate, weather, and geographic location all have an impact on a company's performance.

7. D: The Fair Labor Standards Act (FLSA) separates employees into two main categories: exempt and nonexempt. Nonexempt employees must be paid minimum wage and overtime rates that meet both state and federal regulations.

8. D: The two basic principles of selection that influence the process of making an informed hiring decision are past behaviors and reliable and valid data. Past behaviors are the best predictors for future behavior, and knowing what was done in the past may be indicative of future actions.

9. D: Content validity assesses the skills and knowledge necessary to perform the tasks associated with a particular position.

10. A: A high-performance culture promotes goal achievement by setting clear objectives, clearly spelling out employee responsibilities, encouraging continuous development, and fostering trust.

This culture is characterized by innovation, collaboration, communication, leadership support, and accountability.

Human Resources Expertise: Organization

1. A: Key performance indicators (KPIs) measure specific human resource activities that contribute to the efficiency and effectiveness of a company. KPIs provide a company with quantitative measurements that can be used to examine qualities and actions that contribute to long-term success.

2. B: There are a few group formation theories, including propinquity or proximity theory (based on geography), exchange or benefit theory (based on rewards), balance theory (based on similar attitudes or interests), and activity theory (based on occupational task).

3. A: Storming is the most difficult stage. The team must work through conflicts related to authority, vision and values, personality, and cultural differences. The amount of work often seems overwhelming at this point, and team members struggle to listen to the opinions and experiences of others. If quality improvement processes are implemented and there is good communication, these barriers can become beneficial later on.

4. A: Functional organizational structure organizes firm departments based on their function or what they do for the company. A divisional organizational structure is vertical, and like the functional structure, promotes specialization and expertise. The matrix organizational structure is best for uncertain environments that deal with constantly changing products and/or for a strong focus on the customer experience.

5. B: Long-term forecasting often covers a time frame of 2-10 years and is reviewed on an annual basis for adjustment. There are many techniques for long-term forecasting, such as unit demand, probabilistic models and simulations, or trend projections and regression analysis.

6. C: Attrition, or restrictive hiring, is the act of reducing the workforce by not replacing individuals who leave an organization. Only absolutely essential roles that are critical to strategic business success are filled. Typically, attrition is used to avoid layoffs during times of financial burden.

7. C: The International Labour Organization (ILO) was founded in 1919 to address global working conditions. A part of the United Nations, the ILO comprises 187 member states. Its mission is to promote decent working conditions that include eliminating child labor, ending unlawful discrimination, protecting human rights, and supporting workers' rights to organize.

Human Resources Expertise: Workplace

1. B: There are four methods for calculating global compensation adjustments for international assignments:

- The home country-based approach, which is based on the employee's standard of living in his or her home country
- The host country-based approach, which is based upon local national rates
- The headquarters-based approach, which is based upon the home country of the organization
- The balance sheet approach, which calculates compensation based on home country rates, with all allowances, deductions, and reimbursements before converting into the host country's currency

2. D: The opposite of offshoring, onshoring entails a business moving to its home country to reduce costs.

3. A: There are two main laws, the Family and Medical Leave Act (FMLA) and the Uniformed Services Employment and Reemployment Rights Act (USERRA), that protect the employment of veterans and active-duty military.

4. B: The EEOC defines adverse impact by the four-fifths rule as follows: "A selection rate for any race, sex, or ethnic group which is less than four-fifths (or 80 percent) of the rate for the group with the highest rate will generally be regarded by the federal enforcement agencies as evidence of adverse impact."

5. C: The Occupational Safety and Health Act of 1970 mandates that it is the employer's responsibility to provide an environment that is free from known hazards that are causing or may cause serious harm or death to employees. The only workers who are not protected by this act are those who are self-employed, those on family farms where only family members work, and those in workplaces that are covered by other federal statutes or by state and local government.

6. D: Employers are obligated to keep a log of all incidents on OSHA Form 300 Log of Work-Related Injuries and Illnesses, and a concise report of annual incidents should be reported on OSHA Form 300A Summary of Work-Related Injuries and Illnesses at the end of each year.

7. B: Four of the main challenges to mental health are burnout, anxiety, depression, and boredom.

SHRM-CP Practice Test #1

Want to take this practice test in an online interactive format?
Check out the bonus page, which includes interactive practice questions and much more: **https://www.mometrix.com/bonus948/shrmcp**

SCAN HERE

1. What does the Worker Adjustment and Retraining Notification (WARN) Act require?

a. An employer must provide affected employees with 60-days' notice of an impending layoff of more than 50 employees.
b. An employer must provide employees who are over the age of 40 with a revocation period after signing a severance agreement.
c. An employer must provide affected employees with 60-days' notice of an impending layoff of any size.
d. An employer must publicly release the names of each person affected by a layoff.

Refer to the following scenario for questions 2-3.

> A supervisor reports to you that he/she is having some personality clashes on his/her team. Specifically, there is one employee who is particularly forceful in his/her opinion and tends to dominate the weekly team meetings. He/she openly complains about routine tasks that all human resource team members have to complete because he/she feels that they're "beneath" him/her. Other employees have expressed frustration when working with this individual.

2. What advice would you give to this supervisor?

a. Have a direct conversation with the employee. Explain how this behavior has been putting off others on the team.
b. Be specific in the feedback—explain how talking over others in a meeting makes others feel like they don't have a voice.
c. Tailor the employee's work assignments so that they're more challenging and complex.
d. Provide conflict resolution training to the employee and others on the team.

3. Another employee on the team has poor attendance. He/she always seems to be having one personal crisis after another, from personal medical conditions to taking care of family members to a sick dog. He/she is not private about any of these details and will share these ailments with anyone who will listen. How would you guide the supervisor to handle this employee?

a. Meet with the employee privately and hear him/her out. Understand the issues he/she is facing, and remain empathetic.
b. Try your best to avoid discussing any personal issues in the workplace. Change the subject when the employee begins to over share about his/her personal life and stick to talk about work.
c. Focus on the attendance issue. Hold the employee accountable for being late, and request a doctor's note the next time he/she calls in sick.
d. Facilitate a 360-degree performance evaluation for the entire team in hopes that feedback from others on the team will help give the employee some self-awareness.

4. Which is NOT an example of an unfair labor practice?

a. An employer declining to participate in collective bargaining
b. An employer not making concessions during collective bargaining
c. An employer offering benefits to employees who decline participation in a union
d. An employer closing down a location upon unionizing activity by employees

5. What is one provision of the Affordable Care Act (ACA) regarding preventive care?

a. Characterize all women's health treatments as preventive.
b. Preventive care shall be covered at 100% and is not subject to co-pays, deductibles, or coinsurance.
c. Insured members shall receive $1 million in coverage for preventive care.
d. The out-of-pocket cost for preventive care shall be capped at a percentage of the federal poverty level.

Refer to the following scenario for questions 6-8.

> The CEO of your organization recently decided to launch a comprehensive company-wide employee engagement survey. Included in the survey were questions regarding satisfaction with internal services such as information technology, operations, and human resources (HR). Unfortunately, HR scored the lowest among all internal services, indicating employee dissatisfaction with HR interactions. The CEO is concerned and asked you, the HR director, how you will handle this.

6. How would you respond to the CEO?

a. Explain that although unfortunate, this is a common response from employees when asked how they feel about human resources (HR). HR's role is to be an enforcer of laws and policies, and that is usually not well received.
b. Explain that you will be looking into this further by conducting an audit of all HR processes and protocols to see what needs to be improved.
c. Based on the results it's clear that your HR staff needs to work on their customer service skills—tell the CEO that you'll be mandating customer service training for all HR staff immediately.
d. Tell the CEO that you will be issuing another company-wide survey; this time it will be regarding only HR internal services to identify the exact source of dissatisfaction.

7. What will be your first steps in initiating a human resources (HR) audit?

a. Identify the key HR staff for interviews and feedback.
b. Create a comprehensive audit checklist.
c. Collect benchmark data for comparison to findings.
d. Determine the scope of the audit.

8. Given the original reason for the human resources (HR) audit, what would be the MOST appropriate type of audit?

a. An audit to ensure all HR functions are aligned with best practices
b. An audit to ensure compliance with applicable regulations
c. An audit to ensure HR function is aligned with organizational goals
d. An audit focused on employee relations

Refer to the following scenario for questions 9-10.

> You are a human resources manager for a small software start-up company. The organization is relatively flat with several software engineers reporting to one lead and all five leads reporting to the director. A common complaint among the engineers is that there is no opportunity for advancement. In fact, this is prompting some high performers to look for jobs elsewhere.

9. What approach would you take to address this source of discontent?

a. Spearhead a significant wage increase for all engineers in the company to make up for the fact that they may never receive a promotion.
b. Make it clear to engineers that promotions are difficult to come by in smaller organizations and instead emphasize all the perks that they enjoy by working for a small, dynamic company.
c. Encourage engineers to identify the gaps in their skills in relation to the lead position and improve upon those skills to prepare for a potential promotion.
d. Train the leads to encourage the engineers to assess and communicate their needs and act—pursue learning opportunities and set goals.

10. What types of human resource metrics would you calculate to quantify the severity of the issue?

a. Time since last promotion
b. Turnover rate
c. Retention rate
d. Performance and potential

11. How would you respond to the email?

An employee emails you, as a designated human resources (HR) representative, with a complex explanation of his/her medical history and explains that he/she has an upcoming surgery. It's clear from the tenor of the email that he/she is stressed about missing work time. He/she wanted to know what the next steps are to prepare for the upcoming leave. You don't know the answer to the question off the top of your head, and the HR person who specializes in leaves is out of the office for a week.

a. First, explain that the employee should not send any protected health information over an unsecure network. Request that he/she come into the office and meet with the human resource (HR) specialist face-to-face upon his/her return from vacation.
b. Thank the employee for the email, and explain that the HR specialist who is the point of contact is out of the office. Offer to explain the situation to him/her when he/she is back and have him/her touch base with the employee at that point.
c. Research the information he/she is seeking on your own, and respond back to the employee within the day.
d. Reply to the employee with a CC to the HR leave specialist, explaining that the HR specialist will reach out to the employee upon his/her return to the office.

12. What does PEST stand for in relation to analysis framework?

a. Political, electronic, social, taxation
b. Political, economic, social, technological
c. Pop culture, economy, strategy, technology
d. Political, environmental, social, technological

Refer to the following scenario for questions 13-14.

Late in the afternoon an account manager, Sharon, knocks on your door and asks to come in. It's clear she's been crying: her face is red and her eyes are swollen. She sits down in your office chair and begins sobbing. Through her sobs she explains that she put a lot of work into building a client relationship within a shared account, but her colleague just took all the credit in a team meeting.

13. What would be the most effective way to calm Sharon down?

a. Say, "She should not have taken credit. I'm sorry you had to go through that."
b. Suggest that she talk to her supervisor about it.
c. Suggest that she take some time to calm down, then speak directly with her colleague, and explain how it made her feel.
d. Guess Sharon's feelings and ask if you're correct. For example, "It sounds like you're feeling a lack of recognition and maybe disrespected by your colleague. Do I have that right?"

14. Sharon has calmed down and says, "Thanks. I feel a lot better. I just needed to vent to someone. Now I can go on about my day and put this behind me." What would you do next?

a. Give a warm smile to Sharon, and say, "My door is open any time." Consider it "case closed." Sharon clearly didn't want this conflict to progress into anything more.
b. Give a warm smile to Sharon, and say, "My door is open any time"; however, after she leaves your office, give her supervisor a call, and explain what had just happened and that she should keep an eye on things between the two.
c. Thank Sharon for confiding in you, but diplomatically explain that it is not human resource's role to be a therapist.
d. Explain to Sharon that anything she says in your office is not confidential and that you may be looking into this further.

15. What would be the next course of action for you to get this position filled?

As a recruiter, you are having a difficult time filling a civil engineer position that has been open for a few months. Few qualified individuals have applied, and the passive candidates who you've contacted haven't returned your calls. You've been aggressive in your advertising approach (in fact you've exceeded your advertising budget), but it's proving to be difficult to find quality candidates in this competitive market.

a. Re-assess the salary and benefit package for the position.
b. Work on obtaining additional budget, and post more job advertisements.
c. Have a brainstorming session with the hiring manager, and ask for ideas and suggestions.
d. Change the requirements for the job: it could be that they are hindering potential applicants from applying.

16. Under "coordination of benefits" rules, how are insurance claims processed?

a. Charges are first allocated to the primary payer, and then residual charges are submitted to a secondary payer.
b. Claims are processed only at an "allowable amount" as determined by the insurance company, and any residual cost is an out-of-pocket charge to the employee.
c. Out-of-pocket expenses are deducted directly from the employee's flexible spending account.
d. Charges are split evenly between the primary and secondary payers.

17. How is an organization's vision statement different from the mission statement?

a. It is a set of core principles that guides the organization's decision-making.
b. It is forward looking and higher level, describing the organization's strategic direction.
c. It remains constant throughout the organization's life cycle.
d. It is more specific, describing how business is conducted.

18. Which is the provision that does NOT typically describe a flexible spending account (FSA)?

a. "Use it or lose it"—funds expire at the end of the plan year (or at the end of the grace period).
b. Both employees and employers may contribute to the account on the employee's behalf.
c. Employees may reduce their taxable income by contributing funds to an FSA.
d. FSA enrollment is mandatory for employees with a Section 125 plan.

19. What is the primary difference between coaching and mentoring?

a. Coaching is generally used for a specific reason—either to prepare an individual for a new challenge or to change a specific work behavior.
b. Coaching is generally conducted in a one-on-one setting.
c. Coaching is usually used in the case of pending, or as a result of, a disciplinary action.
d. Coaching is more instructional with job-related training.

20. What is an ineffective approach for a supervisor to deliver feedback to a struggling employee?

a. The supervisor should list each area of deficiency and how it impacts the team and/or organization.
b. The supervisor should provide specific examples of instances in which the employee had a misstep.
c. The supervisor should make performance expectations clear.
d. The supervisor should provide some praise around the things the employee is performing well.

21. Which type of employee must be excluded from bargaining units as per the National Labor Relations Act (NLRA)?

a. Supervisors
b. Employees who work in the private sector
c. Part-time employees
d. Seasonal employees

22. In assessing human resources (HR) technology programs, what is an example of a "best of breed" concept?

a. Selecting an HR/payroll system and a separate third-party learning management system (LMS) with better features
b. Performing a needs analysis internally to determine the optimal system to streamline current processes
c. Selecting an all-in-one, integrated solution with HR, payroll, performance management, and learning management capabilities.
d. Selecting an HR/payroll system that requires the least amount of customization to ensure a fast implementation and simpler future upgrades.

23. What does the SMART goal acronym stand for?

a. Smart, metric-driven, actionable, relevant, and time bound
b. Specific, measurable, accurate, relative, and time bound
c. Specific, measurable, achievable, relevant, and time bound
d. Specific, masterful, achievable, relevant, and time bound

24. Under the Myers-Briggs Type Indicator (MBTI) personality assessment, people are categorized as introverted versus extroverted, sensing versus intuitive, and so on. In total, there are how many different combinations of personality types?

a. 4
b. 5
c. 16
d. 64

25. What is a Performance Improvement Plan (PIP) best suited for?

a. Documentation prior to a termination action
b. Insubordinate behavior
c. Quantifiable performance deficiencies with potential for improvement
d. Unionized workplaces

26. The Fair Labor Standards Act (FLSA) mandates that most employees be paid overtime for more than 40 hours in a week unless they fall under certain criteria. Which is NOT an FLSA exemption?

a. Outside sales exemption
b. Computer employee exemption
c. Creative professional exemption
d. Advanced engineer exemption

27. Why are human resource representatives generally excluded from bargaining unit representation?

a. They often oversee the work of others in a supervisory capacity.
b. They act as an advisor and/or representative of management during collective bargaining.
c. They are responsible for defining organizational policies that may conflict with collective bargaining agreements (CBAs).
d. They are responsible for enforcing the provisions of the CBAs and policies.

28. Critics of utilizing key performance indicators (KPIs) to measure goal attainment say that instead of fostering collaboration, they often times promote

a. competition.
b. micromanagement.
c. slow progress.
d. unachievable standards.

29. What types of organizations are required to maintain an affirmative action program (AAP)?

a. Federal government contractors or subcontractors, as mandated by the Office of Federal Contract Compliance (OFCCP)
b. All organizations with more than 50 employees, as mandated by the Equal Employment Opportunity Commission (EEOC)
c. None, rather it is best practice for all organizations to remain informed of minority and female representation
d. All federal, state and local government agencies

30. In selecting a new human resource information system (HRIS), what is the first step in the process?

a. Determine the available budget.
b. Define organizational needs versus wants in a new system.
c. Determine if the selection process will be conducted by a consultant or internal resources.
d. Collect quotes and proposals from prospective HRIS vendors.

Refer to the following scenario for questions 31-32.

Your organization is opening its first international office in Chennai, India. It will start as a relatively small office with mostly software developers, but there is a need to have a human resource (HR) person located there. You will oversee the work of this India-based HR manager in addition to your U.S.-based team of five.

31. What would be your first step in helping open the India office?

a. Conduct a political, economic, social and technological (PEST) analysis through a human resource (HR) lens.
b. Travel to Chennai, see the landscape, meet the location contacts, and begin recruiting for the HR manager.
c. Conduct a strengths, weaknesses, opportunities and threats (SWOT) analysis through an HR lens.
d. Begin collecting sample employee handbooks, forms, and policies from India companies.

32. Six months later, you have a promising human resources manager on board, and the India office seems to be running smoothly. However, as expected, there are some minor challenges with communication between the two offices. What would be the most effective practice to adopt to improve daily communications?

a. Institute regular video conference calls for all virtual meetings
b. A reminder to the U.S. location to use clear language in emails and eliminate the use of slang
c. A daily 15-minute status call at a time that is convenient for both time zones
d. Training provided at both locations regarding customs of the other culture—India culture training at the U.S. location and American culture training at the Chennai location.

Refer to the following scenario for questions 33-34.

ABC Corp has a large number of millennial employees joining the company in entry-level positions. Most of these individuals show great promise and ambition upon hire, but after a few months, they struggle with the steep learning curve of ABC's complicated product lineup and proprietary sales techniques. They become frustrated and are leaving the organization at a high rate. Because of this, human resources has decided to implement a mentoring program in the hopes that pairing more senior sales leaders and executives with these entry-level employees will help retain millennials. The problem is that a good mentoring program needs a budget, and ABC is conservative with nonessential spending.

33. How would you appeal to senior finance leadership and convince them of the importance of this program?

a. Put together a comprehensive document that defines eligibility requirements, high-potential employees who may participate, a timeline, marketing material, and a communication plan.
b. Put together a succinct, finance-centered document with the total budget needed, how the budget will be spent, the expected impacts on employee retention, and in turn, cost savings.
c. Start a six-month pilot program, which costs much less than the full program, and hope that its success will justify the money spent thus far.
d. Give a presentation to the senior finance leadership, and give several case studies of other organizations that had success with mentoring programs. Explain the employee morale-boosting benefits, and answer any questions they have.

34. Assuming you were given the budget for the mentoring program, you finalize the details and launch the program. So far, you've had plenty of mentors and mentees who are eager participants. What is the LEAST important consideration when pairing mentors and mentees?

a. Similar goals for the mentoring relationship
b. Similar career aspirations and field of work
c. The seniority and experience level of the mentor
d. The mentor and mentee's preference of match

35. 401(k) plan auto-enrollment for new hires

a. is a great strategy to boost participation and encourage financial responsibility among employees.
b. is not legal.
c. is not advisable from an employee relations standpoint; employees tend to feel deceived.
d. is a requirement of most retirement plans.

36. What does Title II of Genetic Information Nondiscrimination Act (GINA) prohibit?

a. Discrimination of employees or applicants based on genetic information
b. Discrimination of employees or applicants based on gender identity
c. Unauthorized sharing of protected health information
d. Discrimination of applicants based on disability status

37. There are many critics of using personality assessments as part of the hiring process. Which of the following is the MOST valid concern that critics have expressed?

a. Assessments can pigeonhole applicants based solely on personality traits.
b. Applicants can usually manipulate the results—they choose the option that the organization wants to hear rather than how they feel.
c. Assessments may ask questions that would identify and exclude disabled individuals.
d. Disparate impact—protected groups of people may be excluded from consideration based on their responses.

38. In which domain is workforce planning and employment a focus?

a. The employee life cycle
b. Organizational strategy
c. Human resource operations
d. Managing performance

39. What is an advantage of hiring externally rather than from inside the organization?

a. It brings a fresh perspective and creativity to the organization.
b. It can be less expensive for recruitment efforts.
c. It causes less conflict among coworkers.
d. External candidates are likely to be more competent.

Refer to the following scenario for questions 40-41.

You are a human resource manager supporting the northwest division of a nationwide electronics store. The majority of your employees work directly with customers, either helping them decide which television to purchase in the store, or they travel to a customer's home to help setup or troubleshoot an electronic product purchased in the store. On occasion, customers will report that they noticed something missing from their home after a visit from an employee. Usually there's no way to definitely prove that an employee stole anything.

40. How would you go about preventing this from happening in the future?

a. Remove the temptation—request that customers secure their valuables prior to a visit from one of your employees.
b. Conduct a thorough background check before hiring, and reject anyone with a criminal record.
c. In new hire orientation, conduct ethics training and threaten criminal prosecution if an employee is caught stealing.
d. Pair up employees who visit customer homes so that they can hold each other accountable.

41. An employee comes to your office one day and nervously tells you he/she has knowledge of another employee who stole an item from a customer's home. He/she doesn't want to tell you who it is until you guarantee him/her anonymity. How would you handle this?

a. Explain that you can never guarantee anonymity and that he/she is obligated to give the name of the accused now that you have knowledge of these events.
b. Promise that his/her name will remain anonymous and the employee in question will never know who complained.
c. Tell him/her that you will do your best to ensure his/her name is kept confidential, but you can't make any guarantees.
d. Explain the importance of finding the person who stole the item and that you need his/her help.

42. Under the Patient Protection and Affordable Care Act (PPACA), an employer may utilize the look-back measurement method to determine

a. if an employee will be expected to work more than 30 hours per week.
b. if an employee has received health insurance coverage over the past year.
c. if an employee has worked more than 130 hours in a month.
d. if an employee's pay is low enough that he/she qualifies for a subsidy.

Refer to the following scenario for questions 43-44.

A team of five customer service representatives (CSRs) works in a call center. They usually sit for the entirety of their eight-hour shifts, answering calls and speaking to customers with a headset. One CSR has severe back issues so has requested a stand-up desk to help with back pain.

43. How would you handle this request?

a. Provide the stand-up desk to the employee as it's a reasonable request.
b. Perform an ergonomic assessment of the workstation before making any determinations if a modification is needed.
c. Ask for a doctor's note. If the doctor states that he/she requires a stand-up desk to perform the essential functions of the job, provide it.
d. Back pain does not qualify as "disability" under the American's with Disabilities Act, so no accommodation needs to be made.

44. After you provide the stand-up desk to the CSR, another employee complains about unfair treatment. He/she would like a stand-up desk as well, not for disability reasons, but for health and wellness. There may be budget to purchase two to three more stand-up desks but not for all five CSRs. How would you handle this request?

a. Explain that the reason the other CSR was given a stand-up desk was for a disability, and this was an accommodation under the Americans with Disabilities Act. For that reason, he/she will not be given one unless he/she too has a doctor's note.
b. Purchase the stand-up desk. If anyone else asks for one, provide it as well until the budget is exhausted. Work to obtain more budget the following year to provide the desks to all five CSRs.
c. Set up a program in which the highest-performing CSR of the quarter is awarded with a stand-up desk until the budget is exhausted.
d. Offer to help set it up if he/she purchases the equipment using his/her own money.

45. A job hazard analysis is a tool that Occupational Safety and Health Administration (OSHA) recommends to prevent workplace injury, illnesses, or accidents. When performing a job hazard analysis, who is it most important to consult with?

a. The employees who are performing the work
b. The supervisor of the employees who perform the work
c. OSHA
d. The organization's safety officer

46. In the instance of Family and Medical Leave Act (FMLA)-protected leave, new mothers' and fathers' rights differ in what way?

a. New mothers can take the entire 12 weeks; new fathers may only take leave for bonding purposes.
b. New mothers can take the entire 12 weeks; new fathers may only take leave to care for their spouse during the period of disability, which ranges from six to eight weeks.
c. They have the same rights; however, they may not take the leave at the same time.
d. They have the same rights—both can take time for bonding with the newborn, and the mother can take time for the period of disability. A new father can take the time to care for his spouse during the recovery period.

47. What is the style of negotiation that aims to meet the needs of both parties and leverage collaboration to come to an agreement called?

a. Principled bargaining
b. Positional bargaining
c. Distributive bargaining
d. Composite bargaining

48. One kind of bias that can occur during an interview is a halo bias. What is a halo bias?

a. Interviewers tend to rank candidates higher when they are similar to themselves.
b. An interviewer observes one negative trait in a candidate, and it negatively influences the perception of other traits.
c. An interviewer observes one positive trait in a candidate, and it positively influences the perception of other traits.
d. Interviewer base a hiring decision immediately upon their first impression of the candidate.

49. Under the North American Free Trade Agreement (NAFTA), what do Canadian professionals need to work in the United States?

a. A TN visa
b. An H-1B visa
c. The appropriate documentation (i.e. offer letter, proof of Canadian citizenship) presented at the U.S. border
d. U.S. permanent residency (green card)

50. What is the practice of storing, managing, and processing data in remote, Internet-based servers commonly referred to?

a. Cloud computing
b. Locally hosted computing
c. Software as a Service (SaaS)
d. E-commerce

Refer to the following scenario for questions 51-52.

You directly manage a team of eight human resource (HR) people, all varying in ages and length of work experience. For example, your senior HR generalist is nearing retirement and has worked in HR for nearly 30 years. Your newest hire, an HR coordinator, is just a few years out from graduating college. As you are aware, managing a multigenerational workforce presents many challenges.

51. What is one challenge that you anticipate your older workers encountering when working closely with younger workers on a high-profile project?

a. The quality of work from younger workers may not be up to the standards of older workers.
b. Older workers tend not to take feedback constructively.
c. Older workers expect more latitude from management, whereas the younger generation needs and expects more guidance at each step of the way.
d. Older workers expect direct, face-to-face communication, whereas younger workers are content with communication via email, text or, instant messaging.

52. What would be the most effective strategy to engage the younger workers?

a. Provide a performance-based bonus.
b. Promote a team-based culture that is heavy on collaboration.
c. Provide a defined career path with training opportunities to achieve the next step.
d. Schedule a once-per-week happy hour with the entire team.

Refer to the following scenario for questions 53-54.

A long-tenured and valued employee has recently been coming to work late, calling in sick on Mondays, and his/her overall appearance is messy and disheveled. He/she has also been behaving strangely and getting agitated more easily than usual. His/her supervisor suspects that he/she has a drug problem.

53. How would you approach the situation as a human resource representative?

a. Call the employee's emergency contact on file, and inquire if something has changed with the employee recently.
b. Pull the employee into a private conference room along with the supervisor. Explain the strange behavior that you and the supervisor have witnessed, and ask for an explanation.
c. Coach the supervisor to have a conversation with the employee privately.
d. Require that the employee complete a drug test before any conversation occurs.

54. Assume the employee admitted that he/she began using cocaine about six months ago. He/she says that he/she started using casually, but recently it's gotten out of control, and he/she needs help. What would be your next course of action?

a. Explain that despite the substance abuse problem, he/she will be held to the same performance standards as any other employee.
b. Your company has a zero-tolerance policy, so his/her employment should be terminated immediately.
c. As an active drug addict, he/she is protected under the Americans with Disabilities Act, so work with him/her to find a reasonable accommodation to help him/her get clean.
d. Offer the employee Family and Medical Leave Act (FMLA)-protected leave to enroll and attend a rehab program.

55. What happens if an employee on leave submits a medical certification and human resources questions the validity of diagnosis and the professional's credentials?

a. Human resources (HR) should contact the medical professional for more information about the employee's medical condition.
b. HR must make the best determination of its validity based on the information provided to maintain the employee's privacy.
c. HR may require a second opinion from another healthcare provider.
d. HR may not contact the medical professional but should contact the employee for more information on the health condition.

56. For an employer to hire an unpaid intern, the internship must meet several criteria. Which option is NOT a criterion to qualify for an unpaid internship?

a. The intern receives academic credit for completion of the internship.
b. The intern's work does not take away work from another paid employee.
c. The intern must work less than 20 hours per week.
d. The intern receives relevant and valuable on-the-job training.

57. How would you handle this situation?

A new father, who has not exhausted his Family and Medical Leave Act (FMLA) leave for the year, has requested the next 12 Fridays off to care for his new baby. He cites "baby bonding time" under the FMLA law and feels that this intermittent leave qualifies. His supervisor has expressed the challenge this will present his department as they usually have a time-sensitive report to submit each Friday.

a. Decline the employee's request as this would clearly present a hardship on his department.
b. Approve the employee's request as he still has Family and Medical Leave Act (FMLA) leave available.
c. Speak with the supervisor to see if other employees in the department would be able to work overtime on Fridays to cover the absence of this employee. If so, allow the request.
d. Require that the employee uses vacation time or paid time off as this would not qualify for FMLA.

58. After a lengthy investigation concludes, a sexual harassment complaint is determined to be unfounded. What is the most appropriate course of action?

a. Disciplinary action for the complainant—there were no grounds for the complaint.
b. Disciplinary action should be taken only if the reason was malicious.
c. Disciplinary action would be considered retaliation if the complainant were to be disciplined for making a complaint.
d. Initiate a gentle conversation with the complainant and subject together to describe the results of the investigation.

59. Which statement does NOT describe unlawful harassment?

a. Unwelcome conduct that is based upon the victim's protected status
b. Behavior that is severe and pervasive enough that a reasonable person would find it hostile or abusive
c. Enduring offensive conduct becomes a condition of employment
d. Any type of bullying or unwelcome conduct from a supervisor

60. How would you deliver the feedback to this employee?

You are a supervisor who manages a small team of three professionals. One in particular is a high performer with a great attitude. Unfortunately, he/she made a huge error on his/her most recent client report, which ended up costing the organization a significant amount of money. It is an error that you need to address with, but you don't want to dampen his/her spirits as he/she tends to be sensitive to negative feedback.

a. Remain neutral and state the facts of the mistake in the report. Ask for feedback on how to avoid these mistakes in the future.
b. Send an email with the details of the mistake to be less confrontational.
c. Explain the mistake and the impact it had on the company. Warn him/her that if it happens again, he/she might be disciplined.
d. Document the event in the details of his/her next performance review.

61. Under Fair Labor Standards Act (FLSA) guidelines, what are employees entitled to?

a. One 30-minute lunch and two 15-minute breaks for every eight hours worked
b. No required lunch or rest periods
c. One hour lunch and two 10-minute breaks for every eight hours worked
d. One 30-minute lunch break for every four hours worked

62. What is a "top-heavy" 401(k) plan?

a. A plan with an average deferral by highly compensated employees at 2% greater than non-highly compensated employees
b. A plan with more than 60% participation by executives
c. A plan with greater than 60% of its total value in the accounts of "key" employees
d. A plan with less than 60% participation by non-highly compensated employees

63. Focus groups are an effective means to gather employee feedback. For what are they best suited?

a. Employees in the same division or department
b. Specific subjects of discussion
c. Fewer than five participants
d. Unstructured brainstorming sessions

Refer to the following scenario for questions 64-65.

Human resources has been tasked with creating a comprehensive and consistent training program in an organization that has never had a structured program in the past. Previously, training was administered and tracked differently across departments according to their specific needs and requirements.

64. What should be human resource's first task in creating the program?

a. Taking inventory of each department's training needs and current processes
b. Researching learning management systems—obtaining quotes, checking references, and so on
c. Becoming familiar with the legal requirements and best practices of training programs in the industry
d. Creating an organization-wide training calendar with scheduled training assignments and due dates

65. What criteria is the LEAST important to consider when deciding on training delivery methods and course durations for the new program?

a. Legal obligations to remain compliant
b. Current training delivery methods and course durations
c. Workplace logistics and preferred learning styles of employees—that is, are there field-based employees who may not have easy access to a learning management system, or perhaps employees aren't able to step away from their desks for long durations
d. The content of the training being delivered

66. When preparing to make an offer to a candidate, recruiters must consider several factors before deciding how much to offer within the applicable pay scale. What factors should NOT be considered?

a. The candidate's expectations
b. Internal equity—how much the other incumbents are being paid for the same job
c. The candidate's current compensation
d. The candidate's potential commute

67. How would you handle this complaint?

A supervisor, John, gives you a call and says, "I have an issue. Another supervisor, Steve, made a joke to one of my employees that made her feel uncomfortable." John goes on to describe the insensitive joke about a "black Santa" that Steve told to the African American employee, Karen. John finishes with, "So what do I do?" Steve is a well-liked supervisor who has never crossed the line before. According to John, Karen and Steve are friends, and she doesn't want him to "get into trouble," but she thought she should at least mention it.

a. Thank John for bringing this to your attention, and ask that he let you know if it ever happens again. Take no further action because this was an isolated incident with Steve
b. Document the interaction between Steve and Karen based on the facts presented by John. Save it in case another questionable scenario with Steve ever comes up.
c. Speak with Karen directly, and document the conversation. Ask her how she wants you to proceed.
d. Have an informal but stern conversation with Steve. Explain that his joke was inappropriate and should never happen again.

68. In the context of Fair Labor Standards Act (FLSA), which statement is true regarding the concept of workers being "engaged to wait" versus "waiting to be engaged"?

a. An employee who is "engaged to wait" is effectively on duty and must be paid for that time.
b. An employee who is "waiting to be engaged" is usually required to remain at the workplace or nearby in case they are needed.
c. An employee who is "engaged to wait" is generally on call and can use his/her time freely as long as they're able to make it to the workplace in the event they are called.
d. An employee who is "engaged to wait" is relieved of duty, so he/she does not need to be paid unless he/she is called to work.

69. Return to Work (RTW) programs are an effective tool to help transition employees back to full duty. When are they used?

a. An employee experiences an on-the-job injury.
b. An employee experiences an injury, whether on the job or off duty.
c. Family and Medical Leave Act (FMLA)-protected leave is denied for the employee.
d. An employee's physician will not give a medical release.

Refer to the following scenario for questions 70-71.

Acme Corp is experiencing a rapid increase in new projects and, in turn, revenue. Because of this influx of new work, the hiring pace has quickened as well. The employee headcount is projected to grow from 500 employees to 600 over the course of the year. Unfortunately, turnover seems to be increasing at the same rate, and it seems to be mostly newer employees leaving the organization.

70. What would be the most impactful action human resources could take to identify the cause of this increase in turnover?

a. Conduct exit interviews with each employee who leaves the organization. Identify trends in the reasons mentioned.
b. Speak with the managers of each exiting employee. Ask if they have any insight on why the individuals are choosing to leave the organization.
c. Analyze the recruitment strategy and interview notes when the employee was hired. Because they're often new employees who leave quickly, it's likely that the wrong hiring decision was made.
d. Send out an employee satisfaction survey to all employees. Identify areas of discontent among current employees.

71. The exit interview comments have shown that employees feel overwhelmed and burnt out—this is causing employees to quit within their 90-day probationary period. What would be a possible solution human resources could take to reduce turnover?

a. Speak with managers and supervisors, relay this information, and request that they lighten the workload for all employees.
b. Introduce every Friday as a work-from-home day to improve work-life balance.
c. Implement realistic job previews during the interview process to give candidates a better idea of what will be expected of them.
d. Improve new hire orientation and training, ensuring that new hires are able to get up to speed quickly.

Refer to the following scenario for questions 72-73.

You are the vice president of human resources for a small start-up software company. The bulk of your employees are young, highly educated hard workers and smart when it comes to technology but not so much when it comes to healthcare benefits, retirement, and other employment-related details. For most, this is their first job out of college. The CEO is a visionary and has expressed that he/she wants the company to always be cutting edge and a desirable place to work to attract only the best software developers in the country.

72. Given the information in the scenario, what proposed initiative or program would you include in your annual strategic human resources plan?

a. Unlimited paid time off (PTO)
b. An onsite health clinic for employees and their dependents
c. An employee recognition program with cutting-edge technology as rewards
d. A structured career path program with learning and development opportunities

73. The career path program was a hit with the software developers. The next step in creating that cutting-edge workplace reputation is embracing flexible/remote work opportunities. Your CEO doesn't like the idea and thinks it would negatively impact productivity. However, you're confident that it's the way of the future. How would you sell the idea to the CEO?

a. Provide positive case studies from other organizations that have embraced remote assignments.
b. Suggest that you allow it for a maximum of once per week as a trial. Monitor the remote work output, and expand the program if successful.
c. Remind the CEO that remote work assignments would expand your recruitment reach into other hot technology markets, not just local to your headquarters office.
d. Remind the CEO that not only is telecommuting cutting edge, but it allows software developers to focus better and in turn produce higher-quality work.

74. How would you describe the most effective approach to diversity recruitment?

a. Hire more diverse employees into the workplace.
b. Alter workplace practices to appeal to multiple generations of employees—leverage technology where appropriate, and train older workers on this technology.
c. Train hiring managers and other interviewers on appropriate, and inappropriate, questions to ask during an interview.
d. Expand advertising sources to include diversity-focused professional organizations and websites.

75. According to Maslow's Hierarchy of Needs, what follows the need for feeling valued and respected as the highest step in the pyramid?

a. Safety and security
b. Love and belonging
c. Physiological (i.e. hunger and thirst needs)
d. Self-actualization

76. What guideline does the "4/5 rule" refer to?

a. Affordability for healthcare insurance under the Patient Protection and Affordable Care Act (PPACA)
b. Potential disparity in recruitment and selection of protected classes
c. Eligibility for labor union membership
d. An employee's ability to perform the essential functions of his/her job

Refer to the following scenario for questions 77-78.

A CEO of a midsized technology company has gained a reputation for berating others in meetings, firing employees who make minor mistakes, and micromanaging his/her senior leadership team.

77. How would you describe the likely culture of the company and its employees?

a. Fear based with minimal contribution from employees
b. Competitive among employees with a cutthroat mentality
c. Tight-knit—employees commiserate about their experiences with the CEO
d. High performing—employees wanting to prove the CEO wrong by doing their best work

78. As a human resource (HR) leader in this organization reporting to the CEO, how would you propose fixing this leadership challenge?

a. Clearly communicate with your own HR staff and other employees in the organization that you're aware of the issue and are working to resolve it. Offer an open door to anyone who needs to talk about their challenges.
b. Hire a third-party consultant to conduct a leadership assessment with the entire executive team, including the CEO.
c. Launch an internal investigation into inappropriate behaviors by the CEO. Interview multiple employees across the organization about their unpleasant interactions.
d. Begin looking for another job. The CEO runs the company how he/she wishes and will likely not be receptive to feedback or any attempts to correct behavior. It's best to begin looking for a better work environment elsewhere.

79. When an employee is injured on the job, what is the first thing supervisors and managers should be instructed to do after stabilizing the employee?

a. Draft a statement of what happened.
b. Contact human resources.
c. Collect witness statements.
d. Address the cause of the injury, and fix it if possible.

80. Dependent enrollment with COBRA continuation coverage

a. is required if the primary beneficiary is enrolled.
b. is allowed even if the primary beneficiary is not enrolled.
c. is only permitted if the primary beneficiary is enrolled.
d. is generally not permitted in any instance.

81. Which is a step that is NOT a part of the evidence-based decision-making (EBDM) process?

a. Identify and frame the situation.
b. Gather evidence from internal and external sources.
c. Ask for factual feedback from stakeholders.
d. Consider the opinions of applicable subject matter experts (SMEs).

82. How would you describe employee engagement?

a. An employee who is satisfied with his/her job
b. An employee with commitment to the organization and motivation to perform well
c. Engagement that is generally higher within the first 30 days after hire but that usually fades
d. An employee who is ambitious and works hard but is always looking outside the organization for new opportunity.

Refer to the following scenario for questions 83-85.

Initech is a healthcare company with 500 employees based out of the home office in Seattle. They have 150 employees working remotely from their homes all over the country. The Initech office is always buzzing with activity and events—company meetings, Friday social hour, summer BBQ, and holiday parties for employees and their families. The remote employees have been complaining because they feel disconnected from the home office. Unfortunately, the budget doesn't allow for frequent visits for the remote employees to visit the home office.

83. What would be a creative solution to help the remote employees feel more included while keeping costs low?

a. Post photos of the events on the company intranet so remote employees can see them.
b. Invite the remote employees to attend the holiday party and summer BBQ; however, they would be responsible for covering the cost of their own transportation and lodging.
c. Organize periodic social meet-ups for remote employees who live near one another.
d. Set up a dial-in/web cam for the company meetings and social events so that remote employees can hear and see the activity.

84. What is the biggest disadvantage of having a remote workforce?

a. Lack of communication between coworkers and employees and managers
b. The possibility for employees to misrepresent their work time
c. Home-based employees being likely to encounter too many distractions and not being as efficient
d. Possible safety and risk concerns for employees to hurt themselves away from the office

85. What could be the biggest advantage of having a remote workforce from a human resource perspective?

a. Lower overhead costs—less office space and equipment required
b. No commute for remote employees, resulting in fewer emissions for the environment
c. No need for child care for remote employees
d. Better overall work-life balance for remote employees, resulting in higher morale and more successful recruitment efforts

86. Which question should interviewers avoid asking candidates during an interview?

a. Are you able to work for our company without immigration sponsorship?
b. Are you able to perform the work duties without accommodation?
c. Do you live close to our office?
d. It sounds like you have an accent. Where are you from?

87. H-1B work visas may only be obtained for employees who

a. reside in either Mexico or Canada and work in a specialty occupation.
b. pass a rigorous test to prove their knowledge of the United States.
c. work in a specialty occupation and have a bachelor's degree equivalency.
d. are a recent college graduate and wish to work in the same field of study.

88. What is an advantage of using a business partner model in an organization rather than the generalist model?

a. A human resources (HR) business partner is able to become more familiar with specific lines of business, thus acting as a strategic partner to the designated group.
b. An HR business partner can focus on a designated area of expertise and become an advanced subject matter expert.
c. An HR business partner has a wide range of skills and abilities, so he/she is able to provide guidance in almost any scenario.
d. The business partner model allows for better consistency in policy application across departments in the organization.

Refer to the following scenario for questions 89-90.

> You are a human resources manager for a midsized technology company with a diverse employee group—there are many employees from India, some are from Russia, and others are American. Employees tend to stay within their own cultural groups for socializing and even for project collaboration. This has created a siloed work environment, resulting in minimal communication and inefficient work processes.

89. What would be a creative and effective way to improve communication across the organization?

a. Pair up individuals from different cultures on specific work assignments.
b. Require language classes for each of the dialects spoken in the organization.
c. Offer cultural sensitivity training for the entire organization.
d. Organize on-site social activities to take place during work hours.

90. What guidance would you give to supervisors/managers for managing teams from different backgrounds?

a. Consider employees' cultural preferences before assigning work tasks.
b. Have weekly team meetings and ask employees to share what they're working on for the week.
c. Get to know each team member and their background to build trust and establish the relationship first.
d. Facilitate face-to-face discussions among team members during times of conflict.

91. When conducting a strengths, weaknesses, opportunities and threats (SWOT) analysis, what portion may be accomplished by a political, economic, social and technological (PEST) analysis?

a. Weaknesses and threats
b. Strengths and weaknesses
c. Strengths and opportunities
d. Opportunities and threats

92. A compensation philosophy is influenced by many factors. Which factor should have the LEAST amount of impact when defining an organization's compensation philosophy?

a. Number of employees in the organization
b. Industry in which the organization works
c. Current employee expectations
d. Availability of talent in the market

93. If an employee requests a day off, citing a religious holiday that he/she wishes to observe, is the employer obligated to grant the request?

a. The employer should if the employee has enough vacation time or paid time off.
b. If it is not a company-observed holiday, the employer is not required to allow the day off.
c. The employer should grant the request if it does not present undue hardship.
d. To avoid claims of discrimination, an employer should allow the request no matter the circumstances.

94. A nine-box grid is an effective tool that compares an employee's performance with his/her potential for advancement. What is it most commonly used for?

a. Disciplinary documentation
b. Succession planning
c. Talent acquisition
d. Compensation planning

95. Which is the provision that does NOT typically describe a health savings account (HSA)?

a. "Use it or lose it"—funds expire at the end of the plan year.
b. Both employees and employers may contribute to the account on the employee's behalf.
c. Employees may reduce their taxable income by contributing funds to an HSA.
d. HSA funds are portable—if an employee leaves the organization, he/she can take the funds.

96. Best practice for initial completion of the U.S. Citizen and Immigration Services (USCIS) Form I-9 does NOT include that

a. the employee should fill out the form no later than the first day of work.
b. the employer may specify that the employee should supply a passport to verify identify.
c. the employee may use a translator for purposes of completing the form.
d. the employer must review the original documentation supplied by the employee.

97. What is the most significant morale destroyer that middle managers often face as a function of their role?

a. Difficult employee relations issues
b. Changing directives from upper management
c. Low compensation relative to the level of responsibility
d. A lack of authority from upper management in application of policies

Refer to the following scenario for questions 98-99.

> In a municipal government workplace, a supervisor oversees a 10-person team of permit technicians who are mostly stationed at the front counter and greet customers. Two permit technicians, Jane and Susan, are like oil and water. They argue in team meetings, roll their eyes at each other, and don't respond to each other's emails. The supervisor is fed up and has come to you for guidance.

98. What would your advice be to the supervisor?

a. Rearrange the counter schedule so that Jane and Susan never work together.
b. Organize a face-to-face meeting between the two with the supervisor acting as a facilitator.
c. Pull Jane and Susan aside separately; explain that the expectation is that their behavior remain professional.
d. Organize a conflict resolution training for Jane and Susan to attend.

99. What is the type of conflict that best describes the interaction between Jane and Susan?

a. Dysfunctional conflict
b. Functional conflict
c. Task conflict
d. Bullying behavior

Refer to the following scenario for questions 100-102.

One of your direct reports, Peter, is quiet, conscientious, and detail oriented. He doesn't speak often in team meetings, but when he does, his responses are logical and fact based. Conversely, another direct report, Jason, almost never stops talking. He likes to exaggerate and always has a funny story to tell. He is creative, easygoing, and excellent at problem-solving.

100. Given Peter's personality, how would you go about delivering a work assignment to him?

a. No different than any other team member, it would be discussed in the regular weekly team meetings.
b. You would bring it up in your next weekly one-on-one meeting with the opportunity for Peter to ask follow-up questions.
c. Send an email with the work assignment details, with the explanation that you will discuss it at your next regularly scheduled one-on-one meeting.
d. In your next regularly scheduled one-on-one meeting, ask for his input on which assignment he'd like to work on. Give him the assignment of his choice.

101. You have a high-visibility performance review overhaul project that you need your team to deliver. How would you go about dividing the work between Peter and Jason?

a. Encourage both Peter and Jason to get out of their comfort zones—assign the research and data analysis to Jason, and Peter can create the communication pieces and deliver the presentations.
b. Determine the overall project plan, strategy, and tasks together. Then let them divvy up the work directly with each other, keeping you apprised of any important decisions.
c. Have Jason determine the overall project plan and the strategy of the program. Peter can conduct best practice research and analyze applicable data.
d. Have both of them work together on the same tasks—both complete research, put together the project plan, and deliver presentations to employees and leadership.

102. While working on this project together, what could be a potential conflict between Peter and Jason?

a. Conflicting roles
b. Competing priorities
c. Conflicting perceptions
d. Conflicting styles

103. Which is NOT a best practice for Form I-9 retention?

a. Retain the form three years after hire date or one year after termination date, whichever is later.
b. Restrict Form I-9 access to supervisors and managers.
c. Shred the forms once an employee reaches the three-year employment anniversary.
d. File terminated employees' forms separately from active employees' forms.

Refer to the following scenario for questions 104-105.

A common recruitment practice of your organization is to attend career fairs to attract a variety of different candidates for multiple open positions. You usually attend the fairs, as well as two to three other recruiters. You enjoy speaking with attendees and sometimes find some quality candidates. The CFO (your boss) has come to you and expressed his concern that the career fairs are very costly, and he's not sure if they're worth it.

104. What metric would you use to either verify the CFO's concerns or prove that the career fairs are worth the expense?

a. Cost per hire
b. Cost per candidate by source
c. Applicants per opening
d. Source of hire

105. Assume you've crunched the numbers and discovered that the career fairs are producing more candidates than other sources such as online job postings or employee referrals. How would you convey to the CFO that he was wrong?

a. Choose your battle. Don't tell the CFO that he was incorrect, but simply stop registering for career fairs and instead focus on improving other recruitment methods.
b. Casually mention it at the next regularly scheduled team meeting when the topic of recruitment comes up.
c. Schedule a meeting with him and bring a print-out showing the data. Ask him what he'd like you to do, given this information.
d. Schedule a meeting with him, and bring a print-out showing the data. Suggest that you continue attending but perhaps reduce the number of other company representatives to reduce the cost.

106. Psychologist Bruce Tuckman developed the "Forming, Storming, Norming and Performing" concept to describe the team formation process. Oftentimes, teams may move back and forth between which two stages when faced with a new task?

a. Forming and storming
b. Storming and norming
c. Performing and forming
d. Norming and performing

Refer to the following scenario for questions 107-108.

A supervisor has reported a situation about one toxic employee in a team of six. His/her work performance is bad, he/she puts others down and rolls his/her eyes in team meetings, and his/her attendance is poor as well. He/she calls in sick frequently and comes in late. He/she has stated that he/she has a medical condition, so the supervisor is afraid to confront him/her about the behavior for fear of a retaliation claim.

107. How would you advise the supervisor to handle this problem employee?

a. The supervisor should send an email to him/her summarizing the disrespectful behavior and specific attendance issues. This would serve as valuable documentation later if needed.
b. The supervisor should focus on the medical condition and refer the employee to human resources to discuss an accommodation or possible Family and Medical Leave Act (FMLA) leave.
c. The supervisor should have a direct conversation with the employee focused on his/her performance and attendance. Going forward, the supervisor should begin documenting each instance of bad behavior.
d. The supervisor should focus on supporting the other team members. Thank them for picking up the slack, and let them know they can stop by any time to discuss concerns.

108. Six months later, the employee is still a challenge. He/she will improve just enough to avoid discipline and seems to be on his/her best behavior around the supervisor, but one team member is reporting "mean" behavior—passive aggressive comments, scoffs and eye rolls, and whispering with other employees. The complainant is shy but well respected and normally has a great attitude. The supervisor doesn't feel a direct conversation between the two will help the situation. What should the next course of action be for the supervisor?

a. Separate the two employees physically. Move their desks, and make it so that none of their work assignments are dependent upon each other.
b. Move forward with a disciplinary action for the offending employee as this is bullying behavior.
c. Pull the offending employee aside privately and explain what has been reported. Inform him/her that bullying is not tolerated in the workplace.
d. Keep a watchful eye on the situation. Check in frequently with the employee who feels targeted and ask the employee to keep a log of each incident.

109. When calculating the rate of turnover in an organization, which is most helpful?

a. Separate out involuntary terminations from voluntary terminations.
b. Include both voluntary and involuntary terminations in the calculation.
c. Consider the prior year's headcount when dividing by the number of employee exits.
d. Consider the prior year's total number of employee exits when dividing by average headcount.

110. To meet eligibility for Family and Medical Leave Act (FMLA)-protected leave, an employee and employer must meet specified criteria. Which criterion is NOT an FMLA qualifier?

a. The employee must have worked for the employer for at least 12 months.
b. The employee must have worked at least 1250 hours in the past 12 months.
c. The employer must employ at least 50 employees within a 75-mile radius.
d. The employee must give the employer at least 30 days' notice of an upcoming leave.

111. What is the model of transactional leadership characterized by?

a. Rewarding high performers with tangible rewards
b. Working to change the organization with innovation and new ideas
c. Leaders "serving" their employees
d. Giving authoritative direction and demanding excellence

112. When presented with a harassment complaint from an employee, which statement should human resources avoid saying to the victim?

a. "Thank you for bringing this to our attention; however, this does not sound like harassing behavior."
b. "Please keep any investigation details confidential."
c. "We do not tolerate retaliation."
d. "The information you're giving me today is completely confidential."

113. The expectancy theory of motivation explains that an individual's choice is driven by

a. an intrinsic desire for personal growth.
b. the desire to avoid the alternative.
c. how desirable the outcome is.
d. the essential needs of the individual.

114. Currently, 28 states in the United States are considered "Right to Work" states. What are Right to Work laws?

a. Legislation that forbids unionizing among employees.
b. Legislation that allows for an employee to be terminated for any reason as long as it is not illegal
c. Legislation that provides a choice to employees with respect to union membership
d. Legislation that ensures employment opportunities for permanent resident aliens

115. What is the most important action to take before initiating recruitment efforts to fill an open position?

a. Determine where the position will be advertised.
b. Build a candidate pipeline.
c. Define the skills needed for the position.
d. Determine the appropriate compensation level for the position.

116. What is the biggest risk in conducting an employee satisfaction survey?

a. Skewed results because only the most satisfied employees respond
b. The potential for employees to not be truthful in their responses
c. The potential for the responses to not be anonymous
d. No employer follow-through on the results gathered from employees

117. To comply with the Age Discrimination in Employment Act (ADEA), what should severance agreements for employees over age 40?

a. A 21-day consideration period plus a seven-day revocation period after signing
b. A seven-day consideration period plus a 21-day revocation period after signing
c. A waiver of any type of complaint to the Equal Employment Opportunity Commission (EEOC)
d. A minimum of 30 days' health insurance coverage

118. When conducting market research for compensation studies, which is a best practice?

a. Consider the job title and level of the position at other organizations.
b. Contact other organizations directly for pay information as the information is more accurate.
c. Leverage employee-reported salary figures through online tools.
d. Utilize at least one market survey with aggregated salary information.

119. If a rejected candidate asks for feedback from the employer on how he/she might improve, what is the MOST appropriate response?

a. A non-specific response like "You just weren't the right fit for our team".
b. Honest and direct feedback with a list of areas to improve upon.
c. A standard, generic response, which is given to all candidates: "We decided to move forward with another candidate".
d. A customized response based on several factors from the level of position, number of candidates interviewed, and whether the candidate is internal or external.

120. According to the Thomas-Kilmann Conflict Mode Instrument chart, as the importance of a goal/assertiveness and the importance of a relationship/cooperation both increase, an ideal conflict resolution style is "collaborating." Under the same model, as the importance of a goal/assertiveness increases and the importance of a relationship/cooperation is minimal, what is the likely response?

a. Avoiding—"I don't want to deal with it"
b. Competing—"It's my way or the highway"
c. Accommodating—"Whatever you want is OK with me"
d. Compromising—"Let's make a deal"

121. Under the Patient Protection and Affordable Care Act (PPACA), what is the period of time during which an employer must offer coverage to those employees who are considered full time called?

a. The measurement period
b. The stability period
c. The administrative period
d. The standard measurement period

122. How long is an H-1B visa valid?

a. An indefinite period of time
b. Three years, then renewable for another three years, for a total of six years
c. Three years
d. One year, then renewable each subsequent year

123. Which is an example of a Bona Fide Occupational Qualification (BFOQ)?

a. A job applicant supplying documentation of his/her college degree
b. A fast-food restaurant with Christian values only hiring Christian employees
c. An airline only hiring attractive female flight attendants to draw in more male passengers
d. A sheriff's office refusing to hire police deputies over the age of 50

124. What is an employee's right to have union representation during a disciplinary interview at the workplace called?

a. Loudermill rights
b. Weingarten rights
c. Garrity rule
d. Right to counsel

Refer to the following scenario for questions 125-126.

> As a human resource manager for a manufacturing organization, you've been noticing a general feeling of low morale among workers on the production floor. There's not a lot of talking among coworkers and no joking or even smiles. Attendance hasn't been stellar, and you've noticed more employees than usual resigning lately. Supervisors have reported that employees are feeling burned out because of the strict deadlines they must meet.

125. Given the fact that these deadlines are nonnegotiable due to client commitments, what could be a creative, low-cost solution to boost morale on the production floor?

a. Conduct "stay" interviews, and give employees an outlet to voice their concerns.
b. Implement an employee recognition program.
c. Hire additional workers to ease the workload of current employees.
d. Encourage coworker relationships by holding on-site social events during work time.

126. What is the most important component of a successful employee recognition program?

a. Plentiful budget
b. Program structure: simple to administer, meaningful rewards
c. Management buy-in
d. Communication and training

127. What is one major differentiating factor that distinguishes an independent contractor from an employee?

a. Independent contractors work for a short, defined duration of time, typically less than six months.
b. Independent contractors work less than 20 hours per week.
c. Independent contractors are usually not located at the employer's site.
d. Independent contractors' work is typically for a defined assignment or project, not ongoing.

128. When an organization assumes direct payment for its employee's medical claims rather than partnering with an insurance provider for coverage, what is it called?

a. Self-funded insurance plan
b. Fully insured insurance plan
c. Disability insurance plan
d. Health maintenance organization (HMO)

129. In the six stages of change readiness, what is the optimal stage for employees during a large organizational change?

a. Indifference
b. Experimentation
c. Neutrality
d. Commitment

130. How would you respond to this request?

An employee makes a request to human resources to hold Bible study during his/her lunch break at work in a conference room. He/she would like to invite other employees who have expressed interest, also during their lunch break.

a. Request that the employee hold the meeting offsite as you don't want it to be perceived as an employer-sponsored event.
b. Allow the request as it is a religious accommodation and does not present an undue hardship on the employer.
c. Allow the request but on the condition that other employees should not be invited as it may make others feel coerced.
d. Allow the request, but post the meeting schedule in a public area so that anyone can attend the meeting if he/she chooses. If attendance is only by invitation, others may feel excluded.

131. When a company uses a matrix organizational structure, what does it mean?

a. The functions of the company are separated into autonomous divisions.
b. There are several layers of authority, and each manager has only one or two direct reports.
c. Employees generally report to more than one supervisor or manager.
d. There are minimal layers of reporting relationships, resulting in the need for more cross-functional teams.

132. What is an important criteria in defining an employee's behavior as insubordination?

a. The threat of discipline up to and including termination
b. The employee yelling or being generally disrespectful toward a direct supervisor
c. The employer making a clear directive to the employee
d. The employee being represented by a bargaining unit

Refer to the following scenario for questions 133-135.

You are the project manager of a large human resources/payroll system implementation at your organization, which is a high-tech digital marketing firm. The implementation is not underway just yet, but you have sent out several requests for proposal, and the responses are coming in from vendors. As part of your role, you must keep the entire organization informed.

133. What type of initial message would you convey to the organization regarding this project to gain buy-in?

a. That a new system will improve efficiencies and ultimately save the company money
b. That there will be lots of training on the new system once it is in place
c. That the executive team is fully committed to replacing the system
d. That the current system is obsolete, and it is a risk to continue to rely on it for human resource and payroll functions

134. To convey the initial message and all subsequent communication, your plan is to issue updates through a variety of mediums. What technique would likely be the LEAST effective method of relaying important information to employees?

a. Sending emails
b. Attending department-wide meetings and giving verbal updates
c. Mailing out a printed newsletter to employees' homes
d. Posting updates on an electronic bulletin board

135. In this organization, employee career levels range from entry-level to advanced software engineers, with several employees fresh out of college and a few gearing up for retirement. Given this wide range in employee demographics, which communication technique should you utilize when giving your next departmental presentation?

a. Tailor the message based on the group you're presenting to.
b. Use stories and real-life examples to be more relatable.
c. Describe the human resource information system project and its intricacies in lay terms.
d. Provide a visual presentation with graphics and charts.

136. In the context of a retirement plan, how is graded vesting defined?

a. The employee receives complete ownership of employer contributions after a certain number of years (no more than six).
b. The employee has elected to fully manage his/her own fund allocations and investments.
c. If a fund's performance drops below a certain threshold, the employer will cease to offer it as an option for employees.
d. The employee's ownership of employer contributions grows partially each year of participation.

137. What is your first priority in your new role?

You are a new human resources (HR) director, reporting to the CEO in a professional services organization. According to the CEO, the HR department has had some challenges with its reputation within the organization. Some specific areas of concern from the CEO include slow response time to employee inquiries, inefficient processes, and poor staff attendance.

a. Conduct an I-9 audit, and ensure there is no legal exposure.
b. Get to know the human resource (HR) staff, and learn all current departmental processes.
c. Send the entire HR staff to customer service training to improve their interactions with other employees in the company.
d. Release a company-wide communication introducing yourself and your role, make the rounds in each department, and get to know as many employees in the company as possible.

138. On which main concept is the interest-based relational approach to conflict resolution based?

a. Find common interests between the two parties.
b. Separate people from problems.
c. Preserve the relationship at all costs.
d. Confront the conflict but only if the relationship is a priority

Refer to the following scenario for questions 139-141.

Sean, a high-performing individual contributor, was recently promoted to be a supervisor and inherited three direct reports. He'd never been a supervisor before.

After several months in his new position, Sean was working 10-hour days but was still falling behind in completing his performance reviews.

139. Given the facts presented, what supervisory skill do you think Sean needs to improve upon?

a. Delegation
b. Time management
c. Giving feedback
d. Communication

140. With Sean not delegating his work, what could be the most damaging repercussion to the organization?

a. His work products would take longer to complete, causing backlogs and delays.
b. If he were to leave the organization, nobody would know how to complete his work tasks.
c. His direct reports would likely feel idle and underutilized, thus reducing engagement.
d. He would not be able to keep up with the workload and may get burned out.

141. Let's assume Sean learns how to delegate and begins feeling more comfortable with assigning projects to his direct reports. What supervisory skill should he work on next, which often goes hand-in-hand with delegation?

a. Time management
b. Accountability
c. Training of work tasks
d. Employee development

142. There are several different types of employees who work on an international work assignment. What is an expatriate, or expat?

a. An employee who permanently relocates back to his/her home country after working abroad
b. An employee who takes on an assignment in a country outside of his/her home country
c. An employee who is brought into an organization from another country
d. An employee who works in the country he/she is originally from

Refer to the following scenario for questions 143-144.

You are a new human resources (HR) director who has inherited a team of 10 HR people. The previous HR director was beloved by the team, and you can already tell that they are not thrilled with your arrival. They are skeptical and resistant to your ideas and suggestions.

143. You've thought of a few ideas to build trust with the team. What is one action item that would likely NOT establish that trust with your team?

a. Communicate often in one-on-meetings and team meetings.
b. Get to know your team outside of work—schedule lunch outings and ask about family, friends, and hobbies.
c. Dive right in and begin to learn about the initiatives in progress: ask questions, review pertinent documents, and provide your insight.
d. Encourage accountability by taking ownership of your own mistakes.

144. Similarly, you're trying to establish a culture of appreciation among your team. What would be the most effective way to set the tone for the group?

a. In the next team meeting, bring up the most recent successful human resources initiative, and thank the team members who did a great job.
b. Bring in donuts on Friday for the team for all their hard work.
c. Send an email to your superior calling out the specific wins in your department and who was responsible.
d. Write simple thank-you notes for a job well done.

145. When an individual's wage amount is "red circled," what does it mean?

a. The wage is above the set range for the position.
b. The wage is below the set range for the position.
c. A cost-of-living adjustment has not been made yet.
d. The wage includes some kind of additional incentive, like a sign-on bonus or educational premium.

146. According to the McKinsey 7S Framework, how do the seven organizational components—structure, strategy, systems, skills, style, staff, and shared values—work together?

a. They are sequential and cyclical—the visual representation is like a wheel.
b. They are interdependent and must be aligned for organizational success.
c. Shared values must be established first, and the other elements can fall into place in any order.
d. The visual representation is like a pyramid with structure, strategy, and shared values at the base, representing the most significant to establish first.

Refer to the following scenario for questions 147-148.

As the human resources (HR) manager for a midsize organization, you have been tasked with spearheading a major new initiative—replacing the outdated HR/payroll system with something more modern and efficient. You feel confident in your project management skills and are excited to begin the process of collecting system requirements and identifying possible vendors. However, the executive sponsor of the project has warned you about some potential resistance from the payroll supervisor. The supervisor has worked for the organization for 12 years, is extremely proficient in the current system, and doesn't like the idea of learning a new system.

147. How would you go about getting buy-in from the payroll supervisor?

a. Meet with the supervisor one on one and hear his/her concerns. Explain the possible risks of the project but also the potential improved efficiencies in the daily work.
b. Show the supervisor the project schedule and explain all the important upcoming milestones. Ask for initial thoughts and feedback.
c. Request that direct manager have a conversation with the payroll supervisor. Clarify that he/she will be expected to participate and provide expertise when needed.
d. Ask the supervisor to draft a wish list—everything he/she would like in a new payroll system.

148. As the project is in full swing, you are hearing that some of the human resource (HR) staff is unhappy with being left out of making important decisions. The project requires many meetings over several months, and it's difficult to accommodate all six of the HR staff's schedules. As it stands now, waiting to schedule meetings when all can attend is delaying the entire project. How would you approach this discontent with the HR staff?

a. In the next staff meeting, explain that if people want to be involved in the decision-making, they must be in attendance at all the project meetings.
b. Organize a human resources (HR) retreat, and provide change management training to the entire team.
c. Each week, summarize the decisions that need to be made and bring that list to each HR staff meeting for discussion.
d. Select a small HR project team—two other employees besides yourself—to attend all meetings. Explain to the others that this small team will have the authority to make decisions on HR's behalf.

149. Which statement is true about COBRA?

a. Employers may charge a 2% premium in addition to the original insurance premium cost.
b. The employer may terminate COBRA coverage at any time and for any reason.
c. COBRA insurance plans generally have a higher deductible than the base employer plan.
d. A divorce disqualifies a participant's beneficiary from coverage.

150. What could be an effective active listening skill that Jennifer could leverage in her meetings with Rhonda?

> Jennifer, a newer employee, is meeting with her supervisor, Rhonda, for their weekly one-on-one meeting. Rhonda has a thick accent, and Jennifer has a hard time understanding her. Jennifer often leaves their meetings feeling confused and concerned that she doesn't know what is expected of her. Rhonda is also getting frustrated with Jennifer as she doesn't feel that Jennifer is listening to her when she talks.

a. Request that Rhonda speaks a little slower.
b. Take notes throughout the meeting to show that she is engaged and listening.
c. Maintain eye contact, smile, and nod.
d. Ask for clarification and confirm understanding such as, "So what I'm hearing is XYZ. Is that correct?"

151. Which of the following statements BEST describe active listening?

a. A listener is able to eliminate distractions and fully comprehend the information being delivered by the speaker.
b. A listener is able to memorize the majority of the facts provided by the speaker.
c. A listener gives verbal and nonverbal cues of listening such as nodding and saying "uh-huh."
d. An individual silently listens to a speaker and does not provide any type of verbal or nonverbal reaction.

152. How is position control defined?

a. A process by which positions are created, maintained, and tracked according to budgetary constraints.
b. A process by which only the highest human resource leader has authority to add new positions.
c. A process by which all recruitment activity is paused, and no new employees will be hired.
d. A process by which a position is defined by the person in it.

153. What is the first step in the strategic planning process?

a. Develop S.M.A.R.T. goals.
b. Define desired outcome.
c. Identify potential risks that would threaten the goal.
d. Analyze the applicable data.

154. Which of the following scenarios would NOT result in a COBRA-qualifying event for an employee?

a. A reduction in hours below plan eligibility requirements
b. Voluntary termination of employment
c. Family and Medical Leave Act (FMLA) protected leave
d. Involuntary termination of employment for reasons other than gross misconduct

155. Which is an expense that a flexible spending account (FSA) may NOT be used for, as governed by the Internal Revenue Service (IRS)?

a. Acupuncture
b. COBRA insurance premiums
c. Child care costs
d. Electric toothbrush

156. What is one major difference between a cost-benefit analysis (CBA) and a return on investment (ROI) calculation?

a. ROI is displayed as a dollar value, whereas CBA is displayed as a percentage or ratio.
b. CBA is generally conducted before the expense is made, whereas ROI is generally calculated after the investment is made.
c. CBA is displayed as a dollar value, whereas ROI is displayed as a percentage or ratio.
d. CBA tends to focus on tangible financial gains, whereas ROI is more in depth and takes into account tangible and intangible gains.

157. A job applicant who was invited to interview with your organization requests to have the questions in print format during the interview so that he/she can read along as the questions are asked. The applicant mentions that he/she is hard of hearing, and this will help him/her respond appropriately to the questions. But you have not done this for the other candidates in the process. What do you do?

a. Offer to read the questions loudly and slowly during the interview.
b. Decline the request as it is important to treat every candidate consistently and interview candidates do not have the same Americans with Disabilities Act (ADA) protections as employees.
c. Accommodate the candidate, and print out the interview questions for him as it is an accommodation request under the ADA.
d. Provide a special hearing device for the candidate to use during the interview.

Refer to the following scenario for questions 158-159.

At a recent management meeting, during one manager's presentation, he/she made a joke that others reported later as being insensitive. Apparently, he/she had laughed when he/she saw a "he-she" at the grocery store the evening prior and "ran the other way." Two employees have now come to you with a similar account of what happened and asked what will be done to handle this situation.

158. What would you say in response to the complainants?

a. "This is completely unacceptable. We do not tolerate insensitive remarks at our organization. We will address this right away, and the manager will be dealt with appropriately."
b. Ask clarifying questions such as these: "What was the context of discussion when the remark was made? Was it said in a joking manner?"
c. "Thank you for bringing this to my attention. You are not the only person who has reported this incident. We will be launching an investigation shortly regarding this matter."
d. "Thank you for bringing this to my attention. We will look into this immediately. Is it OK if I contact you again for questions or clarification regarding the facts of the situation if needed?"

159. Assuming you launch an investigation and confirm the comments were made in the meeting, what would be your course of action with the manager who made the offensive comments?

a. Create a performance improvement plan (PIP) with a six-month plan for addressing his/her biases.
b. Enroll the manager in a diversity and inclusion-focused coaching program.
c. Rather than focus on the individual manager, explore cultural sensitivity training for the entire organization.
d. This individual should not be in a leadership role in the organization—demote him/her to be an individual contributor.

160. How long is the COBRA election period?

a. 45 days
b. 90 days
c. 60 days
d. 30 days, unless the employee or dependent is disabled, then it is 60 days.

Answer Key and Explanations for Test #1

1. A: The Worker Adjustment and Retraining Notification (WARN) Act requires that for a layoff affecting 50 or more employees at one location, employees must be given 60 days' notice prior to their employment ending.

2. B: Feedback is best delivered in a specific format. Describe the exact behavior that needs to stop and what needs to start happening. In this case, the employee needs to stop talking over people in meetings. Providing more complex work assignments to the employee may further alienate others on the team as they'd see the poor behavior rewarded with more advanced assignments.

3. C: Although this employee may be going through a series of personal crises, it's important to focus on his/her work performance and attendance issues. If the attendance issues are not addressed, they can have a negative impact on the others on the team.

4. B: Both the employer and the union must participate in the collective bargaining process and display good faith bargaining efforts; however, neither party is required to make concessions.

5. B: As part of the Affordable Care Act (ACA), preventive care, vaccines, and screenings are no longer subject to copayments, deductibles, or coinsurance. There are also expanded protections for women's health services.

6. B: In this instance, you should gather more information before instituting a plan of action. The cause of the poor ratings could be anything from bad internal customer service to inefficient processes. Another survey would probably give employees survey fatigue, so it's best to launch an internal audit.

7. D: The first step in a human resources audit is to determine the type and scope of the audit. Will you focus on one specific function, such as recruiting or employee relations? Or will it be more exhaustive of all processes? Will it be strategic or compliance-oriented, or will it identify best practices?

8. A: This audit should address all human resource (HR) functions, not just employee relations. The poor survey results could be prompted by other processes such as performance reviews, benefits enrollment, promotional opportunities, and so on. Although compliance is important, it is not the goal of this audit. Industry best practice will provide a useful benchmark to identify deficiencies in the HR function.

9. D: In this situation, you don't want to imply that the engineers only need to improve upon their skills to get a promotion, but you also don't want to stifle their ambition. The leads should work with the engineers to identify exactly what they need—is it just more money? More recognition? More responsibility? More autonomy? Perhaps some of these needs can be met with a creative solution rather than a promotion.

10. A: The best way to quantify this situation is to calculate the time since last promotion for each employee and average it out across the organization. Whereas a turnover rate may indicate a problem with higher-than-average employee exits, it will not identify the reason for exits.

11. C: As the employee is noticeably anxious about the health condition and missing work, it is best to respond to the email with a response as soon as possible rather than deferring to the HR Specialist who is not in the office.

12. B: A PEST analysis is conducted as part of a strategic market analysis of several factors: political, economic, social and technological.

13. D: When an individual is in the "red zone," an effective technique is to guess an employee's feelings and/or needs that aren't being met. This can help them articulate his/her feelings while focusing on the facts. Advice in any form to an individual in this state is usually not well received. Once he/she has calmed down, you might ask if you can give them some advice.

14. B: This conflict does not rise to the level of any type of harassment or even bullying; it sounds like normal workplace conflict between two colleagues. For this reason, there is no need for a formal investigation; however, the supervisor should be made aware of the situation so that the conflict does not escalate.

15. C: The hiring manager knows the position and the industry best, he/she can give expert insight into the next steps in the recruitment strategy.

16. A: Coordination of benefits rules require that the insurance plan listed as primary will be charged first, and any residual charges will be processed by the secondary payer.

17. B: A vision statement should be aspirational and strategic, describing where the organization wants to be in the future and how they plan to achieve that goal.

18. D: FSA participation is optional for employees. During open enrollment, each employee decides how much money, if any, to contribute to an FSA. Employers may contribute to a flexible spending account (FSA) on behalf of their employees. The funds generally do expire at the end of the plan year; however, many plans offer a three-month grace period that allows employees to access the funds into the following year.

19. A: Coaching is used in specific instances for individuals—to help them prepare for a leadership role or an upcoming assignment or to help them develop a specific skill or stop exhibiting a certain behavior. Mentoring is usually in the case of a formal or informal program and can help individuals pursue their personal or professional goals.

20. A: When providing feedback, a supervisor should limit the focus to one or two areas of deficiency. Otherwise, it tends to make the employee feel defensive.

21. A: Supervisors are to be excluded from bargaining units under the National Labor Relations Act (NLRA) if they have independent judgment to make personnel decisions such as hiring, terminating, or promoting.

22. A: "Best of breed" is a term used to describe the process of selecting only the best software system for a specific need of the organization, which often means not choosing an all-in-one system, which may have system limitations in various areas.

23. C: A SMART goal is specific, measurable, achievable, relevant, and time bound.

24. C: There are 16 different personality type combinations using the four pairs of Myers-Briggs Type Indicator (MBTI) preferences: introverted versus extraverted, sensing versus intuitive, thinking verses feeling, and judging versus perceiving.

25. C: PIPs are best for specific and measurable problems with an employee's performance that may be turned around with guidance and training. Insubordinate behavior is not generally resolved with a PIP. And last, although PIPs are sometimes the final step before a termination, it is best for managers and supervisors to issue a PIP with the intent that the behavior can be improved.

26. D: There is no specific advanced engineer exemption. The Fair Labor Standards Act (FLSA) exemptions apply only to white collar-type employees who fall under the salary and duties test that include executive, administrative, professional (learned and creative), computer, outside sales, and highly compensated employees.

27. B: Human resources is usually in the role of preparing for, and participating in, collective bargaining. This falls under the "confidential employee" exemption with the National Labor Relations Act (NLRA).

28. A: Key performance indicators (KPIs) are relatively controversial, with some experts claiming they foster competition rather than collaboration.

29. A: Federal contractors and subcontractors are required by the OFCCP to annually review and update their AAPs, which include a report and documentation of affirmative actions such as outreach efforts and training programs.

30. C: The first step in the process of selecting a new human resource information system (HRIS) is to determine if the organization will conduct the vendor selection process internally or if a third-party consultant will be hired to perform the search. Once that decision is made, the other steps will follow.

31. A: Before traveling to Chennai or collecting sample documents, a political, economic, social and technological (PEST) analysis should be conducted from a human resources viewpoint. Political, economic, social and technological factors will influence most decisions that need to be made, so thorough research and analysis is critical.

32. C: The most effective approach to improving daily communication is a short status call that occurs every day. The attendees can discuss pressing topics for the day or just catch up, and this allows attendees to build relationships and feel connected.

33. B: Senior leaders who are focused in finance are usually most interested in how much things will cost and what the return on investment will be. Furthermore, usually their time is short and valuable, so a more succinct delivery of this information is better.

34. C: A successful mentor does not necessarily need to be the most senior. Even a less experienced mentor can provide insight and guidance to a mentee in an area the mentee is not familiar with.

35. A: Automatic enrollment in a 401(k) for new hires, although not a requirement, is a recommended strategy to boost participation in the plan. There is not usually backlash from employees against this provision; however, communication to new hires and current employees is essential to avoid mistrust.

36. A: Under Title II of the Genetic Information Nondiscrimination Act (GINA), it is illegal for employers to base any type of hiring decision (promotions, hiring, and/or firing) based on genetic information such as family medical history or the likelihood that they may contract a disease or illness.

37. A: The other concerns listed can usually be assuaged with a legitimate assessment provider. But no matter how buttoned up the assessment tool is, great applicants might be eliminated from the process based solely on their personality type.

38. C: Workforce planning and employment are a human resources domain that is operationally focused, with emphasis on recruitment/selection, retention, and separation. Although similar to the employee life cycle, workforce planning and employment are less comprehensive.

39. A: External candidates can bring new ideas and approaches to an organization, whereas an internal candidate is influenced by the current organizational mind-set.

40. D: Pairing up employees when they visit customers' homes is a creative solution that would provide a safer situation for everyone—customers and employees. It is unwise to make a uniform disqualification for anyone who has a criminal record as this can result in disparate impact. Although it is a good idea to inform new hires of the organization's expectations when it comes to ethics, threatening criminal prosecution is not exactly a warm welcome! Last, telling customers to secure their valuables prior to a visit conveys that they should not trust the employee visiting the home, which may have a negative impact on future business.

41. B: Generally, in the case of a harassment complaint, you cannot promise anonymity. However, this is a complaint regarding criminal activity of the accused, and there is no need for the complainant's name to be disclosed.

42. A: The look-back measurement period is a method of determining eligibility for coverage. The employer looks at a defined period of time that the employee has worked and averages the weekly hours. If the average is 30 hours or more per week, the employee would likely be eligible for coverage.

43. C: The CSR's medical professional should make the determination of the need for the stand-up desk. You should not try to determine the legitimacy or severity of a disability; rather, focus on the reasonableness of the accommodation request. And in this case, the request is reasonable.

44. B: Employers should never divulge another employee's personal health information, even to justify the reason for an accommodation. Although the performance-based program is creative, an employee's comfort should not be dependent on how well he/she performs on the job. The best course of action in this case is to work to obtain a budget to eventually offer stand-up desks to all employees who sit for extended periods of time. This can be treated as a perk of the job and may end up preventing future health issues for employees.

45. A: Although a supervisor may also be a good resource in assessing the dangers of the job, employees have the best familiarity with the potential hazards of their everyday responsibilities.

46. D: Both new mothers and new fathers have the same rights under Family and Medical Leave Act (FMLA)—that is 12 weeks of job and benefit protection following the birth or adoption of a child. This includes bonding time, physical incapacity from the delivery, and/or care for the spouse who is recovering.

47. A: The principled negotiation style is an interest-based bargaining technique that aims to identify a mutually beneficial agreement, also known as "win-win."

48. C: A halo bias is when interviewers or recruiters base their assessment of a candidate solely on one positive characteristic. A horns bias is the opposite: one perceived negative trait sours the entire interaction. A similarity bias is when interviewers are drawn to a candidate who is similar to themselves, and a first impression bias is when interviewers makes a hiring decision based solely on their initial thoughts and feelings of the person.

49. C: Canadian citizens, unlike Mexican citizens, do not need a TN visa to work in the United States. They need only present proof of Canadian citizenship, a written job offer from the prospective employer, and proof of qualification for the position at the U.S. border. They are generally then admitted as a TN nonimmigrant.

50. A: Cloud commuting is a practice of storing, managing, and processing data in remote servers rather than a locally hosted server.

51. D: Older workers tend to value direct communication and lengthier, personal-type conversations. This can present challenges with a younger generation, who tend to prefer quick, work-related conversations to accomplish the objective. They also tend to be more familiar with modern communication technology like texting and instant messaging.

52. C: The millennial generation wants to know how to get to that next step in their career and feel engaged when they are provided with development opportunities.

53. B: Suspected drug users who are acting erratically should never be confronted alone. Also, supervisors are often not trained to handle a conversation of this magnitude, so it is best to have both a human resource representative and the supervisor present. Also, presenting the employee with a drug test prior to any conversations could cause the employee to panic and risk a negative outcome for the situation.

54. D: The most appropriate course of action would be to offer Family and Medical Leave Act (FMLA)-protected leave so the employee can attend rehab. You might also verify with your insurance to see if, and how, it is covered. Although it is true that he/she could be held to the same standards as other employees, it is important to first provide the tools for the employee to get clean. Once he/she is recovered, you may hold him/her to that standard. Additionally, current drug users are not protected under the Americans with Disabilities Act, but recovered addicts are.

55. C: Although human resources (HR) may contact the medical professional to confirm the validity of the certification and ask clarifying questions, to protect the employee's privacy, they may not ask for more information about the condition. HR may require a second or third opinion at the employer's expense.

56. C: The Department of Labor has issued seven criteria that qualify an internship to be unpaid. There are no restrictions for weekly hours.

57. A: Intermittent Family and Medical Leave Act (FMLA) leave is not mandated for baby bonding time; however, an employer may allow it. In this particular instance, it would present a hardship on the department, and asking others to work extra hours to fill in for this employee would likely be perceived as unfair.

58. B: A harassment claim that is found to be malicious should result in discipline for the complainant. It is never a good idea to discuss an investigation and its results with the complainant and subject in the same room.

59. D: According to the Equal Employment Opportunity Commission (EEOC), petty slights, annoyances, and isolated incidents will not rise to the level of illegality.

60. A: Direct, timely feedback is always the best approach with employees. Asking for feedback on how to avoid mistakes in the future makes him/her feel invested in the solution.

61. B: Federal law does not require lunch or rest periods for employees; however, many states do have these provisions.

62. C: A "top-heavy" 401(k) plan is one in which more than 60% of the entire plan's value resides in the accounts of "key" employees. A key employee is defined as an employee with major ownership of the company and/or in a decision-making role.

63. B: Focus groups with employees are optimal when they pertain to specific topics, such as feedback on the benefit plan or succession planning. Around eight to 10 participants are best, and they should be a diverse group of employees to more accurately represent opinions across the organization. Although employees should feel free to voice their opinions openly, the facilitator should bring some semblance of structure to the focus group. He/she should give an introduction, ask open-ended questions to participants, and be prepared to summarize the discussion at the conclusion.

64. A: Understanding the current state of training and the needs for each department will help human resources (HR) determine where the gaps are and what training needs to be eliminated, added, changed, or maintained. At that point, HR can verify that legal obligations are being met and best practices are being followed, and a plan can begin to take place.

65. B: Current training delivery methods and course durations should not be an important factor in deciding how to structure the new training program. Human resources should factor in legal obligations and logistical requirements. In addition, some training content is best delivered in person rather than online—for instance, training that needs discussion or opportunities for learners to ask questions.

66. C: Many states and local legislatures are banning the practice of asking for a candidate's current compensation as basing an offer on current pay can have disparate impact on protected classes. The salary offer should be based primarily on the candidate's level of experience, but other factors such as potential commute, candidate requirements, internal equity, and others may be considered as well.

67. C: Based on the facts that Karen and Steve are friends, Steve is in good standing with the company and has never been in trouble before, and Karen clearly has a desire to maintain the friendship, it would be best to let her make the decision on the next course of action.

68. A: An employee who is "engaged to wait" is one who must stay at the workplace until his/her work assignment is given; therefore, he/she must be paid for that time as he/she is effectively on duty. An employee who is "waiting to be engaged" is relieved of his/her work duties, and can use his/her time freely, but must return to the workplace if a work assignment requires his/her presence.

69. B: Return to Work (RTW) programs can be used for on-the-job injuries or off-duty injuries as well.

70. A: Although each option presented could help identify different causes of turnover, the best way to pinpoint the top reason would be to conduct exit interviews with each exiting employee and identify trends.

71. C: Realistic job previews would give candidates a realistic glimpse into what the job would entail on a daily basis. It would encourage them to self-select out of the hiring process if they aren't a good fit rather than waiting until after they're hired.

72. D: The software developers in this scenario are young and hardworking, so unlimited paid time off (PTO) may not resonate with them as much as other perks. Additionally, unlimited PTO has plenty of pitfalls and risks, so ultimately it may not be worth the potential issues. These employees also seem to have minimal interest in anything related to health care or insurance benefits. Millennials typically have a strong desire to remain challenged and advance quickly in their careers—a career path program would allow them to constantly learn, evolve, and move to the next level when the time is right.

73. B: The most effective method of gaining leadership buy-in is to show, rather than tell. If the CEO is willing to agree to a trial period, he/she will see the intangible benefits of allowing employees to work from home. Trial periods are effective methods of testing out a workplace program without a full commitment. The CEO is more likely to agree to this.

74. D: Organizations should never base any hiring decision on race, gender, age, or any other protected visual attributes, even if the intent is to "hire for more diversity." Also, whereas the other two suggestions would help create a more inclusive workplace, the most effective strategy is to expand the reach of recruitment efforts toward underrepresented groups.

75. D: The need for self-actualization is the final stop in the pyramid. Once an individual has met his/her basic hunger and thirst needs, he/she looks to fill the need for safety, then feeling a sense of belonging. Next is the need for feeling esteem from others and, finally, the need for a sense of purpose, or self-actualization.

76. B: The "4/5 rule" and "80% rule" are commonly used phrases that describe the ideal selection rate for protected classes, as defined by the Equal Employment Opportunity Commission (EEOC). The selection rate of minorities should be at least 80% of the selection rate of nonminorities.

77. A: The most likely resulting culture in the organization would be fear based. Employees would likely be fearful of making contributions as they may make a mistake and would be fearful of losing their jobs or speaking up in meetings.

78. B: It's best to hire a neutral third-party expert to come in and make an unbiased assessment. The CEO is more likely to be receptive to feedback from a professional who has made a thorough analysis of the organization's leadership.

79. B: Once the injured employee is helped and stabilized, the first call should be to human resources (HR) before taking any witness statements or writing up a summary of events. It could be dangerous to fix the cause of the injury, so again, it is best for supervisors to consult with HR before handling anything themselves.

80. B: Dependents may enroll with COBRA continuation coverage even if the primary beneficiary (employee or former employee) is not enrolled.

81. D: The evidence-based decision-making (EBDM) process is a concept that is based solely on research and facts, so thoughts and feelings, even from a subject matter expert (SME), are not generally factored in when making a management decision.

82. B: An engaged employee is one who is loyal to the organization, speaks highly of the organization to friends and family, knows what work needs to be done to make a positive impact, and does it. Job satisfaction and employee engagement are not the same thing; job satisfaction is usually driven by extrinsic factors such as pay, benefits and time off, whereas intrinsic motivators and strong leadership drive engagement.

83. C: Organizing a social meet-up for remote employees to connect with one another would encourage strong working relationships and a kind of support group where they can share remote working experiences and tips. Posting photos would probably make remote workers feel even more left out of the fun. Also, if given the choice, remote workers would probably prefer not to attend the company party if it meant paying for travel and lodging. The dial-in and webcam would not be a bad idea but, again, may make the remote workers feel more left out.

84. A: Although the other options could be potential downsides of having a remote workforce, the biggest disadvantage is the impact on communication and work relationships. Employees and managers must be more proactive in communication efforts with remote workers—a simple face-to-face chat is not an option.

85. D: The biggest advantage is offering a better work-life balance for employees. Overhead costs may be slightly less for a remote worker; however, the employer should still pay for home office supplies and equipment. A lack of commute does have a positive impact on the environment, but that is not necessarily the focus from a human resource perspective. Last, a remote work arrangement is not a substitute for child care as the employee's focus should be on working, not tending to other responsibilities.

86. D: Even if a candidate appears to be originally from the United States, interviewers should not ask where the candidate is from, as national origin is a protected class. If not selected, a candidate could claim discrimination based on this criterion.

87. C: H-1B visa applicants are eligible if they possess a bachelor's degree or foreign equivalent and work in a specialty occupation as defined by the U.S. Citizen and Immigration Services (USCIS).

88. A: Answer B describes a specialist role, answer C describes a generalist role, and answer D is actually a common disadvantage of utilizing the business partner model. Different business partners across the organization who support different divisions tend to reflect inconsistency in practice as compared to their counterparts.

89. D: Encouraging social connections will help work interactions as well. If the social activities occur on site during work hours, employees are more likely to attend than if they are offsite or on employees' own time.

90. C: Direct confrontations and group meetings where people are expected to share updates can be uncomfortable for some cultures. Supervisors and managers should focus their time and energy on establishing trust with each individual on their team.

91. D: A political, economic, social and technological (PEST) analysis is a method of obtaining and reviewing data from external influences to the organization.

92. C: Current employee expectations should not be a driving factor when defining an organization's compensation philosophy. Although it is important to pay a fair and equitable amount for the work being performed, employee expectations are often higher than the wage commensurate with the work performed.

93. C: It is a good idea to grant the employee's request but only if it does not present undue hardship to the employer. Some examples of undue hardship could be cost, staffing shortages, or a decrease in workplace efficiency.

94. B: A nine-box grid is a matrix with three degrees of performance on one axis and three levels of potential on the other axis. Names are generally plotted in the different grid squares to identify individuals who have potential to move into leadership roles in the organization.

95. A: HSA funds never expire, and employees who leave the organization do not lose access to the funds.

96. B: The employer should provide a comprehensive list of acceptable documentation to an employee and allow him/her to choose the documentation that meets the criteria. Requiring a new hire to supply a passport would discriminate against those who are not U.S. citizens.

97. D: According to research, middle managers are among the most unhappy in the workplace, and a primary reason is a lack of authority from upper management and having to enforce policies that they may not agree with.

98. B: A direct, facilitated conversation is best in the instance of workplace conflict. That way Jane and Susan can hear each other's perspectives and make strides in repairing the relationship. It is best to address the situation before it continues to get worse.

99. A: Dysfunctional conflict among employees is a detriment to the workplace and can cause absenteeism and/or turnover—this is the best descriptor of the interactions between Jane and Susan. Functional conflict is actually a beneficial type of conflict and can actually promote problem-solving and creative ideas. Bullying behavior is generally one-sided, and task conflict is isolated to a certain project or task.

100. C: Individuals who are thoughtful and fact based typically prefer to "digest" information before asking questions or responding. Sending an email ahead of the one-on-one meeting would allow Peter the time to consider all his questions or concerns before having a direct conversation. Also, it is not always feasible or equitable to dole out work assignments based solely on employee preference.

101. B: As the manager of the group you should be involved in the strategic discussions and overall project plan. From there, if Jason and Peter are able to decide collaboratively which tasks they feel most comfortable with, they will have more buy-in for the project itself.

102. D: Peter and Jason have different working styles. Peter may resent Jason's attention-seeking and flashy style, and Jason may feel that Peter needs to speak up if he has questions, concerns, or generally any information to share.

103. C: Forms for active employees should never be destroyed. The retention requirement is three years after hire date or one year after termination date, whichever is later.

104. B: Cost per candidate by source is calculated by dividing the total cost of the source (in this case, the total cost of the career fairs) by number of candidates generated by the source. This metric can then be compared to the cost of alternate sources of generating candidates to prove its efficiency.

105. D: Because you report to the CFO, you should tread lightly when telling him he's wrong but still have a direct and private conversation about it. It's obvious that he's concerned about cost, so it's best to provide a solution to mitigate those costs while still meeting your objective of attending the career fairs.

106. B: Teams often will relapse from the norming stage back into storming when faced with new challenges.

107. C: The supervisor should focus solely on the employee's performance and attendance. A blend of direct face-to-face feedback and documentation is best to illustrate that the supervisor is following protocol and no unfair treatment based on his/her medical condition is taking place.

108. A: This employee's bad behavior is just under the radar and is not quite egregious enough to rise to the level of discipline. A direct conversation from the supervisor may only make matters worse for the other employee. In this case it would be best to separate the two employees in hopes that the situation can be diffused over time.

109. A: When determining the cause of employee turnover, it is best to separate out involuntary terminations from voluntary terminations. Counting involuntary terminations in the calculation will skew the separation rate and will not help determine the cause for attrition.

110. D: Although 30 days' advance notice of an upcoming leave is ideal, in many instances it will not be feasible for an employee to give any advance notice. If no advance notice is given, it is not an adequate reason to deny Family and Medical Leave Act (FMLA) leave.

111. A: Transactional leadership is a style of leadership that is objective driven, in which leaders incentivize wanted behavior with tangible rewards and discourage unwanted behavior with punishment. Transactional leadership is an opposing model from transformational leadership, in which leaders look to inspire and motivate to change the status quo. Transactional leadership is best in the instance of emergency operations or when there is a high-priority objective.

112. D: Human resources should never guarantee confidentiality to complainants. In the case of an investigation, details of the complaint will likely need to be shared with the accused and/or witnesses.

113. C: The expectancy theory of motivation hypothesizes that individuals make the choices that they do based on the likelihood and importance of the outcome.

114. C: In a Right to Work state, employees are able to decline union membership if they choose.

115. C: The most important first step before beginning a recruitment process is defining the needed skills an incumbent should have to be successful in the role. Once this list is established, that will help define compensation, optimal advertising sources, and finally, qualified candidates.

116. D: The biggest organizational risk when conducting an employee satisfaction survey is the potential for not taking any action based on the findings of the survey. This may backfire and create ill will among employees.

117. A: The Age Discrimination in Employment Act (ADEA) requires an employee over 40 to receive 21 days to review a severance agreement before signing. Once the employee signs the agreement, he/she has seven days from the date of signature to change his/her mind and revoke the agreement. Agreements should not contain any type of language that would prevent employees from filing a complaint with the Equal Employment Opportunity Commission (EEOC).

118. D: Organizations should not contact other organizations directly for specific compensation amounts as this may lead to antitrust violations. Also, job titles and levels can vary across organizations; the actual duties and responsibilities should be taken into account when determining the similarity of positions. Last, employee-reported salary amounts are not always accurate.

119. D: A response to a candidate asking for feedback on how to improve can vary based on multiple factors. If there is a reason to foster a relationship with a candidate, it can be worthwhile to provide constructive but carefully worded and concise feedback.

120. B: During a conflict between two individuals, when the relationship is of minimal importance and the goal is of high importance, often the response between the two parties is competitiveness.

121. B: The stability period is the duration of time that coverage must be offered to all full-time employees. This period of time must be at least six months and not less than the defined measurement period.

122. B: The initial issuance of an H-1B visa is valid for three years and is renewable for another three years for a total duration of six years.

123. D: A Bona Fide Occupational Qualification (BFOQ) is only legitimate if it is a criterion (e.g., gender, religion, or national origin) that is required for business operations. There is a business need and safety consideration for hiring police officers and deputies who are younger than 50.

124. B: A union member has the right to union representation in an investigatory interview that may result in discipline, and this right is known as "Weingarten."

125. B: An employee recognition program can vary from formal and structured to inexpensive and casual and generally promotes positive results from employees with minimal expense. It would be an effective approach to ensure that employees feel appreciated for working hard without significantly altering the working conditions.

126. C: Leadership buy-in is critical to create a culture of appreciation, not only as it relates to the tangible rewards in a formal recognition program but setting the tone of direct verbal kudos and thank-yous for a job well done.

127. D: Independent contractors' work is independent—specifications are provided by the employer with a required deliverable, and they determine how, what, and where the contractor performs the work to complete the task.

128. A: When an organization is self-funded, or self-insured, it typically purchases stop-loss coverage for larger claims over a predefined amount but pay for all other claims directly.

129. D: Under several change management models, employees' reaction to large organizational changes evolve from indifference to rejection, then doubt, neutrality, experimentation, and finally commitment. When employees are in the commitment phase, this is the optimal stage to implement the change.

130. B: The on-site Bible study is a religious accommodation and does not present an undue hardship on the employer. Additionally, allowing the request will help contribute to a more inclusive work environment.

131. C: A matrix organizational structure is one in which employees may report to multiple supervisors or managers; often one is a functional relationship and the other may be project based.

132. C: Defining an employee's behavior as insubordination must meet three criteria: the employer gives a clear directive to the employee, and the employee acknowledges the directive in some manner then refuses to follow directions.

133. D: To gain buy-in for a large change management initiative, the first step is to create a sense of urgency with your audience so that they understand the importance of the project.

134. C: Given the fact that this is a high-tech digital company, a printed newsletter would likely be the least effective. Newsletters mailed to employee's homes are generally best for messages that need to be delivered to employee's spouses and/or family members, such as open enrollment for benefits or retirement plan updates.

135. A: Using lay terms about a human resource information system in a room full of software engineers may elicit a few eye rolls. Similarly, a complex presentation with acronyms and tech jargon may confuse the less tech-savvy employees. It is best to tailor the message based on the audience you're speaking to. That could mean explaining a concept in several different ways to ensure comprehension.

136. D: Vesting is the process by which employees receive ownership of the employer contributions made into their retirement savings plans. Graded vesting is a common plan design strategy and allows employees to earn an increased portion of the employer contributions each year of their participation.

137. B: The first order of business should be to learn the landscape for yourself—get to know your staff and what they do on a daily basis—before making any sweeping changes in the department.

138. B: The interest-based relational approach emphasizes a fact-based approach to conversations about conflict. The two parties should practice active listening, remain calm, and focus on the facts of the conflict at hand rather than letting emotions influence the discussion.

139. A: Based on the fact that Sean is a new supervisor and started out as an individual contributor, he is likely still holding onto some of the tasks that he had as an individual contributor. The fact that he is working long days and still not completing his required objectives also suggests a lack of delegation. This is a skill that is often difficult for new managers and supervisors.

140. C: Although these could all be negative impacts of not delegating work, the most damaging is the impact on Sean's direct reports. If they feel idle and underutilized, this could prompt poor morale and increased turnover across the team.

141. B: After a leader delegates high-priority tasks and projects to his/her direct reports, it's important for the leader to remain accountable for the successes or failures of the outcome. For this reason, the leader should hold regular check-ins with individuals to understand challenges they're facing, milestones completed, and anticipated completion dates.

142. B: An expatriate, or expat, is an employee who takes on an international assignment, usually for three to five years.

143. C: Mistrustful employees may view this behavior as second-guessing their past work efforts. In the early stages of managing a team, leaders should refrain from giving advice on projects that are in process and instead focus on developing relationships and establishing trust.

144. A: A practice of publicly acknowledging a job well done will set the tone with the team and establish a culture of appreciation in the group. Although the other actions would contribute to a sense of team appreciation, they would not have the same widespread effect as a more public acknowledgement.

145. A: When a wage is "red-circled," it means that the individual is paid above the set salary range for the position. Red-circled wages are often either frozen or reduced to be in the correct range for the position.

146. B: The McKinsey 7S Framework is a tool to analyze organizational effectiveness in times of change. The concept of the model is that all seven elements are interdependent and must work in a cohesive manner for optimal performance. The framework can identify areas that are not performing to standards and need to be improved.

147. A: As soon as you hear about potential concerns from the payroll supervisor, it's best to meet with him/her privately and hear those exact concerns. It's important to be honest and explain the challenges he/she may face and the organization may face as well. Allowing him/her to feel heard will help solidify his/her commitment to the project. The other approaches may end up backfiring, causing him/her to feel overwhelmed and that the project is moving forward with or without his/her endorsement.

148. D: Because the project schedule is at risk, a small human resource (HR) project team should be organized to participate in all the pertinent meetings for the sake of efficiency. The other HR staff should have trust in the project participants to make configuration decisions that are best for their group. The project team should provide regular updates to the others but waiting to make important decisions after an internal discussion will only further delay the project.

149. A: Employers may charge up to 102% of the original insurance premium to COBRA participants to help cover administrative fees.

150. D: Asking Rhonda for periodic clarification and confirming understanding will accomplish both goals: helping Jennifer better understand Rhonda and convey to Rhonda that she is listening and engaged.

151. A: Active listening is a concept that suggests that a listener suspends judgment, eliminates distractions and fully focuses on the details and concepts being conveyed from the speaker. This often results in verbal and nonverbal cues of comprehension, but those alone do not constitute active listening. Passive listening is when a listener provides no reaction whatsoever to the speaker.

152. A: Position control is often a feature of a human resource information system (HRIS)/financial tool within which employees are tracked separately from positions. Positions are often approved according to available budget and then maintained and tracked in the position control system.

153. D: According to several strategic planning process models, the first step is always to collect and analyze the applicable data prior to setting goals, defining the desired outcome, or identifying potential threats and risks.

154. C: All the other scenarios listed are qualifying events that allow an employee to elect into Family and Medical Leave Act (FMLA) to continue health insurance coverage for employees who are on a protected leave.

155. D: Flexible spending account (FSA) funds may not be used to purchase an electric toothbrush. The other items are eligible expenses according to the Internal Revenue Service (IRS), and an FSA may be used for those purchases.

156. C: Cost-benefit analysis (CBA) is calculated by subtracting costs from benefits, and the result is potential profit as a dollar value. Return on investment (ROI) is costs subtracted from benefits divided by costs, resulting in a ratio or percentage.

157. C: The Americans with Disabilities Act (ADA) protects job applicants as well as employees, and this candidate's request is a reasonable one; the employer should provide this reasonable accommodation so that the candidate has a fair opportunity to compete for the position.

158. D: In the instance of an employee complaint, it's important to remain calm and professional toward the complainant and all other parties involved. Asking follow-up questions is a good idea; however, neither the context nor the manner of delivery would change the severity of the offensive remarks. Also, the fact that others have complained is best kept confidential.

159. B: Performance improvement plans (PIPs) are best used when the behavior that needs correction is quantifiable. This seems to be an isolated incident with multiple employees reporting that the comments were inappropriate, so organization-wide training is likely not the best avenue, and neither would demotion be the best choice if this is not a recurring problem.

160. C: Employees or former employees who are eligible for COBRA must be offered 60 days to elect COBRA continuation coverage.

SHRM-CP Practice Test #2

1. How should a risk that is slowly but surely going to happen be handled?

a. Prepare
b. Act
c. Park
d. Adapt

Refer to the following scenario for questions 2-4.

> The CEO of a growing software company has been noticing a recent decline in productivity. When talking to the project directors, they learn that the majority of junior developers are not living up to their anticipated potential.

2. In a meeting with the executive leadership team, a strict performance management system with the goal of terminating underperforming employees is being discussed. How should the HR manager, who is attending the meeting, react when asked to implement the new system?

a. The HR manager should discuss employee engagement initiatives that can improve employee performance.
b. The HR manager should implement the system as asked by the executive leadership team.
c. The HR manager should address the lack of communication between the developers and their managers as a potential reason for the performance issues.
d. The HR manager should point out the difficulty of hiring new developers, and challenge management to look at the underlying reasons for the low performance.

3. The senior management team agrees that one of the steps to address the performance issues is to update their current performance management system, which is based on annual reviews. The CEO tasks the HR manager with developing a new performance management system based on continuous feedback and regular check-ins with the employees. What is the first step that the HR manager should take?

a. Conduct a company-wide employee opinion survey to determine the reason(s) behind the junior developers' low performance.
b. Meet with the project directors to develop an understanding of what improvements they want to see as a result of the new performance management system.
c. Develop a thorough communication plan to inform all employees of the upcoming changes to the performance management system.
d. Gather data, including the projected return on investment, to demonstrate the value of rolling out a new performance management system.

4. After implementing a new performance management system and other changes, the company sees an increase in productivity. The performance of most of the developers has improved significantly. However, four developers were terminated for continuously failing to meet performance standards. The HR department is now tasked with filling the four open positions. What is an important step the HR team should take?

a. Meet with the project directors to determine the knowledge, skills, and abilities a candidate needs to be successful.
b. Update current job descriptions to reflect the implementation of the new performance management system.
c. Utilize internet recruiting to build a large pool of both active and passive candidates.
d. Build a strong employment brand to position the company as an employer of choice.

5. What was the court ruling in Lechmere, Inc. v. NLBR?

a. If an employee misses time worked due to union-related activities, the company cannot hold it against him in his attendance record.
b. A company does not have to allow union representatives to campaign on company property if they are not employed by the company.
c. A company is allowed to continue business operations during a strike by hiring new employees or temporary workers.
d. Employees have the right to bring a third person into the room if they are being questioned as part of an investigation.

6. A consulting firm determines that the average annual salary for project analysts in their area is $60,000. They are looking to hire a new project analyst and post the position with an annual pay rate of $70,000. What pay strategy does the company pursue?

a. Top market competition
b. Match market competition
c. Lead market competition
d. Lag market competition

7. What are the three key qualities of a leader that are crucial for leading a learning organization, according to Peter Senge?

a. Designer, steward, teacher
b. Mentor, change agent, motivator
c. Manager, trainer, strategist
d. Planner, visionary, communicator

Refer to the following scenario for questions 8-10.

> Over the last decade, a telecommunications company has been struggling financially as the demand for landline phones continues to diminish. They have been incorporating other business lines, some more successful than others, but have not been able to turn around their financial performance as much as they had hoped. The executive team decided to implement significant organizational changes that include a number of layoffs, department restructuring, and moving the administrative offices to a smaller location.

8. They are discussing ways to implement the changes successfully. What is the first thing that they should do?

a. Communicate a clear vision to the workforce.
b. Encourage employees to take action.
c. Behave with urgency on a daily basis.
d. Ask the workforce for feedback on the proposed changes.

9. The information technology (IT) department is not affected by any of the layoffs. One employee was recently terminated for poor performance. Despite management assuring the IT staff that the department is not participating in the layoffs, rumors circulate that the terminated employee was laid off and that there might be more terminations coming. One employee questions the IT manager about the reason for their coworker's termination. How should the manager respond?

a. Explain that the coworker's termination was due to performance issues.
b. Inform the employee that he is unable to discuss his coworker's termination.
c. Direct the employee to the HR department for an answer.
d. Request that the employee stop spreading rumors within the department.

10. The majority of the company's software developers are contractual employees from the Philippines. Based on their distinct cultures, should the change initiative be communicated differently to them than to their US counterparts?

a. Yes, because US employees tend to be more open to change than their Filipino counterparts.
b. Yes, because the Filipino employees tend to be more open to change than their US counterparts.
c. No, because cultural differences do not influence how employees perceive change.
d. No, because they both perceive change similarly.

11. A call center is looking to fill some of their open management positions. They receive a total of 250 applications, of which 100 are from female candidates. What is the yield ratio of female applicants to total applicants?

a. 20%
b. 25%
c. 40%
d. 60%

12. A company introduces a new product and needs its call center employees to go through extensive product training so that they can answer customer questions. The training is conducted through an online learning portal, set up as a labyrinth, that employees have to navigate through. Along the way, they learn about different aspects of the product, take quizzes, collect points, and move up levels to access more information. What type of learning is this?

a. Scenario-based learning
b. Maze product training
c. Gamification
d. Play-based learning

13. While at work, two employees get into a serious argument that results in a physical altercation on company property. The employees have a clear understanding that this violates company policy. The manager pulls both employees in the office to terminate their employment. What step should the manager have taken beforehand?

a. Establish a baseline for the termination.
b. Review the company's performance management system.
c. Interview the employees as part of an investigation.
d. Consult with legal counsel.

14. What would indicate that a company's business manager has a global mindset?

a. The manager recommends a cultural seminar to the staff.
b. The manager is not afraid of change and welcomes it.
c. The manager trusts that the company's structure will produce the desired results.
d. The manager has experience applying headquarter policies to subsidies.

15. What approach can be used to evaluate HR's performance and alignment with organizational strategy?

a. Internal customer satisfaction rate
b. Employee retention rate
c. Human capital return on investment
d. Balanced scorecard

16. Why is it essential that a company works hard to build a comprehensive diversity and inclusion program?

a. Because it has a direct impact on the company's profitability
b. Because it is necessary for building a positive company reputation
c. Because it helps employees and managers approach situations from different perspectives
d. Because it is difficult to change deeply held beliefs, assumptions, and habits

Refer to the following scenario for questions 17-19.

> The new CHRO of an insurance agency notices that the company is struggling to hire, develop, and hold onto its human capital. In particular, she notices low retention, low employee morale, excessive absenteeism, and a lacking talent pipeline.

17. The CHRO studies recent exit interviews and conducts a series of stay interviews that all point to a lack of management support. She is convinced that the managers would benefit from training but heard that the CEO does not want to spend money on training and development initiatives. What could the CHRO do to address the problems?

a. Use the data and insights gained to present a business case to the CEO indicating the importance of investing in managerial training and development.
b. Develop a cost-efficient employee engagement initiative to address low employee morale.
c. Meet with managers one-on-one to review the company's performance management process.
d. Research literature on management best practices, provide it to the managers, and encourage them to study the material.

18. The new CHRO is aware that hiring top talent in the insurance sector is a challenge because it is often not the industry of choice for many recent graduates. She also knows that unemployment is low and the labor market is highly competitive. What can the CHRO do to improve hiring efforts?

a. Research and study recruiting metrics for the insurance sector.
b. Review job postings and rewrite ads to attract more candidates.
c. Build rapport with local college career services personnel.
d. Sign up for several local job fairs to meet candidates in person.

19. The company recently introduced a new state-of-the-art software program that transforms the way insurance agents put together portfolios, calculate rates, and create presentations for customers. Due to the complexity of the new software, the company had all insurance agents go through a one-day training to become familiar with the new tool. After a couple of weeks, the CHRO notices that some of the more tenured agents are struggling with using the new software program and have decreasing sales. What should the CHRO do?

a. Hold agents accountable for their decreased performance, setting clear expectations.
b. Prepare for increased turnover by building a talent pool.
c. Arrange for all agents to attend a second day of training on the new software program.
d. Offer additional training to agents whose performance has decreased.

Refer to the following scenario for questions 20-22.

A growing online travel agency has 1,500 employees in three offices working in a fun, but fast-paced environment. The small HR team is trying to keep up with the demands of a busy and growing company.

20. Each year, for compliance purposes, the HR team instructs all employees to review and sign a one-page sexual harassment policy. Their managers are supposed to review the information with them in a one-on-one meeting before they sign the document. The HR business partner is well aware that the managers do not spend time reviewing the information, and most employees do not read it before signing and turning the document in. She is concerned about the lack of effective harassment prevention training the company is conducting. But when she raises her concerns, the leadership team makes it clear that they cannot spend any extra time on this. What can the HR business partner do?

a. Advise the leadership team of the significance of the training, and insist on improving the current process by conducting in-person trainings for all employees.
b. Instead of the managers, have the HR generalist review the document with employees one-on-one before asking them to sign.
c. Eliminate the training because it wastes valuable resources but does not yield the desired outcome.
d. Develop a series of short online training modules that employees are asked to complete each year.

21. As part of their flexible working environment, the company put all employees on salary and classified them as exempt. This allows them to complete their work on a flexible schedule. The HR business partner reviews results of an internal audit, and discovers that not all employee groups meet the requirements to be exempt. For example, the customer service partners do not fall into any of the exemptions and often work overtime. What is the next step the HR business partner should take?

a. Set up a meeting with the leadership team, inform them of the findings, and present a solution to change the compensation structures.
b. Because the current pay structure emerged from the company's culture, it is not subject to the exemption rule, and no further steps are needed.
c. Inform employees and their respective managers that no one is allowed to work any overtime going forward.
d. Modify the job duties of the employees in question so that they meet the exemption requirements.

22. After growing for the last couple of years, the company is now considered to be in the maturity state of its life cycle. What should the HR business partner focus on during this stage?

a. She should conduct job assessments to improve and correct job descriptions.
b. She should help maintain the company's agile and creative spirit.
c. She should contribute to creating a compelling company culture in alignment with its mission and vision.
d. She should provide support to employees who experience stress due to ongoing change.

23. How should diversity and inclusion (D&I) strategies be put into effect?

a. Strategies should be put into effect identically.
b. Strategies should be put into effect justly.
c. Strategies should be put into effect simultaneously.
d. Strategies should be put into effect consecutively.

24. What tool can you use to make sure all of the firm's risk management strategies and processes are compliant with local laws?

a. Attestation
b. Audit
c. Risk analysis
d. Security report

25. A company operates in an area that is subject to a reoccurring tornado and earthquake risk. As part of their disaster preparedness plan, they set up an employee text alert system that will allow the company to quickly communicate information to all employees in case of emergency. What is this risk strategy called?

a. Transfer
b. Alleviate
c. Mitigate
d. Enhance

Refer to the following scenario for questions 26-28.

A bank, who had a conservative image in the past, decides to update their employment brand to attract a younger and more diverse customer and candidate base. The CHRO is in charge of updating the recruiting website. To gather ideas, she holds a brainstorming session with the HR team.

26. What is the best idea that the CHRO should look into further?

a. Highlight the bank's affirmative action plan in the new employment brand.
b. Conduct a series of stay interviews to gather managers' views on diversity within the organization.
c. Ask several employees to each make a short video showing what diversity in the workplace means to them.
d. Launch a quick diversity and inclusion project that can be used as the basis for the new employment brand.

27. The CHRO asks the HR manager to work together with the marketing manager on one aspect of the new recruiting website. The HR manager is from New York, direct, task-focused, and efficient. The marketing manager is from Peru, creative, relationship-oriented, and enthusiastic. They set up a meeting to discuss the project, but are both frustrated afterward. The HR manager feels like they did not make any progress and wasted time. The marketing manager is offended by his harsh tone and feels like he does not like her. After a couple of meetings with no success but growing frustration on both sides, the HR manager seeks the advice of the CHRO. What should she do?

a. Break up the project. The HR manager and marketing manager will each work on one aspect of the website without having to collaborate.
b. Sit in on their next meeting, and mediate between the two parties by having each of them explain the other's perspective.
c. Explain to the HR manager that this behavior is unacceptable. In his position, he needs to show more cultural sensitivity.
d. Inform both parties that even though they are not friends, they are still expected to work together professionally and complete the assigned project.

28. The marketing department consists of eight employees who have been working together for many years. They are very tight- knit. A new content marketing lead is hired and joins the department. The marketing manager notices that there is tension between the old employees and the new hire. The tension disrupts their work and resulted in a missed deadline. How should she handle the conflicts within her team?

a. Talk to employees one-on-one to understand what causes the tension.
b. If the new employee does not fit into the department's culture, it is best to reassign her to a different team.
c. Schedule a team meeting, and facilitate a team discussion to solve the problems.
d. Wait to intervene until the team moves from the storming to the norming phase.

Refer to the following scenario for questions 29-31.

> A transportation company operates shuttle buses that bring guests from the airport to a number of hotels. The company has 60 employees. There are four buses running at any given time, picking guests up every 10–15 minutes.

29. Bus driver A, whose personality is to operate very much by the book, always sticks to the exact bus schedule. Bus driver B, who is known to be more of a free spirit, keeps his bus going with the flow, often ends up well ahead of schedule, and occasionally overtakes the other shuttles. This leads to regular conflict between the two drivers. Bus driver A decides to report the situation to the HR generalist. What should she do?

a. Arrange a meeting with both bus drivers to facilitate communication.
b. Observe both bus drivers by spending time riding on each of the buses.
c. Prepare a written warning for the bus driver not following the exact bus schedule.
d. Collect data on customer satisfaction regarding their shuttle service.

30. The company is planning to change the bus routes to service the hotels more efficiently. The general manager asked the HR manager to inform all company employees of the changes. The majority of bus drivers are well-tenured and older. Most of the sales representatives are newer to the workforce. The company's management team oversees both groups. What is the best way for the HR manager to roll out the new information?

a. Create a short video that illustrates the new bus routes, and send it to all employees via email.
b. Set up a conference call for the managers, send an email to the sales representatives, and schedule a workgroup meeting for the bus drivers.
c. Meet with each employee one-on-one to discuss the new routes and answer their questions.
d. Utilize the company's intranet, and create a space for all information regarding the new routes. Then, send an email to all employees directing them to check the intranet.

31. One bus driver, who has been working for the company full-time for 25 years, is clearly unhappy about the introduced changes to the routes. A week later, he meets with the HR generalist, and informs her that he needs to take a leave of absence due to a serious health condition. He turns in an FMLA medical certification form that his doctor completed. The HR generalist reviews the information, determines that he qualifies for the leave of absence, and informs his manager that he will be out for a certain amount of time. The manager responds that the bus driver only requested the time off because he is unhappy with the changes and HR should not approve his leave. What should the HR generalist do?

a. Tell the manager that the employee qualifies for FMLA and therefore has a right to take the requested leave.
b. Deny the employee's leave request based on the manager's argument.
c. Advise the manager to terminate the bus driver's employment. That way, he can fill the position with a new employee.
d. Decide to compromise. Inform the employee that the maximum amount of time he can be off is two weeks.

32. New procedures are being rolled out from the company headquarters to offices located all over the country. The communications director created a detailed slide show presentation to share with all general managers virtually. What type of groupware is intended to be used for this purpose?

a. Web conferencing
b. Video presence
c. Virtual meeting
d. Network seminar

33. A technology company hires three new information technology professionals. To fill the positions, the company incurs both internal and external costs totaling $60,000. The total first-year compensation of the three new hires is $300,000. What is the Recruitment Cost Ratio?

a. 2%
b. 5%
c. 20%
d. 50%

34. What is an example of a business outcome that can be measured to gauge the effectiveness of an employee engagement initiative?

a. Employee problem-solving abilities
b. Employee motivation
c. Managerial skills
d. Employee absences

Refer to the following scenario for questions 35-37.

> A local grocery retailer employs 2,000 employees in its 25 stores. The company is family owned, and the current CEO is the founder's son. Many of the managers and employees are related to the CEO and his family.

35. The company recently hired a new HR manager. The CEO briefs the HR manager that the company is looking to cut costs where possible. Therefore, he would like him to find a more affordable benefits vendor as premiums have been steadily increasing. The HR manager, who has many years of experience in managing employee benefits, reviews the current benefits package. He concludes that premiums are already on the low-end and there would be no significant cost savings by switching vendors. What alternative can he suggest to the CEO?

a. Inform the workforce of rising benefits costs and ask them to use their benefits wisely.
b. Continue research until a more affordable benefits vendor has been located.
c. Organize a reoccurring health fair for employees where vendors offer free BMI measurements, blood pressure checks, and tips for a healthy lifestyle.
d. Consider reducing the employees' hours so that they are no longer eligible for benefits.

36. The new HR manager spends time observing different employees to learn about the business. He notices that the maintenance supervisor, who is the CEO's cousin, appears unqualified when working on a defective fridge. When talking to the maintenance supervisor, the HR manager finds out that he has no training in performing the work required by his position. He further hears other employees saying that the maintenance supervisor often calls in favors from friends when he cannot complete the job himself. The HR manager is concerned about the maintenance supervisor's performance but also knows that he is close to the CEO. The CEO does not like to hear his family members being criticized. What should the HR manager do?

a. He should give the CEO a hint to observe the maintenance supervisor's work himself.
b. Because the maintenance department and the HR department are separate from each other, the HR manager does not need to act.
c. He should conduct an investigation to find out how the maintenance supervisor got his position without having the necessary qualifications for it.
d. He should inform the CEO of his findings and concerns.

37. One day the HR manager is informed that a department of labor representative is at the reception desk looking to talk to her. What should she do?

a. Talk to the representative and provide the information the department of labor is requesting.
b. Ask the representative to have a seat in her office while she calls the company's attorney.
c. Ask the representative to come back later so she has time to collect files and find out if there is any potential legal exposure.
d. Inform the representative that she is happy to meet with him, but he would first need to schedule an appointment.

38. After a diversity council has been established, what is part of the next step in the Diversity and Inclusion (D&I) Strategic Process by Gardenswartz and Rowe?

a. Build a diverse candidate pool through targeted recruiting initiatives.
b. Assemble an employee resource group.
c. Assess the results achieved by the diversity council.
d. Develop a diversity immersion program for managers and employees.

Refer to the following scenario for questions 39-41.

A car rental company offered only two-way rentals in the past, where customers pick up and drop off their rental car at the same location. The company's strategic goal is to expand business to include one-way rentals so customers can return their car at a different location from where they rented it. The vice president of HR is tasked with preparing branch employees for the new business process. He is aware that each branch currently operates independently and in competition for profit with each other. Therefore, they are likely to resist the change. The new one-way rental program will require branches to work collaboratively and communicate frequently.

39. Since the vice president of HR has significant experience with leading change initiatives, the executive team asked him what they can expect from employees once this change initiative is rolled out. What advice can he give?

a. There is likely to be an initial drop in performance.
b. There is likely to be an initial increase in turnover.
c. There is likely to be an initial decrease in customer satisfaction.
d. There is likely to be an initial lack of trust in leadership.

40. What suggestion can the vice president of HR make that will help prepare the teams working at the different branches for the new business process?

a. Schedule in-person meetups between each of the branches so teams can build relationships.
b. Host a video conference to roll out the new process and introduce the teams to each other.
c. Encourage the different branches to communicate via the company's intranet, and develop an app that connects employees on the go.
d. Communicate strict performance management steps for employees who do not cooperate with other branches.

41. After the new process has been rolled out, the vice president of HR conducts an assessment of how well it has been implemented and embraced. He finds out that all branches are working together well with the exception of one region called region X. Region X is managed by a senior regional manager who is known for being the cause of conflict and ongoing disagreements among the other regional managers. How should the VP of HR handle this?

a. Advise the CEO to restate clear expectations of how branches and regions are to collaborate with each other.
b. Take performance management steps to correct the regional manager's behavior.
c. Reintroduce the change initiative to region X, and work alongside the regional manager to roll out the new process.
d. Meet with regional managers to determine the underlying issues for the disagreements, and encourage communication to find solutions.

Refer to the following scenario for questions 42-44.

A brewing company employs 1,200 people across four breweries. The VP of HR works at the headquarters and has four HR generalists reporting to her. There is one HR generalist on site at each of the breweries. One of them recently got promoted to training manager, and a new HR generalist was hired for the position.

42. The VP of HR asks the new HR generalist to prepare a 30-day action plan and then meets with her for an initial development meeting. What should the HR generalist include in her action plan?

a. Schedule a one-on-one meeting with each manager she will be supporting.
b. Observe current processes instead of asking too many questions.
c. Make suggestions to improve work processes and procedures.
d. Implement best practices learned from her previous positions.

43. During her first week, the new HR generalist spends time observing different workgroups to understand the business better. She overhears a supervisor say to a pregnant employee that she's been forgetful lately because of her "baby brain." The comment stays on the HR generalist's mind, and she is unsure if she should say something. What is the BEST thing for her to do?

a. Consult with a peer to determine if the comment is acceptable or not.
b. Report her observations to the VP of HR.
c. Continue learning about the company culture to understand the context.
d. Approach the pregnant employee to ensure the comment did not upset her.

44. The supervisor of the pregnant employee comes to the HR generalist with a request for a written warning. Despite multiple verbal warnings, the employee keeps using her cell phone during work time for personal text messaging and playing games. The HR generalist has also had several conversations with the employee about this. However, the HR generalist is sympathetic because the employee reminds her of herself when she was pregnant. She does not think that the employee should receive a written warning and consults with her supervisor, the VP of HR. What should the VP of HR do?

a. Allow the HR generalist to deny the manager's request for a written warning if she does not agree with it.
b. Ask the HR generalist to prepare a written warning according to the manager's request.
c. Review the employee's file to determine if there have been previous performance management issues.
d. Find out why the HR generalist does not agree with the written warning.

45. What is an example of cultural relativism?

a. An organization's goal to contribute to social justice
b. Not utilizing a vendor because they engage in child labor
c. Expressing that ant soup offered in the employee cafeteria sounds unappetizing
d. A company built on values of respect and honesty

Refer to the following scenario for questions 46-48.

> A satellite communication firm recently added specialty broadband services to their line of offerings. As a result, they have been growing rapidly. This has led to a number of internal promotions, bringing in many new hires, and extending contracts with third-party staffing partners.

46. A former assistant manager was promoted to lead his own department. One of his first goals is to get to know his team and find out ways to motivate individual employees. What can the manager do to motivate one of his employees who he regards as affiliation-oriented?

a. Create a collaborative work environment.
b. Create a competitive work environment.
c. Create an innovative work environment.
d. Create a flexible work environment.

47. The HR manager attends a legal seminar that covers recent lawsuits involving third-party staffing arrangements. Because the company has been increasingly using third-party employees, he is concerned that some of the arrangements could potentially pose a legal risk for the firm. What steps should he take?

a. Recommend that the company not sign any further agreements with third-party contractors.
b. Extend company benefits to all third-party employees.
c. Research the company's use of third-party employees, and seek clarification from legal counsel.
d. Ensure that no third-party employee works more than twenty hours per week.

48. With the growth of the company, the executive team is discussing changing the organizational structure to group departments under its main product divisions. How can the HR manager best support this effort?

a. Research types of organizational structures, and present the advantages and disadvantages of each to the executive team.
b. Communicate the restructure to all affected employees, addressing any questions and concerns.
c. Meet with department heads to hear their opinions and concerns regarding the company's restructure.
d. Develop employee engagement initiatives for each step of the change process.

Refer to the following scenario for questions 49-51.

> A pharmaceutical company motivates its employees to work hard through offering big sales incentives. With sales booming, many employees work 60 to 80 hours per week to earn the bonuses.

49. The HR business partner becomes aware of high turnover throughout the organization. It has created so many vacancies that the recruiting team is not able to keep up with filling them. However, the CEO is pleased with the company's sales performance and says the turnover is the nature of the business and the recruiting team needs to work harder to fill the openings. What should the HR business partner do?

a. Focus all efforts of the HR team on filling the open positions.
b. Outsource recruiting requests that the in-house recruiters are unable to fill.
c. Review exit interviews to determine the root cause of the retention problem.
d. Provide training and development opportunities for employees to improve retention.

50. The CEO announces plans to expand the company and gathers data to draft a business plan for the expansion strategy. What should the HR business partner do because he is aware that the company is already short-staffed?

a. Advise the CEO to hold off with expansion efforts until the staffing situation has been improved.
b. Set up an employee referral program with strong incentives to boost talent acquisition efforts for the expansion strategy.
c. After assessing the current workforce, research temporary staffing agencies that can provide the needed talent, and provide a cost estimate to the CEO.
d. Motivate employees with the CEO's vision for the expansion, showcasing all of the new career opportunities that will come with it.

51. The HR team checks in with the different sales teams to gather feedback on implemented changes as a result of the expansion efforts. Although most teams give positive feedback, one team displays low employee morale. To find out more, the HR team conducts interviews with representatives from this team. They find out that the sales team manager often makes inappropriate comments and derogatory remarks about older employees. The HR business partner reports these findings to the head of sales. In their discussion, the head of sales urges the HR business partner to not upset the team manager because he has close relationships with major accounts that the company cannot afford to lose. What should the HR business partner do next?

a. Provide coaching and training to the manager to improve his communication and leadership style.
b. Report the findings to the CEO, conduct an investigation, and take the necessary steps to stop the manager's behavior.
c. Recommend hiring additional sales staff to decrease stress and pressure on the team.
d. Keep a close eye on the manager to see if further incidences occur.

Refer to the following scenario for questions 52-54.

> Previously, a car manufacturer has been successful in hiring managers in training and then quickly promoting them after the training period. However, they recently noticed a majority of the managers in training leaving the company as soon as their training was complete, often taking positions with competitors. The talent manager reviews the reasons behind the resignations, and concludes that the majority of employees left because they were dissatisfied with their rate of pay.

52. The vice president of human resources meets with the talent manager to discuss the retention challenges. What's the best course of action?

a. Ensure that a realistic job and pay preview is provided to candidates during the hiring and onboarding process.
b. Research competitor pay rates, obtain other market compensation data, and establish new, more competitive pay plans.
c. Give all employees a cost-of-living pay increase and add nonmonetary incentives to pay plans.
d. Position the company as an employer of choice by offering perquisites such as company cars, a wellness program, and gym memberships.

53. The headquarters of the car manufacturer is located in the United States, whereas the manufacturing units are spread across different countries. A manager with a successful career at headquarters receives a promotion to vice president and will run the company's motor vehicle assembly plant in India. He is popular amongst his direct reports for being engaging and for sharing both responsibilities and recognition with them. What challenges is he likely to face in his new position?

a. He might have to adjust project deadlines because employees tend to be late.
b. His new direct reports might not appreciate him distributing important tasks within the team.
c. His new employees are likely to challenge his authority.
d. He might experience difficulties creating harmony within the new team he is leading.

54. What can the new VP do to be successful in running the company's motor vehicle assembly plant in India?

a. He should attend social events outside of work to build relationships.
b. He should create a competitive work environment.
c. He should only expect employees to participate in company events during the regular workday.
d. He should expect that employees will be productive in their roles, despite any personal differences.

55. Data is being gathered during the strategy implementation phase of a project. What is the BEST way to communicate the results to senior managers after analyzing the data?

a. By organizing the data in a spreadsheet
b. By providing the full raw data
c. By presenting bulleted slide show presentation slides
d. By telling a story backed by the data

56. In what type of interview would the following question MOST likely be asked? "Tell me about a time when your team failed to accomplish a goal. How did you lead your team to achieve the goal in the end?"

a. Behavioral interview
b. Stress interview
c. Case interview
d. Unstructured interview

57. An HR manager wants to determine if there is a correlation between an employee's score on a pre-hire assessment test and their sales performance as measured by the number of closed sales in the last quarter. What tool can he use?

a. Trend diagram
b. Pie chart
c. Scatter diagram
d. Pareto chart

58. A company recently went through an organizational and employee development (OED) intervention. How can HR help the company promote and support adherence to the new processes?

a. Utilize HRIS to track data.
b. Support leaders through ongoing training and development initiatives.
c. Ensure new processes and goals are reflected in performance reviews.
d. Establish a mentorship program.

59. What is a key benefit of conducting stay interviews?

a. Improved retention
b. Development of performance objectives
c. Not needing exit interviews
d. Data gathered for performance appraisals

60. What is one advantage of a group interview?

a. More candidate comfort during the interview
b. Elimination of unqualified candidates
c. Increased control for the interviewer
d. Time-savings for both companies and job seekers

61. Two employees sit on the board of directors and have full voting power. What system is that?

a. Mixed system
b. Single-tier system
c. Matrix system
d. Dual system

Refer to the following scenario for questions 62-64.

> A company that develops and sells household products is going through firm-wide change initiatives. Their goal is to become a leader in corporate sustainability by developing green, nontoxic household products and using recycled packaging.

62. The CHRO keeps a pulse on how the employees feel while changes are being implemented. At first, she hears positive feedback. But later, employees start to express that the company is not doing enough. Digging deeper, she finds out that employees feel like the company is talking a lot about sustainability but not really living up to their vision. What should the CHRO do with this information?

a. With the approval of the CEO, gather employee feedback and ideas, and organize them to formulate suggested solutions.
b. Sell the employees on the company's vision, and engage them more in the change initiatives.
c. Ask employees to be patient and wait for the changes to be completed before making judgments.
d. Improve communication to employees through frequent updates on the company's internal website.

63. The company decides to focus on utilizing the creativity, skills, and knowledge of its employees to achieve their long-term goal of becoming a leader in corporate sustainability. To accomplish these goals, the company needs to retain their top talent. The CEO asks the CHRO to develop a retention strategy and wonders if offering substantial pay increases will be necessary. What suggestion should the CHRO make?

a. Give employees a pay increases each time the company reaches one of their strategic goals.
b. Develop an aggressive lead market compensation strategy.
c. Improve company benefits in addition to a moderate pay increase for all employees.
d. Conduct an employee survey and focus group to determine what motivates the team.

64. In a meeting with the executive team, the CEO lays out the revised second phase of the change initiative aligning their day-to-day business operations with the company's vision of becoming a leader in corporate sustainability. The CEO asks each department head how they will support the upcoming changes. What contribution can the CHRO make?

a. Implement changes within the HR team before they are rolled out to the rest of the company.
b. Review the change proposal to streamline processes and remove any redundancies.
c. Analyze the effects of the change initiative on employees and departments.
d. Build a candidate pool focusing on candidates with experience in corporate sustainability.

65. A company decides to outsource part of the human resources function. What is the next step after a contractor has been selected?

a. Monitor the project schedule
b. Negotiate a contract
c. Define goals
d. Create an RFP

Refer to the following scenario for questions 66-68.

A home improvement retailer has been reporting negative cash flow due to low sales numbers and high expenses. The senior leadership team develops a new organizational strategy to turn around the company's financial performance, and all departments are asked to take immediate action.

66. The CEO asks the CHRO how the HR department will contribute to the strategy. What is the best suggestion the CHRO can make after brainstorming with the HR department?

a. Because the HR department does not generate revenue, they will provide their support to the revenue-generating segments of the company.
b. Suggest a reduction in force, and develop severance packages for laid-off employees.
c. Analyze current sales commission thresholds and evaluate company spending on perquisites and employee appreciation initiatives.
d. Temporarily enact a hiring freeze of all nonessential positions to reduce costs.

67. The new organizational strategy affects all employees, and the executive team is discussing ways to communicate it to the store and warehouse personnel. They decide to hold staff meetings with each workgroup. What can they do to ensure that the meetings are successful?

a. Start the meetings off with an icebreaker activity.
b. Provide lunch for employees while presenting a detailed slide show presentation.
c. Conduct focus groups within the meetings.
d. Choose a presenter who understands the audience's needs and perspectives.

68. One of the store managers in charge of implementing a number of changes is known to be a "country club manager." What kind of advice can the HR manager give him to be successful?

a. Create a collaborative team environment.
b. Delegate tasks to the team as much as possible.
c. Hold employees accountable.
d. Encourage employees to accomplish goals.

Refer to the following scenario for questions 69-71.

A local coffee shop chain has a promote-from-within culture. The company hires management trainees that are later promoted to assistant store managers after successfully completing the training program. A formal mentorship program is part of the training program.

69. An employee has successfully passed the training and is getting ready for his new role as assistant store manager. He meets with his mentor to get advice on how to lead the team of the new store he has been assigned to. The mentor knows the team well as he previously managed that exact location. What advice can the mentor give when asked by the mentee how he should approach his new employees?

a. Because the mentor has in-depth knowledge of the particular store, he should pass as much knowledge as possible on to the new assistant manager.
b. The mentor should review situational leadership theories with the mentee to prepare him for his new leadership role.
c. The mentor should ask the mentee to take the employees' perspective, and think about how he would want a new assistant manager to approach him.
d. Because the mentee has completed the training program, the formal mentorship relationship is ending. Therefore, the mentor should spend the last meeting celebrating the promotion and closing the mentoring relationship.

70. A new trainee is hired at the store, and the assistant manager is put in charge of her training. What should he focus on first?

a. Support the new trainee in making decisions and finding solutions.
b. Provide guidance and direction, keeping a close eye on her.
c. Delegate tasks to the new trainee and empower her.
d. Coach and motivate the new trainee.

71. The assistant manager has four trainees directly reporting to him. His trainees attend quarterly training seminars at the corporate office and are asked to prepare for the next one by setting a professional goal. The assistant manager meets with each of them before the training to review the goals that they set. Which of the employees should the assistant manager encourage to change their goal?

a. Employee A: My goal is to successfully complete the training program by September.
b. Employee B: My goal is to increase my add-on sales by 10% over the next three months.
c. Employee C: My goal is to submit three employee referrals to talent acquisition before the end of the year.
d. Employee D: My goal is to double the store's profitability over the next six months.

72. A company was recently certified as a B Corp. What stage of the corporate social responsibility (CSR) maturity curve is the firm in?

a. Adaptation
b. Integration
c. Assimilation
d. Transformation

73. What is a feature of an asynchronous learning environment?

a. Employees can access learning modules using different types of technology.
b. Employees receive real-time feedback.
c. Employees can study anywhere and anytime.
d. Employees interact with each other in real time.

74. A new marketing manager is assigned a mentor by the human resources (HR) department. The mentor is a senior business partner of the company with many years of experience. They are meeting once a month, and the mentor prepares for the meetings by setting learning objectives and creating training material for the mentee. Why might this mentorship NOT be successful?

a. Meetings should take place weekly.
b. Communication should be a two-way street and objectives set together.
c. The mentor should be a peer and not a senior colleague.
d. The mentor should not be assigned by HR, but selected by the mentee.

75. A company is experiencing low productivity and therefore plans to restructure its workflows. A team of organizational and employee development (OED) specialists develops a plan for the restructure and implements it. After the change initiative has been completed, the company notices employees resisting the changes. What is likely to be the reason for their resistance?

a. The changes were implemented too quickly.
b. The restructure was developed with insufficient data.
c. Employees were not included in the development.
d. No feedback was provided after the implementation.

76. What conflict resolution technique aims to find a solution that both parties view as a success?

a. Integrate
b. Compromise
c. Accommodate
d. Collaborate

77. What is an important task of the HR department when a company expands outside of its home country?

a. Prepare the workforce for global transfers and assignments.
b. Balance the need of standardization with the necessity for localization.
c. Research and identify HR vendors in each country.
d. Restructure the HR department to mirror the global business structure.

78. A person is described as being single and a recent college graduate from San Francisco. What layer is this description referring to?

a. Internal dimension
b. Organizational dimension
c. External dimension
d. Personal dimension

79. What is an important prerequisite for successful networking?

a. Firm handshake
b. Elevator speech
c. Business cards
d. Having expertise

80. What protects a company from having to pay for legal costs and settlement fees in case an employee sues?

a. COBRA
b. ADR
c. EPLI
d. EAP

81. What can someone improve on to become an impactful communicator?

a. Giving feedback
b. Multitasking
c. Vocal qualities
d. Emotional intelligence

82. An organization decides to partner with two employment service agencies for a temp-to-lease program. HR is asked to write the staffing contract. What best practice should they keep in mind?

a. Refrain from pricing negotiations.
b. Utilize a standard contract.
c. Consult with legal counsel.
d. Specify an end date of service in the contract.

83. What is the C-suite?

a. Cloud that stores human resources data
b. Coaching seminar
c. Employee appreciation celebration
d. Executive management

Refer to the following scenario for questions 84-86.

> The new CEO of a clothing retail store is looking to increase sales. The company has storefronts in twenty different US states. At the moment, all associates are paid hourly and there are no sales incentives. The CEO finds out that sales performance has not been tracked in the past. Each store has its own sales techniques, and product knowledge varies vastly.

84. The HR manager is asked to develop a sales incentive plan. What should he do first?

a. Conduct a series of sales trainings to increase the product knowledge and sales abilities of the associates.
b. Communicate the new sales incentive plan to associates and address their questions and concerns.
c. Develop an incentive program with monetary as well as nonmonetary sales incentives.
d. Analyze the current sales performance of individual stores and associates, and benchmark it against market data for other retail stores.

85. In order to effectively lead the new sales-driven culture that the general manager wants to see in stores, the store managers need some sales and leadership training. The CEO comes across free online training modules that he wants the HR team to roll out to the store managers. However, the HR manager believes an in-person custom training would be the best option to achieve the desired results. What should he do?

a. Gather information about the free online training, and develop a plan to roll it out to the store managers.
b. Research different training options, conduct a cost-benefit analysis of the top choices, and then meet with the general manager to recommend the most effective training option.
c. Meet with the store managers to find out which training option they would prefer to participate in.
d. Develop an in-house training program that is cost-effective but delivers more value than the free online training modules.

86. The company decided to change the current employee pay structures to a competitive sales incentives-based pay structure. What would be the best way for the HR manager to communicate the new pay structure to all employees?

a. Conduct a conference call with store managers to prepare them to answer employee questions and concerns. Then, send a concise, but comprehensive email to all associates.
b. Conduct face-to-face meetings with associates in each store to address their questions and concerns in person.
c. Because the individual store managers know their associates best, put them in charge of communicating the changes to their employees.
d. Send a detailed letter to each associate that explains the changes, including the rationale behind them. Make sure that the associates have ample time to review the letter.

87. What should organizational and employee development (OED) specialists be aware of during the entire OED process?

a. Organizational structure
b. Employees' emotional reactions
c. Leadership succession plans
d. Institutionalized practices

88. What can be said about good governance at an organization?

a. It is introduced by the governance board.
b. It is free of any contradictions.
c. It originates at the leadership level.
d. It applies equally to the host and home country of the organization.

89. What task is performed by a leader compared to a manager?

a. Schedule and plan the open enrollment benefits meetings.
b. Design informational handouts to be distributed at the open enrollment benefits meetings.
c. Organize speakers on health topics for the open enrollment benefits meetings.
d. Motivate the team to exceed benefits enrollment goals.

Refer to the following scenario for questions 90-92.

> It is the busy holiday season for a hotel, so the hotel's CEO wants to see strong sales and steep profits. As an incentive, front desk receptionists receive a commission whenever they sell a room upgrade to a customer. The hotel front office manager

noticed that some of the receptionists are giving customers vouchers for a free night's stay when they purchase an upgrade. Those vouchers should only be given out to address serious customer complaints. The hotel front office manager, who tends to avoid confrontation, is content that sales numbers are looking good. They do not want to address the issue and possibly upset their employees.

90. What should the HR manager do when he becomes aware of this practice?

a. Because the hotel front office manager is aware and approves of the practice, HR does not need to act.
b. The HR manager should talk to the front desk receptionists to find out how common the practice is.
c. The HR manager should make the hotel front office manager aware that the practice is problematic and needs to be addressed.
d. HR should recommend eliminating the voucher program to prevent misuse.

91. During the busy holiday season, many high-performing employees resign. This time of year is especially stressful for front desk employees who have to serve a large number of customers quickly. The HR manager overhears some of the best-performing front desk receptionists say that they are thinking about resigning. What should he do after informing the front office manager about what he just heard?

a. Identify the exact reasons for the high turnover, and develop strategies to eliminate them.
b. Hire employees with high stress tolerance, and build a candidate pool in case of further resignations.
c. Help the front office manager create employee schedules to ensure that there is enough coverage for adequate rest breaks.
d. Train the front office manager on strategies to increase employee engagement during the busy season.

92. The HR department is in the process of filling an open front office lead position. Two candidates made it to the final interview stage and are scheduled to meet with a panel of managers next week. The front office manager approaches the talent acquisition manager and hands him a résumé. He says that he found a highly qualified candidate that he thinks would be a much better fit for the open position than the other two candidates. The talent acquisition manager reviews the résumé and agrees that the candidate appears to be highly qualified. When he asks the front office manager where he received the résumé, he says that the candidate is his cousin. How should the talent acquisition manager handle this situation?

a. The manager should interview the candidate.
b. The manager should inform the front office manager that all candidates need to complete an online application in order to be considered for a position.
c. The manager should schedule a phone screen with the candidate to determine if he truly is as qualified as his résumé seems to indicate.
d. The manager should inform the front office manager that he is unable to consider the candidate.

93. What are the three components of sustainability?

a. Social, economic, environmental
b. Local, regional, international
c. Resources, infrastructure, production
d. Equality, justice, ethics

94. A group of seven managers is meeting to discuss restructuring the geographic areas that their sales teams support. They make a list of factors that will support the restructure as well as a list of what might hinder it. They then rate each factor depending on its importance. What kind of decision-making tool are they using?

a. Cost-benefit analysis
b. SWOT analysis
c. Multi-criterion decision analysis
d. Force-field analysis

95. Which organization focuses on challenges brought about through globalization?

a. Organization for Economic Co-operation and Development
b. UN Global Compact
c. World Trade Organization
d. International Labor Organization

96. What pay system rewards long-term employment instead of high performance?

a. Merit pay
b. A straight piece-rate system
c. A differential piece-rate system
d. Time-based step-rate pay

97. A company introduces a new human resources system that allows managers to view and generate reports, write employee reviews, and process transfers, leaves, and terminations in one application. What kind of system is this?

a. Decision-maker service
b. Employee self-service
c. Service point application
d. Manager self-service

98. A pharmaceutical company that employs 1,000 sales representatives determines during a supply analysis that its current attrition rates are at 16%. Conducting a demand analysis, they set a future goal of attrition rates being at 6% or less. What is the attrition gap that they need to close to accomplish their goal?

a. 6%
b. 10%
c. 16%
d. 37.5%

99. What is a characteristic of a polycentric talent acquisition orientation?

a. Each country has its own unique talent acquisition approach.
b. Headquarter staffing policies are mimicked in other countries.
c. The company has a global talent acquisition plan.
d. Each region establishes its own staffing policies.

Refer to the following scenario for questions 100-102.

A federal credit union prides itself on creating a positive workplace culture for its 600 employees. They offer benefits like a free gym membership, paid volunteer opportunities, movie nights, and excellent health insurance. The CEO meets with the VP of HR to discuss the costs of the employee perks. While he wants to maintain the benefits, the company also needs to find cost savings. After further discussion, they decide that renegotiating their benefits premiums will be the best strategy to lower costs.

100. The VP of HR is under pressure to negotiate lower benefits premiums and is preparing for a tough price negotiation with the benefits vendor. What will be the BEST strategy to start off the negotiation?

a. Convey the company's firm position on reducing costs.
b. Create a welcoming atmosphere that makes the benefits vendor feel comfortable.
c. Set goals for the meeting and lay out the company's negotiation strategy.
d. Focus on understanding the benefits vendor's side.

101. As the VP of HR prepares for the negotiation meeting, she reviews some points with the company's controller. At the end of their meeting, the controller wishes her good luck and jokes that she should wear her sexy, low-cut blouse for the negotiation. How should the VP of HR react?

a. Smile and walk away because it is important to maintain a good relationship.
b. Follow his recommendation because he knows the vendor and what it will take to win the negotiation.
c. Ask the controller to please refrain from making sexual jokes.
d. Schedule a follow-up meeting with the controller to address the situation.

102. To find further cost savings, the VP of HR wants to eliminate the benefits and perquisites that employees rarely use. The company has not been tracking usage data. How should she go about determining which ones are underutilized?

a. Conduct a company-wide employee survey.
b. Conduct interviews with individual employees.
c. Review statistical data on what company benefits employees generally use and do not use.
d. Review stay and exit interviews to determine which benefits are most frequently and infrequently mentioned.

103. What is an important part of administering an employee survey to avoid employees becoming disappointed and disengaged?

a. Conducting surveys at regular intervals, for example, annually
b. Using online surveys for higher response rates
c. Communicating the results to the employees
d. Asking primarily open-ended questions in the survey

104. A manager interviews a candidate who demonstrates that she possesses the knowledge and skills required for the position. However, the interviewee has a large tattoo on her arm. The manager doesn't hire her because he feels that she appears irresponsible. What bias is this?

a. Contrast effect
b. Halo effect
c. Cultural noise
d. Nonverbal bias

105. What is the final step when putting a knowledge management system in place?

a. Training employees on how to access and use the knowledge database
b. Integrating the knowledge database into the company's information technology system
c. Creating a dashboard for easy information access
d. Revising and adding new information on an ongoing basis

106. What are the four common phases of the employee life cycle according to the Society for Human Resource Management (SHRM)?

a. Attraction, onboarding, retention, separation
b. Recruitment, integration, development, transition
c. Application, selection, training, compensation
d. Talent acquisition, performance, payroll, offboarding

107. An employee has been selected for a global assignment and is getting ready to move in the coming weeks. What is an important step in preparing the assignee for departure?

a. Determining a competitive pay rate for the employee while on assignment
b. Analyzing the return on investment
c. Identifying how the assignment fits with the employee's career aspirations
d. Attending a cultural awareness training program

108. A recently formed team is beginning to develop good working relationships. Employees are starting to work together and help each other. What should the manager do to support the team?

a. Promote communication and assist in decision-making processes.
b. Communicate expectations clearly.
c. Motivate employees and give praise for achievements.
d. Establish guidelines for team interactions.

109. Which of these is most important for having a successful focus group?

a. Encourage discussion.
b. Have an agenda.
c. Recognize conflicts early on.
d. Summarize statements.

110. What is a common reason behind an employee's resistance to change?

a. Because it is outside of the employee's comfort zone
b. Worry that change will result in unexpected costs
c. Belief that change is not possible
d. Fear that he or she will not be able to meet new performance expectations

111. A manager tells his employee that he will be demoted if he votes for the union. What are possible consequences if the employee reports the incident?

a. The National Labor Relations Board (NLRB) will investigate the charge.
b. The union and employer will engage in mediation.
c. The NLRB will file a complaint on behalf of the employee.
d. There will be no consequences because the employer can demote, but not terminate, the employee.

112. As a step to reduce workplace accidents, a company assesses how many workers are wearing personal protective equipment. What kind of indicator are they studying?

a. A preceding indicator
b. A leading indicator
c. A dominant indicator
d. A lagging indicator

113. A company aims to reduce occurrences in which employees violate company policy and have to be disciplined. What steps can they take?

a. Implement strict disciplinary actions as a deterrent.
b. Monitor employees closely throughout their shifts.
c. Take away employees' company discounts if violations occur.
d. Create a company culture of open two-way communication.

Refer to the following scenario for questions 114-115.

> An electric utility company operates four petroleum-fired power plants that provide the majority of the electricity for the region. Recent legislative changes require the company to make substantial shifts away from petroleum and towards renewable sources of energy. Although the CEO has a future vision for the company and is ready to lead the company through the transition, many of the company's managers are set in their ways and reluctant to change.

114. In a meeting with the upper management team, opinions are voiced that the company should resist change and stick to the old ways that have been working for so many years. The CEO and the CHRO meet separately after this meeting to discuss how to move forward. The CEO is concerned that the company does not have leaders with experience in the renewable energy sector or the ability to lead related change initiatives. What initial suggestion should the CHRO make?

a. Start building a talent pool and hiring managers with knowledge in the renewable energy sector.
b. Develop leadership training seminars to prepare the managers for leading change initiatives.
c. Review the performance of each manager, and suggest which managers should be terminated because they are unlikely to support the upcoming change initiative.
d. Conduct an assessment of the current talent within the organization, and forecast which talent will be needed to determine hiring and training needs.

115. The CHRO wants to make sure the HR team is prepared to fully support the change initiative. What steps can she take to prepare her team?

a. Ask her team to review job descriptions in preparation for necessary revisions and updates.
b. Delegate one initiative-related responsibility to each member on the team.
c. Enroll HR employees in a refresher seminar on employee communications.
d. Identify how the individual HR employees will be affected by the changes.

116. What is arbitration?

a. A third party assists in the decision-making process.
b. An executive employee makes a decision.
c. A neutral agent determines a resolution.
d. Negotiation among the involved parties.

117. In what stage of a workforce analysis would a flow analysis be conducted?

a. Supply analysis
b. Demand analysis
c. Gap analysis
d. Solution analysis

118. What contributes to an employee's motivation, according to Vroom?

a. Likelihood to get promoted if one puts in effort
b. Transparent communication from managers to employees
c. Working in a motivated and driven team environment
d. Having a manager with good leadership skills

119. A manufacturing company produces finished goods for a multinational technology company with whom they have an agreement. The technology company incorporates these goods into its product lines and owns the marketing, customer service, and all sales. What type of growth strategy is this for the technology company?

a. Contract manufacturing
b. Joint venture
c. Strategic alliance
d. Greenfield operation

120. What tasks needs to be performed continuously throughout the entire risk management process?

a. Invest and set direction
b. Reevaluate and direct
c. Monitor and review
d. Engage and motivate

121. What is an advantage of a functional human resources (HR) structure?

a. Alignment with organizational strategy
b. Ensuring compliance and confidentiality
c. Consistency across the entire organization
d. Accessibility of the HR department for employees

122. Which of the following contains an instruction for how the federal government should operate?

a. Administrative protocol
b. Agency guideline
c. Statute
d. Executive order

123. An Indian citizen moved to the United States for a job in the information technology industry. What is the term for money he regularly sends back to his family in India?

a. Global diaspora
b. Global disbursement
c. Global remittances
d. Global support payments

124. What is the MOST significant reason why a company would want to invest in leadership development and succession planning?

a. It results in higher employee engagement and lower turnover.
b. A competitive labor market makes it difficult to hire leaders externally.
c. Employees are more likely to meet and exceed performance expectations.
d. Sharing leadership responsibilities allows companies to succeed in a rapidly changing environment.

125. The corporate social responsibility (CSR) strategic process starts with a committed leadership team. What is the second step?

a. Assessment
b. Plan development
c. Brainstorming
d. Communication

Refer to the following scenario for questions 126-128.

> A food manufacturer owns several production facilities in the United States, where workers earn an average of $13 per hour and work 40 hours per week. To cut production costs, the company is planning to expand into a developing economy and acquire an existing production facility there. The factory the company acquires currently pays its workers $0.75 per hour, and the employees work 14 hours per day, 7 days a week.

126. The CEO asks the CHRO to find out if the workers' current pay rates violate the host country's laws, planning to keep pay rates the same if they are not unlawful. The CHRO determines that the current pay rates are not in violation of the host country's laws. However, they do violate the company's ethics policy. What should he do?

a. Rewrite the company's ethics policy to accommodate the host country's compensation laws.
b. Explain to the CEO that the host country's employees should be paid the same as their US counterparts.
c. Develop a step-rate pay system that gradually increases the host country's employees' pay rates.
d. Advise the CEO that the host country's employees should be paid a living wage that meets the company's ethics policy.

127. The CEO further tasks the CHRO with introducing the company culture, mission, vison, values, and policies to its newly acquired workforce. What is the most important thing the CHRO should do?

a. Roll out the communication plan once the newly acquired employees are well-integrated.
b. Work with specialists from the host country to develop a communication plan.
c. Task local managers with communicating the information to their respective employees.
d. Hold a factory-wide staff meeting so information can be communicated to all employees at the same time.

128. After the acquisition is complete, the company rolls out a number of change initiatives that affect many work processes as well as team structures and chains of command. The employees appear to not have any reaction to the introduced changes. What conclusions can the leadership team draw from that?

a. They should consult with someone well-versed in the local culture on how to interpret the workforce's reaction.
b. They can be confident that the change initiative was implemented successfully.
c. They should communicate directly with the employees to find out how they feel about the introduced changes.
d. They can conclude that the host country's culture is one that is open, comfortable, and accepting of change.

129. Which recruitment method takes into account an employee's desire to move into a certain position even though there are no current openings?

a. Intraregional recruiting
b. Job bidding
c. Open house
d. Inside moonlighting

130. What best practice increases employee engagement during onboarding?

a. Implementing a "buddy program"
b. Conducting an employee engagement survey
c. Providing positive feedback to new employees
d. Reviewing company policy documents with new employees

131. A food and beverage manufacturer has four open account manager positions that they asked the recruiting manager to fill. After posting the position, the company receives a total of 240 applications, of which 80 applicants meet all minimum qualifications. After the final interviews, the company extends offers to four candidates. What is the yield ratio of offers extended to qualified applicants?

a. 2%
b. 5%
c. 12%
d. 20%

132. A women's shoe designer advertises a job seeking two female models for catalog photos. Is this considered discrimination?

a. Yes, because basing a hiring decision based on an applicant's gender is considered discriminatory.
b. No, because the gender is a bona fide vocational criterion.
c. No, because the gender is a reasonable accommodation.
d. No, because the gender is a bona fide occupational qualification.

133. A male manager demoted one of his female employees because she turned him down when he asked her out on a date and tried to kiss her. What type of harassment is this?

a. Offensive conduct
b. Quid pro quo
c. Forced arrangement
d. Hostile environment

134. An organization is changing organically. Where does the change originate from?

a. From the top
b. From numerous separate origins
c. From the bottom
d. From multiple coordinated origins

135. What guideline should an organization follow when it keeps employment records electronically?

a. Files must be able to be converted into a paper version.
b. Files must be audited at regular time intervals.
c. Files must be organized alphabetically and chronologically.
d. Files must be made available to employees upon request.

Refer to the following scenario for questions 136-138.

A local bookkeeping company has a total of 80 employees, mainly bookkeepers and accountants, working in two relatively small open office spaces. HR duties were handled by the office manager in the past. However, because the HR responsibilities increased, the company decided to hire an HR manager.

136. The new HR manager reviews the company's current processes and learns that they utilize a lengthy skill test as the first step in the hiring process. Looking at the data, she sees that a reasonable number of candidates apply to open positions, but only few complete the skill test and move on to the next stage of the hiring process. What can she do to improve the recruiting process?

a. Eliminate the skill test because it leads to too many applicants dropping out of the hiring process.
b. Assess the skill test's validity.
c. Review the skill test to see if it is biased in favor of certain candidate groups.
d. Remove a number of questions to shorten the skill test.

137. The HR manager notices high employee turnover. She conducts a number of stay interviews that point to a lack of career opportunities as the main reason employees leave the company. When she approaches the general manager with her findings, he argues that there are plenty of people looking for a job, and anyone who leaves can be replaced. What should the HR manager do next?

a. Show the general manager how developing a career path with advancement opportunities will help the company's retention and performance.
b. Make sure that the general manager understands the reason for the high turnover.
c. Identify what HR concerns the general manager prioritizes, and focus on addressing them before revisiting the retention concerns.
d. Compare the company's retention rate to that of their competitors to determine if it is truly a concern or within the industry average.

138. A worldwide pandemic starts to spread, quickly threatening the health of people from all over the globe. The state in which the company operates recommends that all employees work from home, but has not issued any mandatory rules yet. The general manager meets with the HR manager to review the situation. The general manager says that even though it would be possible for employees to work from home, he does not trust them to do so. He prefers to keep an eye on them and suggests moving the desks farther apart. How should the HR manager respond?

a. Present a plan on how to rearrange the open offices space so that employees sit as far away from each other as possible.
b. Recommend that they gather their employees' input on how safe they feel coming to work, and find out if they would prefer to work from home.
c. Point out that there is no reason to not trust employees to be productive, and advise that they should work from home.
d. Suggest that employees continue to report to work as usual for now, but the company should prepare in case remote work becomes mandatory.

139. What is the difference between a multidomestic multinational enterprise (MNE) and a global MNE?

a. Multidomestic MNEs adjust their business practices depending on local circumstances, and global MNEs have universally consistent practices.
b. Multidomestic MNEs own operations outright, and global MNEs have franchised operations.
c. Multidomestic MNEs focus their operations on one continent, and global MNEs have operations spanning the entire globe.
d. Multidomestic MNEs apply the same principles in all of their subsidiaries, and global MNEs vary their approaches depending on local conditions.

140. Which of the following scenarios is covered by FMLA?

a. Care for the employee's grandmother who needs ongoing medical care
b. Care for the employee's aunt with a serious health condition
c. Care for the employee's brother who is recovering from a surgery
d. Care for the employee's child after adoption

141. What can be a possible downside of extending the use of technology in a human resource department?

a. Discourages teamwork
b. Potential employee lack of computer literacy
c. Difficult to use for employees with disabilities
d. Cost intensive for the company

142. What is considered a breach of confidentiality?

a. Granting an employee's request to view his or her personnel file
b. Disclosing an employee's drug test results
c. Sharing the hire and termination dates of a former employee
d. Providing employee data to the company' benefits vendor

143. The executive team of an organization is selecting employees for succession planning. What should they look for in potential candidates?

a. Readiness to take on responsibilities of aspired position right away
b. Display of growth potential
c. A current management employee
d. Participation in the company's mentorship program

144. What is an example of HR's strategic role?

a. Anticipating the knowledge, skills, and abilities needed in the future
b. Conducting background and reference checks for new hires
c. Utilizing HR's information system to maintain employee data
d. Conducting team-building initiatives to reduce turnover

145. An organization is assessing the compliance program it put in place. As part of the program, all employees watch a short video and then take a quiz to ensure understanding of the information. What type of evaluation takes place when the HR team looks at the number of completed quizzes?

a. System evaluation
b. Process evaluation
c. Method evaluation
d. Outcome evaluation

146. What are examples of perquisites a human resources manager might receive?

a. Life insurance and disability benefits
b. Company car and Society for Human Resource Management (SHRM) membership
c. Paid time off and 401(k)
d. Flexible work hours and parental leave

147. An organization provides company cars with full insurance coverage to their management employees. An employee drives faster than usual with the company car because he would not be responsible for any costs should something happen to the car. What is this an example of?

a. Moral hazard
b. Loss expectancy
c. Ethical dilemma
d. Principal-agent problem

148. A car rental branch employs 40 customer service employees. Four of the employees leave the company and are replaced. What is the turnover rate?

a. 1%
b. 9%
c. 10%
d. 90%

Refer to the following scenario for questions 149-151.

A hotel concierge desk is responsible for making activity and dinner reservations for the hotel guests. There are more than 50 restaurants in the area, and their goal is always to find the best dining experience based on the guest's preferences.

149. One of the concierges has a good friend who owns an upscale Italian restaurant and often brings him free lunch. In return, the concierge sets up as many reservations as possible for hotel guests at his restaurant. The concierge manager has been noticing that an unusually high number of reservations are made at this Italian restaurant. What should he do?

a. Remove the Italian restaurant from the list of restaurants that guests can choose from.
b. Report findings to HR, and conduct an investigation.
c. The manager does not need to take action if there are no complaints from hotel guests.
d. Utilize the performance management process to correct the concierge's behavior.

150. There is only one concierge working at the concierge desk at any given time. Because the desk should not be left unattended, concierges are asked to stay at the desk during their 30-minute lunch breaks. The HR manager, who is studying for the SHRM exam, learned that breaks have to be paid if the employee performs any work during that time. Concierges generally do work during their lunch breaks because guests approach the desk even while the concierges are eating. What should the HR manager do?

a. Display awareness between theory and practical implications of the law, and recognize that the current process does not pose a violation.
b. Observe concierges to determine how much work they actually perform during their breaks.
c. Inform concierge managers that employees have to be paid if they stay at the desk during their lunch breaks.
d. Explain to concierges that they can no longer take breaks during their shifts.

151. The concierge manager has been receiving customer complaints regarding the service of one of his employees. Customers are complaining that this concierge is pushy, talks them into buying activities that they do not want to do, and is so persistent that it makes them uncomfortable. The manager schedules a training session with the concierge, reviewing acceptable sales techniques and customer service expectations. However, the complaints continue. What should the concierge manager do?

a. Terminate the concierge's employment.
b. Place the employee on suspension while the complaints are being investigated.
c. Wait to see if his performance improves over time after the training session.
d. Provide more training, and then observe the concierge's interaction with customers.

152. A CHRO is working on the HR budget for the next year and uses the current year as a baseline plus a 3% increase. She also requests additional funds for a new upcoming project. What form of budgeting is this?

a. Activity-based
b. Incremental
c. Zero-based
d. Formula

153. What do you call the sum of all interrelated actions, inputs, and processes that create a company's product until it ends up in the hands of a customer?

a. Supply channels
b. Logistic cooperation
c. Value chain
d. Production system

154. The Age Discrimination in Employment Act forbids discrimination against people over what age?

a. 40
b. 50
c. 55
d. 60

155. In the 2012 Q12 Engagement Survey, Gallup researchers found that certain company performance measures correlate with employee engagement. What did they find in organizations with high employee engagement compared to those with low employee engagement?

a. Increased number of applicants per job posting
b. Fewer employee safety incidents
c. Increased brand value recognition
d. Fewer involuntary employee terminations

156. A company is planning to redesign its organizational structure. What is one of HR's responsibilities during this process?

a. Develop the company's pay structure, and set pay rates for all positions.
b. Analyze organizational problems through structural diagnosis.
c. Lead a workforce committee on organizational change.
d. Develop succession plans for all key positions.

157. An organization restructures itself and removes some management layers. Having fewer levels of middle management between staff and executives give individuals more autonomy in their decision-making. What kind of pay structure is a probable result of this restructure?

a. Broadband structure
b. Graded structure
c. Market-based structure
d. Hybrid structure

158. Which piece of legislation regulates when travel time that occurs during working hours has to be paid?

a. Fair Labor Standards Act
b. Sarbanes-Oxley Act
c. Portal-to-Portal Act
d. Equal Pay Act

159. What is an example of a structural issue HR should recognize during a merger and acquisition?

a. Compliance provisions
b. Use of different technologies by the two companies
c. Existing labor contracts
d. Conflicts of culture in the two organizations

160. Which environmental scanning tool considers a thriving line of business a "star"?

a. Scenario analysis
b. SWOT analysis
c. Growth-share matrix
d. PESTLE analysis

Answer Key and Explanations for Test #2

1. D: In the PAPA model, this risk falls in the adapt category because the event is approaching slowly but surely. The organization is certain that it is going to happen but has time to adapt to the circumstances.

2. D: The HR manager displays the leadership and navigation competency by guiding the senior management team to look at the problem from a different angle, considering factors they might have previously overlooked. Even though the HR manager should aim to align the HR strategy with the company's strategic goals, he has to evaluate the decisions of the executive leadership team to be sure that they are in the best interest of the company. The HR manager does not know if low employee engagement or a lack of communication are reasons for the low performance, so addressing these would not be helpful.

3. B: By meeting with and listening to the project directors, the HR manager displays the relationship management competency. The first step is to understand the needs of the project directors to make sure that the new performance management system achieves their desired results. Conducting an employee survey is not a necessary step in developing a new performance management system. Communicating the change to the performance management system should take place after it has been developed. Because the decision to update the performance management system has already been made, there is no need to make a case for doing so.

4. A: The HR team displays the business acumen competency by seeking information about the position that they are asked to fill. Knowing exactly what knowledge, skills, and abilities are needed helps HR recruit the right candidates. After the HR team has gained an understanding of what the ideal candidate looks like, they can utilize recruitment strategies including internet recruiting. The question does not indicate that job descriptions are outdated or whether the company already has an employment brand in place.

5. B: In Lechmere, Inc. v. NLBR, the court ruled in favor of the company. Lechmere, Inc. did not allow union representatives on company property to solicit and distribute materials because they were not employees of the company and had no other business reason to be on the property.

6. C: To attract the best talent, the company pursues a lead market strategy and offers higher wages than the market. A match market strategy would be to offer pay rates similar to other companies. A lag market strategy would aim to save on personnel costs by offering lower-than-average wages.

7. A: In a learning organization, leaders are designers, stewards, and teachers. As designers, they create the vision, values, and processes of the organization. They have a sense of stewardship for their employees as well as for the company's mission. As teachers, they encourage others to discover and seek new possibilities.

8. C: The first step in Kotter's Change Model is to create a sense of urgency. Establishing a sense of urgency will demonstrate the need for change. Providing a clear vision is the third step. Over-communicating and encouraging feedback are part of the fourth step.

9. B: The information technology manager displays the ethical practice competency by maintaining confidentiality. Neither he nor the HR department should share any details regarding an employee's termination. Asking the employee to stop spreading rumors would not address his question.

10. D: Both the US and the Philippines generally have a short-term orientation in Hofstede's dimensions of culture. Therefore, people in both countries typically value tradition and resist change. They also tend to focus on quick, short-term results in both their professional and personal lives.

11. C: The yield ratio is calculated by dividing the number of female applicants by the number of total applicants: 100/250 = 40%.

12. C: This is an example of gamification, a form of mobile learning (m-learning), where educational material is delivered in the form of a game. It is intended to make learning more fun and the material more engaging.

13. C: The company should conduct a thorough investigation before making the decision to terminate an employee. As part of the investigation, the manager should interview each of the employees to hear their side of the story. The employees should then be suspended pending investigation. This will give HR time to research and review all relevant information, including any prior similar instances, before making a final decision.

14. B: One characteristic of someone who acquired a global mindset is that they are not afraid of change and uncertainty. They welcome it and see it as a chance for improvement.

15. D: A balanced scorecard shows if the HR strategy is in alignment with and supports the company's strategic direction. It can be used to assess the performance of the HR department and gauge the value it provides for the organization.

16. D: It is important for a company to invest in a comprehensive diversity and inclusion program because the goal is to change deeply held beliefs, assumptions, habits, and processes, which is a difficult undertaking. If the company does not truly care about making these difficult changes and putting in the necessary effort, the initiative will not be successful. Further, the company will not be able to profit from the advantages of a diverse workforce.

17. A: The CHRO displays the critical evaluation competency by using the data and insights she gained to build a business case. A business case that is well-researched and backed up by solid data has the best potential to convince the CEO to invest in the necessary training and development for his managers. Properly trained managers will have a positive impact on the company's operations. A cost-efficient employee engagement initiative, one-on-one meetings, and literature for self-study can be quick fixes in the interim. However, they do not adequately address the manager's training needs.

18. C: The CHRO displays the relationship management competency by building rapport with external contacts that can help create a talent pipeline for the company. Working directly with colleges and their career services centers will improve hiring efforts in the long term.

19. D: The CHRO displays the ethical practice competency by promoting fairness when she notices that the new technology has become a disadvantage for the more tenured and less computer-savvy employees. She shows awareness that new technology can lead to performance gaps between the younger and older workforce. To give all employees a fair chance, the company needs to offer more training and support to the less computer-savvy employees.

20. D: The HR business partner displays the leadership and navigation competency by recognizing and modifying ineffective practices. Converting the training from paper forms to online training modules is a creative solution to promote compliance while accommodating business needs. The proposed training design gives employees the flexibility to complete the training modules when they find time to do so. It also ensures that they actually receive the information instead of signing a document without reading it.

21. A: The HR business partner displays the consultation competency by recognizing an area of improvement the company has and advising the leadership team of solutions to remedy the problem. Falsely classifying employees as exempt can have serious legal consequences for a company. Therefore, the HR business partner has to research and present lawful alternative compensation options that will align with the company culture to the leadership team.

22. B: The HR business partner displays the business acumen competency by being aware of where the company is in its life cycle. A company's life cycle includes: introduction, growth, maturity, and decline. One of HR's responsibilities during the maturity stage is to keep the company's agile, competitive, and creative spirit alive, which can be challenging due to its larger size.

23. B: Diversity and inclusion (D&I) strategies need to account for differences in cultural backgrounds, organizational departments, and geographical locations. Therefore, they should not be put into effect identically across the entire organization. It is important that the implementation is adaptable, just, and fair, taking into account the uniqueness of individuals and teams.

24. B: Conducting a compliance audit at the last step of the risk management process will ensure that all implemented changes comply with applicable regulations and laws.

25. C: This is an example of risk mitigation. The company reduces the severity of the potential consequences by creating a plan to quickly communicate with employees and share information that will help keep them safe.

26. C: This suggestion displays the global and cultural effectiveness competency by taking advantage of the diverse perspectives that exist within the organization and involving employees in the development of a new employment brand. Efforts and views should come from the employees and managers themselves and not originate solely within the HR department. Diversity and inclusion programs generally take time to develop and cannot be expected to bring quick results.

27. B: The CHRO displays the global and cultural effectiveness competency by recognizing the cultural differences as the root cause of their problem working together. Therefore, she is able to mediate between both parties and use the situation as a learning lesson about how to overcome cultural differences by seeing the other person's perspective. This will allow them to understand each other better and improve their working relationship going forward.

28. A: The marketing manager displays the communication competency by having one-on-one conversations with all team members to find out why the new employee does not fit in with the rest of the team. If the current employees are a close group that has worked together for a long time, they might need support to adjust to the new team member. It is important to get to know the new employee to see if they have any conflicts with the company culture.

29. A: The HR generalist displays the relationship management competency by mediating between the two bus drivers and guiding them to find a solution to their disagreement. Instead of imposing a solution, the HR generalist allows the employees to come to one on their own, helping them gain a better understanding of their coworker's perspective. This understanding will lead to better collaboration in the long term.

30. B: The HR manager displays the communication competency by adjusting the communication method depending on the audience. Managers need to be informed through a communication medium that allows them to ask questions and prepares them to address issues that their bus drivers might bring up. A conference call would be ideal for this. The sales representatives also need to know about the change. However, since they are tech-savvy, and the change does not affect them much, an email is sufficient. The bus drivers are most affected by the change and should be informed in person. A workgroup meeting is a good choice because all of their questions and concerns can be addressed in real-time.

31. A: The HR generalist displays the ethical practice competency by granting the employee his right to take FMLA. He protects the company from legal exposure by complying with the law. Terminating the bus driver's employment would be against the law. The employee has a right to take up to 12 weeks of leave if he qualifies for it due to a serious health condition.

32. A: Web conferencing allows a presenter to share presentation slides on each participant's computer. The participants can see the slide show presentation slides on their device and can hear the presentation over their computer's speakers or headphones. They also have the opportunity to directly communicate with the presenter through a webchat or their computer's microphone.

33. C: The Recruitment Cost Ratio is calculated by dividing the total amount of recruitment costs ($60,000) by the total first-year compensation of new hires in a given time period ($300,000) and then multiplying the result by 100. $60,000/$300,000x 100 = 20%.

34. D: The employee absence rate is a measure that can be calculated and used to assess the effectiveness of an engagement action plan. Problem-solving abilities, employee motivation, and managerial skills are not outcomes that can be measured explicitly.

35. C: The HR manager displays the critical evaluation competency by recognizing that switching to a cheaper vendor, if available, would not have the desired results. That's because the new vendor's premiums are likely to increase year after year as well. He knows that there is a direct link between the health of the employees and how much the company is paying in healthcare premiums. Therefore, his strategy of focusing on preventative health is a good long-term solution to reduce premium increases.

36. D: The HR manager displays the leadership and navigation competency by speaking up even if it is something that the CEO would rather not hear. It is necessary for the HR manager to voice his concerns because improper maintenance can have costly consequences for the company.

37. B: The HR manager is displaying the communication competency by knowing when to talk to someone and when to seek expert advice first. Even though the company has nothing to hide, it is important to follow the attorney's recommendations when dealing with the department of labor. The attorney can provide guidance regarding what information has to be shared and what files need to be turned over.

38. A: Establishing a diversity council is part of the third step of creating a diversity and inclusion (D&I) infrastructure. The next step (fourth step) is taking action and implementing the planned initiatives. This includes making changes to talent acquisition, onboarding, career advancement opportunities, and remuneration.

39. A: When change is introduced, there is likely to be some initial decline in performance, which is known as the "J curve." Employees often react to change with resistance and rejection. As a result, productivity declines. If the change initiative is managed well, then employees will come to accept the change, and performance will ideally increase above the initial level.

40. C: The VP of HR displays the business acumen competency by using his understanding of the business to identify solutions to organizational challenges. His suggestion to utilize the intranet for communication aligns HR strategy with the company's strategic goals by enabling employees to communicate and collaborate on a daily basis. A one-time meeting in person or virtually would be a good start. However, it does not support the need for ongoing interaction and collaboration. Strict performance management steps would not be appropriate at this time because the company first needs to create a platform that enables employees to successfully collaborate with each other.

41. D: Because the working relationship with Region X's manager is an ongoing problem, the VP of HR needs to get to the bottom of the issue. He does this by displaying the relationship management competency which involves meeting with each regional manager to gain a full understanding of the problem. Once the root of the problem is uncovered, he can encourage open communication among the regional managers and find a permanent solution. Solving this disagreement and improving the relationships between the regional managers will result in improved cooperation and better overall performance.

42. A: The HR generalist displays the relationship competency by focusing on getting to know the managers and department heads she will be supporting in her new position. To successfully support the locations, she needs to build strong relationships with the leaders and get to know them to build mutual trust. The meetings will also help her learn about the business and build her business acumen competency.

43. B: The HR generalist displays the global and cultural effectiveness competency by recognizing that the pregnant employee is being stereotyped by her supervisor. The HR generalist should take action. Since she is new in her role, she should consult with her supervisor, the VP of HR, on the company procedure to address these kinds of inappropriate comments.

44. D: The VP of HR displays the critical evaluation competency by being aware of biases that can occur and asking further questions to determine if the HR generalist's sympathy is due to a similar-to-me error. If the reason for not agreeing with the written warning turns out to be because she sees herself in the employee, then the VP of HR can address the bias. Then, they can train the HR generalist on how to act objectively and identify and remove bias in similar situations.

45. C: This is an example of cultural relativism because a judgment is made based on the person's own cultural perspective. Someone from Laos is likely to regard it as tasty, whereas a European visitor might find the idea disgusting. The other answer choices are examples of ethical universalism.

46. A: According to McClelland's Three Needs Theory, there are three intrinsic needs that determine how an employee can be motivated: achievement, affiliation, and power. An affiliation-oriented employee is motivated by teamwork and building relationships. An achievement-oriented employee is motivated by meaningful and challenging work. A power-oriented employee is motivated by competition.

47. C: The HR manager displays the business acumen competency by applying information he learned in the legal seminar to improve the company's operations. Conducting further research on the company's use of third-party employees and seeking the assistance of a legal counsel shows that he takes the necessary steps to limit the company's legal exposure.

48. C: The HR manager demonstrates the relationship management competency by meeting with each department head and listening to their concerns. The meetings give the HR manager a broad understanding of how the restructure will impact the different departments, including what they will need in terms of support during the process. Involving leaders on different levels of the organization in the decision-making process will contribute to a successful restructure and ensure that their concerns are addressed early on. One possible need could be developing employee engagement initiatives, but it is too early to determine this yet. Communicating the restructure to employees should take place once the plans are concrete. Because the executive team has already decided on the organizational structure, there is no need to research alternatives.

49. C: The HR business partner displays the critical evaluation competency by collecting and reviewing data and using it to identify the root of the problem within the organization. Once the core of the problem has been identified, he can develop solutions to improve the company's retention. He knows that solving staffing shortages in the long term requires improving retention - not hiring more employees who will likely leave quickly.

50. C: The HR business partner displays the business acumen competency by collecting data, analyzing the current workforce, identifying solutions that will support the company's strategy, providing a recommendation, and supplying the CEO with the necessary data for the expansion business plan.

51. B: The HR business partner displays the ethical practice competency by reporting and investigating the accusations right away. Unethical behavior and inappropriate comments can damage the company's reputation, result in employees leaving the organization, and lead to costly legal ramifications. Even though the head of sales is hesitant to address the issue, the HR business partner does the right thing by stopping the inappropriate behavior.

52. B: The VP of HR and the talent manager demonstrate the critical evaluation competency by seeking out market pay rate data that allows them to evaluate how their company's pay system compares to other companies. This data has to be collected before determining if employees should be given pay increases, incentives, or perquisites. The lack of a realistic job preview does not seem to be the cause for the retention problem.

53. B: According to Hofstede's dimensions of culture, the United States is a country with low power distance, whereas India is a country with high power distance. The VP's approach of sharing responsibilities and recognition with his employees is not likely to be well received because Indian employees would expect a manager to complete important tasks himself.

54. A: According to Trompenaars's and Hampden-Turner's cultural dilemmas, India has a diffuse culture, which means that their personal and work lives intertwine. Therefore, to be successful, one has to attend work-related social events and build relationships. The United States is the opposite and has a specific culture, where work and personal lives are kept separate. In the United States, forming relationships is unnecessary to work together successfully. The US is also an individualist culture that values competition, and India is not.

55. D: The best strategy to communicate results is to tell a story based on the data. A large quantity of data that is presented in bulleted slides or pages of spreadsheets can overwhelm many audiences.

56. A: This question is asking how the interviewee handled a particular situation in the past. The idea behind a behavioral interview is that you can predict how a candidate will behave in the future based on how he behaved in the past. A stress interview aims to put a candidate on the defense to determine how he responds to pressure. In a case interview, a candidate is given a business problem and asked to solve it. An unstructured interview is characterized by casual, spontaneous, and open-ended questions.

57. C: A scatter diagram is used when one wants to determine if there is a correlation between two variables. One axis would be the test scores, and the other axis the number of closed sales. The diagram will show a dot for each employee. If the dots resemble a line, it would suggest that there is a correlation between the two variables.

58. C: HR professionals can support adherence to new processes by incorporating goals that reflect those processes into performance reviews. Performance objectives should be transparent and easy for employees to understand. They should also reflect the new goals and responsibilities that resulted from the change initiative.

59. A: Stay interviews can improve retention by allowing managers to find out early on if an employee is happy and satisfied or unhappy and disengaged. If the employee is unhappy or disengaged, the manager has an opportunity to address their concerns. With exit interviews, it's usually too late to prevent the employee from resigning.

60. D: In a group interview, one or several managers interview a number of job candidates. They can be conducted as either team interviews or panel interviews. The main advantage is that they reduce the time spent on the interview and candidate selection process.

61. B: Involving employees in the company's decision-making process is called codetermination. One form of this is the single-tier system in which one or more employees sit on the board of directors and have the right to vote. Other possible forms of codetermination are a dual system or a mixed system.

62. A: The CHRO displays the leadership and navigation competency by seeing potential for the company to improve, finding innovative solutions, and taking action to implement them. Through keeping a pulse on the employees, the CHRO finds out early on that employees feel like the company is not walking their talk. The CHRO takes their input seriously and uses it to develop solutions that can support the company's strategy and contribute to organizational success.

63. D: The CHRO displays the communication competency by not assuming that the rate of pay is the only thing that motivates employees. Instead, the CHRO seeks to develop an understanding about what employees truly want. Focusing company resources on what truly motivates employees will be more successful in retaining them than just increasing their pay. An employee survey and interviews will be a good foundation to develop a successful retention strategy.

64. C: The CHRO displays the consultation competency by showing awareness how the HR team can best contribute to the successful implementation of the proposed changes. One responsibility of the HR department in managing change is to keep a pulse on the workforce and analyze the effects that the changes have on employees and departments. This allows the HR department to identify if there are additional training needs and to determine if there is effective communication to and from employees.

65. B: There are nine steps in the outsourcing process. Choosing a contractor is the sixth step, followed by negotiating a contract. Defining goals is part of the first step. Creating an RFP (request for proposal) is the third step. Monitoring the project schedule after the project has been implemented is the eighth step.

66. C: These projects demonstrate the CHRO's business acumen competency by taking steps to align the HR strategy with the organizational strategy. They demonstrate that the CHRO understands how the HR department can contribute to cost savings and improving the company's financial performance. Supporting the revenue-generating sections of the company does not necessarily lead to improved financial performance. Laying employees off or enacting a hiring freeze might not be in the best interest of the company.

67. D: An impactful communicator is most likely to successfully communicate the message. He should be engaging and credible, understand the employees' needs and perspectives, and communicate a clear message. An icebreaker activity would not be appropriate for this kind of meeting. Providing a detailed slide show presentation can overwhelm the employees with information. Focus groups are also not the right medium to communicate the change because they are used to gain information rather than disseminate it.

68. C: According to Blake-Mouton's theory, a "country club manager" is highly concerned about his people but has a low concern for tasks. He tends to be encouraging and creates a collaborative environment. But he often fails to hold employees accountable and avoids giving negative feedback to his subordinates. In order for him to become a team leader, he would need to develop an equal amount of concern for tasks. "Impoverished managers," with a low concern for both tasks and people, tend to delegate their work.

69. C: The mentor displays the communication competency by giving his mentee tools that will allow him to find his own solution. Instead of giving him the answer, the mentor assists him in discovering the answer for himself. This helps prepare him for his new leadership role. Passing on knowledge is helpful, but teaching the mentee how to find solutions and develop his own leadership style will have a bigger impact. Ending the training program does not necessarily end the mentoring relationship. If both parties agree, they can continue the mentoring relationship.

70. B: According to the Hersey-Blanchard Situational Theory of Leadership, employees go through different stages, and leaders should adjust their leadership style accordingly. The first stage is "telling," in which the leader should provide guidance and direction, keeping a close eye on the new employee. The second stage is "selling," in which a leader should focus on coaching and motivating. The third stage is "participating," in which the leader should provide support when the employee is making decisions and finding solutions. The fourth stage is "delegating," in which a leader should empower the employee.

71. D: According to the goal-setting motivation theory, goals need to be precise, clear, measurable, challenging, and attainable. The goals of employees A, B and C fit this criterion. Employee D's goal is not likely to be attainable by a trainee, and therefore the assistant manager should encourage him to rephrase the objective.

72. D: There are three stages on the corporate social responsibility (CSR) curve: compliance, integration, and transformation. The company is at the transformation stage. They have successfully integrated sustainability into their core strategy by receiving the B Corp certification. A company can obtain this certification if they meet a number of environmental and social performance standards.

73. C: E-learning, which is learning conducted via electronic media, can be either synchronous or asynchronous. Asynchronous learning means that employees can access the material anytime and anywhere. With synchronous learning, employees go through the training material at the same time and communicate with each other in real time.

74. B: A successful mentorship is a two-way street in which both parties exchange knowledge and learn from each other. The mentee must help shape the overall mentoring relationship, and goals should be set together. The frequency of meetings can vary. Generally, a mentor is a senior colleague or a peer. In a formal mentorship, the mentor and mentee are usually paired by HR. In an informal mentorship, the mentee often selects someone as a mentor for themselves.

75. C: The employees affected by the change were not included in the development of the restructure, which can lead to resistance.

76. D: A collaborative conflict resolution seeks to find a mutually agreed-on solution that both parties view as a success. This process can take time and effort, but it allows for maintaining a valuable relationship.

77. B: Finding the right balance between standardization and localization is an important part of HR's role in supporting the company's globalization efforts. Some policies, processes, and procedures will be consistent across the entire company. However, others will need to be adjusted to reflect the local culture of the host country.

78. C: According to the layers of diversity model by Gardenswartz and Rowe, the external dimension includes a person's marital status, education, and place of residence.

79. D: Keys for successful networking include meeting people that can help you, having expertise or other resources that you can contribute, and the willingness to put in time and effort to maintain the relationship.

80. C: EPLI (employment practices liability insurance) is insurance for companies that protects them in case they get sued by an employee. It covers legal costs and settlement fees related to the suit.

81. C: Being an impactful communicator involves effective listening, integrity, trustworthy appearance, good eye contact, good posture, a well-projected voice, and appropriate gestures.

82. C: HR should consult with legal counsel when writing a staffing contract. They should avoid setting end dates in the contract so it can be terminated in case of dissatisfaction. They should also stay away from generic contract forms. Finally, they should negotiate the price of the staffing company's service.

83. D: The C-suite refers to the executive management team of the company and often includes the CEO, CFO, COO, CHRO, and CIO.

84. D: The HR manager displays the critical evaluation competency by first gathering and analyzing the data. He needs to determine where sales numbers are currently at and then set realistic goals by comparing those numbers to market data. This enables him to develop a sales incentive plan that challenges the sales associates while still being achievable. Developing an understanding of this data and setting realistic goals is the foundation for creating and communicating the new sales incentive plan. That understanding is also critical for developing effective training programs.

85. B: The HR manager displays the relationship management competency by researching and gathering data before meeting with the CEO to make a recommendation. By looking at the problem through the CEO's eyes and comparing options for cost and effectiveness, he can prepare to answer any questions the CEO might have. Then, the HR manager can gain the CEO's support in choosing the best available training option for the management team. Rolling out the free online training modules might not be in the best interest of the company. Asking the store managers for their preferences also does not help HR find the most effective training option. It's unknown if the HR team has the resources and abilities to develop an in-house training program.

86. A: Impactful communication starts with understanding the audience's perspective, drafting a clear message, and delivering it effectively. A conference call gives managers the opportunity to ask questions and prepare answers to questions they might get. A concise but comprehensive email communicates the message consistently to all associates. Conducting face-to-face meetings is not realistic with a dispersed workforce. The company would want the message to be consistent across all stores and therefore would not want to leave all communication up to the individual store managers. The message should be understandable and complete but at the same time brief and to the point. Providing too much information in a letter can lead to a communication overload for many employees.

87. B: During the entire OED (organizational and employee development) process, the specialists should be aware of the employees' emotional reactions to proposed and implemented changes. They should also find ways to improve their ability to adapt to the changes.

88. C: Good governance starts with a company's leadership team. The top company officials need to exhibit it in everything that they do. It then must be obviously displayed at all other levels of the organization.

89. D: A leader has a strategic vision. They motivate and encourage a team to reach and exceed goals. A manager focuses on transactional activities. They schedule, organize, plan, and compile resources.

90. C: The HR manager displays the ethical practice competency by recognizing the behavior as unethical and taking the necessary steps to investigate and address it. The receptionists receive a commission percentage for a successful upgrade sale. However, enticing customers to buy an upgrade with a voucher that is not intended for that purpose should not be rewarded with a sales incentive.

91. A: HR displays the consultation competency by identifying the reasons for the high turnover and working with the team to address the issue. This can involve developing strategies to help the employees reduce stress and deal with the large workload during the season. It has not been determined if a lack of breaks or low employee engagement are the reasons for the high turnover. Before building a candidate pool, the HR manager should find out what kind of skills and abilities a qualified candidate needs rather than assume that high stress tolerance is the most important characteristic.

92. D: The talent acquisition manager displays the ethical practice competency by explaining to the front office manager that he is unable to consider the candidate. It would be unethical towards the two candidates that made it to the final interview to add in another candidate who did not have to go through the same initial selection process. It would also be unethical to give preferential treatment to a family member of the front office manager.

93. A: There are three main parts of sustainability: social, economic, and environmental. The social aspect addresses social inequalities and advocates for the fair treatment of all individuals. The economic aspect focuses on how to operate a business and use resources conscientiously to achieve profits. The environmental aspect addresses the consequences of one's actions on the environment, to include climate change.

94. D: The managers are conducting a force-field analysis and identifying factors that help and hinder the proposed restructure. As a result, the team can determine which possibilities they should pursue further and which ones to stay away from.

95. A: The Organization for Economic Co-operation and Development (OECD) sets goals, formulates policies, and supports its member states on issues brought about through globalization and global trade.

96. D: Time-based step-rate pay rewards tenure over performance. Pay increases are granted on a previously established timeline. On the contrary, merit pay, also called performance-based pay, grants pay increases based on an individual's performance. With a straight or differential piece-rate system, an employee is paid a base wage plus additional pay for completed work up to an established standard. They may receive a premium for work accomplished that exceeds this standard.

97. D: This is an example of a manager self-service (MSS) application. It allows managers to handle the HR part of their role through one portal. It can be used for reporting and the performance management process. Tasks that are traditionally handled by the HR department can now be performed by the managers themselves.

98. B: The company has determined that 16% of their sales representatives are leaving the firm. Their goal is to reduce this number to 6%. Therefore, the gap between the current attrition and the future targeted attrition is 10% (16%-6%). Given that the company has 1,000 sales representatives, this change would result in only 60 employees leaving the organization (6%), rather than 160 (16%).

99. A: In a polycentric organization, each country has its own unique talent acquisition approach. In an ethnocentric organization, headquarter staffing policies are mimicked when expanding into other countries. A geocentric organization has a global talent acquisition plan. Each region establishes its own staffing policies in an egocentric organization.

100. B: The VP of HR displays the relationship competency by preparing for a successful negotiation. Before going into a negotiation, it is important to prepare and be clear about what one would like to accomplish. Upon starting the meeting, one should create a welcoming and comfortable atmosphere to build a trusting relationship with the negotiation partner. This forms the foundation of a successful meeting and discussion.

101. C: The VP of HR displays the global and cultural effectiveness competency by recognizing this comment as an inappropriate gender stereotype. The right thing for her to do is to speak up, make the controller aware of the implication of his joke, and ask him to refrain from gender stereotyping in the future.

102. A: The VP of HR displays the critical evaluation competency by being knowledgeable on how to best gather data. The best data collection method in this case is an employee survey. Conducting interviews is too time intensive and would not survey the entire workforce. Reviewing stay and exit interviews is unlikely to provide the needed information. Reviewing data from outside the organization would not answer the question of which benefits the company's employees are using and not using.

103. C: Employee surveys are a tool to increase employee engagement. But it is important that managers communicate the results honestly to their employees, take the feedback seriously, and respond in a meaningful manner. The greatest mistake companies can make with employee surveys is ignoring or not responding to the survey results. This can lead to frustrated and disengaged employees.

104. D: This is an example of a nonverbal bias. The manager draws conclusions based on her personal appearance and interprets her tattoo as a sign that she is irresponsible.

105. D: The final step in creating a knowledge management system is to update, revise, and add information on an ongoing basis to keep the database relevant and current.

106. B: The recruitment phase is the beginning of the employee life cycle (ELC). Then comes integration, which includes onboarding and the employee's introduction to their new role. The third phase, development, includes training and performance management. The last phase, transition, is when the employee leaves their position due to a promotion, termination, or transfer.

107. D: Once the employee has been selected for the global assignment, it is important for him to learn about the local culture. This will prepare him for a successful start overseas. Setting pay rates, analyzing the potential return on investment, and assessing fit with the employee's career aspirations should take place well before selecting an employee for the assignment.

108. A: The team is in the norming stage of Tuckman's ladder of team development. The leader's role is to promote communication among the team members and guide them in decision-making processes. In the forming stage, leaders need to communicate expectations clearly. In the storming stage, it is important for leaders to establish guidelines for team interactions. Once the team moves past the norming stage to the performing stage, leaders should motivate employees and give praise for achievements.

109. A: The leader of a focus group should put his emphasis on drawing out information from the participants. He can do this by involving all of them equally and encouraging deep discussion of the topic.

110. A: One common reason an employee might express resistance to change is that he fears new and unfamiliar processes that are outside of his comfort zone. This is called the fear of the unknown.

111. A: Telling an employee that he will be demoted if he votes for the union is an unfair labor practice (ULP). After the employee reports the ULP to the NLRB, the NLRB will investigate the allegation.

112. B: Wearing personal protective equipment is considered a leading indicator because it affects the rate of future workplace accidents. The opposite is a lagging indicator, which had an impact on the number of workplace accidents that occurred in the past.

113. D: Companies that want to minimize having to discipline their workforce should practice open communication with their employees. It allows employees to develop a good understanding of company policies and expectations. And, managers who are in regular communication with their employees understand reasons for their behavior and can correct it before a violation occurs.

114. D: The CHRO displays the business acumen competency by studying the talent and knowledge that exists within the organization and forecasting what will be needed in the future. Assessing the company's current talent resources is an important first step, followed by forecasting what the company will need to successfully implement the upcoming changes. By contrasting these two, the

CHRO can put together a recommendation for the CEO about which talent gaps need to be filled through either hiring or training.

115. C: The CHRO displays the consultation competency by knowing what skills are needed to successfully support organizational change. Expertise in channels of communication will be critical for the HR team to support the company changes.

116. C: Arbitration is a contract negotiation tool available to both the union and the company. If the two parties cannot reach an agreement, a third party, the arbitrator, is tasked with determining a resolution. Both parties must adhere to the arbitrator's decision.

117. A: A flow analysis looks at how employees move around in the company. It follows each team member throughout the employee life cycle, including any promotions, demotions, or transfers. It is a critical part of evaluating the skill and talent that exists within the organization (supply analysis). The demand analysis forecasts future talent needs of the company. The gap analysis contrasts the demand against the supply to identify possible talent shortfalls. During the solution analysis, a company identifies ways to fill any talent gaps.

118. A: According to Vroom's expectancy theory, an employee is motivated by three factors: expectancy, instrumentality, and valence. For example, an employee will be motivated if he can expect to get a desired promotion by working hard.

119. A: Contract manufacturing is characterized by one company having another company manufacture its products as a means of controlling costs. In a joint venture, two companies set up a new company that they own together. A strategic alliance is formed when companies share resources. A Greenfield operation is building a new facility altogether.

120. C: Throughout the entire risk management process, it is important that strategies are monitored and reviewed to ensure alignment with the process' goals and the organization's overall strategy.

121. C: An advantage of a functional HR structure is that HR practices are uniformly applied throughout the entire organization. Accessibility of the HR department for employees is an advantage of a decentralized HR structure. No matter what the structure of the HR department is, it should be in alignment with the organization's strategy while maintaining compliance and confidentiality.

122. D: An executive order issued by the US president is an order for how the federal government is to act, operate, or collaborate.

123. C: Global remittances are funds that migrant workers send to support their families back in their home countries.

124. D: Succession planning and leadership development are imperative because the environment in which organizations operate changes rapidly. Shared leadership, in contrast to having single leaders, allows for quicker and more efficient responses to external change.

125. A: The second step of the corporate social responsibility (CSR) process is to conduct an assessment of the organization's current state. The assessment will review company structure, strategy, and processes.

126. D: The CHRO demonstrates the ethical practice competency by advising the CEO to act in accordance with the company's ethics policy. Increasing the pay rates gradually could be a possible consequence, but the company could also decide to implement a different pay system. A fair living wage in the host country is likely to be different than current US pay rates. The company's ethics policy should not be rewritten in response to this situation.

127. B: By working with a local specialist, the CHRO displays the communication competency because he will communicate the information in a manner that is respectful of the host country's culture. He demonstrates cultural sensitivity and takes his audience's perspective into account when developing the communication strategy. Once the communication plan has been established, it could be communicated by local managers if they have the required skill set. Communication should be timely and ongoing. A single meeting will not be sufficient to relay all of the information.

128. A: Some cultures avoid expressing their feelings or concerns to someone in power. To prevent widespread resistance later on, the leadership team should find out how the change initiative has been perceived by the workforce. To ensure cultural sensitivity, they should consult with a local expert on how to read the lack of employee reaction to the change initiative.

129. B: Job bidding allows current employees to express interest in positions even though there might not be any openings at the moment. Inside moonlighting means that an employee works a second job at the same company before or after his regular working hours. Intraregional recruiting and open houses are external recruiting sources.

130. A: Implementing a "buddy program" increases employee engagement. The company assigns the new employee a "buddy" who has been with the company for a significant amount of time. The "buddy" can provide guidance and help the new employee settle into his new role.

131. B: The yield ratio is calculated by dividing the number of offers extended by the number of qualified applicants: 4/80 = 5%.

132. D: Hiring females to model women's shoes is a bona fide occupational qualification (BFOQ). This hiring practice is not discriminatory because only females would be able to model women's shoes.

133. B: This is an example of quid pro quo (this for that). The manager asks for a sexual favor in return for the employee's continued employment. Quid pro quo and hostile work environment are two types of harassment that can occur at a workplace.

134. B: There are three approaches to change: cascade, progressive, and organic. When a company changes organically, the change comes from numerous separate origins. These changes spread gradually and naturally throughout the organization.

135. A: When a company keeps electronic employee files, they have to be able to produce paper versions in a timely manner if a request is made. This could occur as part of a compliance audit or a lawsuit.

136. B: The HR manager displays the critical evaluation competency by being knowledgeable about statistical principles such as validity. High validity of the test means that it successfully measures how well the applicant will perform in the position he is applying for. The HR manager should determine if every question on the skill test is producing data that can predict a candidate's future performance. If questions do not meet these criteria, they can be eliminated from the test. Assessing the test's overall validity will help determine if the test should be used going forward.

137. A: The HR manager displays the consultation competency by making recommendations that benefit the company as well as its employees. She identified the lack of career opportunities as a roadblock in the company's success. By proposing to develop a career path that gives employees advancement opportunities, she not only addresses the retention problem but also suggests a solution that will improve the company's performance. Since the general manager is concerned with company performance, this argument may help win their support.

138. C: The HR manager displays the ethical competency by recognizing that the company has a duty of care to keep employees safe and healthy. If it is possible to have employees work from home, this should be done during a pandemic to keep them safe. Potentially exposing them to the virus by having them come into the office violates the company's duty of care.

139. A: Briscoe, Schuler, Tarique, Bartlett, and Ghoshal distinguish multinational enterprises (MNEs) by their degree of global integration and local responsiveness. Multidomestic MNEs are high in local responsiveness but low in global integration. Global MNEs are high in global integration but low in local responsiveness.

140. D: The Family and Medical Leave Act (FMLA) grants unpaid time off to an employee who is caring for a newborn or a child placed for adoption or foster care. The employee may also use this time to provide care for immediate family members that are experiencing a serious health condition. Immediate family members are limited to the employee's spouse and parents. Finally, if the employee is unable to work due to their own serious health condition, they may apply for FMLA to take care of themselves. FMLA does not apply to extended family members such as grandparents, aunts, uncles, or siblings.

141. B: One concern companies have to take into consideration when moving parts of the HR function to an online portal is that not all employees are computer literate. Therefore, they might need training on how to use a computer and access different functions.

142. B: HR must protect confidential employee information. Data that cannot be shared includes medical information, such as drug test results.

143. B: Succession planning builds a talent pool of potential future leaders within the company. Therefore, it is important to select candidates with growth potential. Candidates can come from all levels of the organization. After candidates have been selected, they receive training and development, which for example, can include a mentorship program.

144. A: Anticipating and developing the knowledge, skills, and abilities needed for the organization's strategic direction is an example of HR's strategic role. Maintaining employee data in the HRIS and conducting background and reference checks are examples of HR's administrative role. Team-building initiatives are an example of HR's operational role.

145. B: This is an example of a process evaluation, which looks at the details of the conducted program and assesses which activities have been completed. The opposite would be an outcome evaluation, which looks at the effects of the program. These effects could be changes in behavior as a result of the newly acquired information.

146. B: Perquisites are company perks provided to employees in addition to their regular salary and benefits. Examples include company car, cell phone, laptop, discounted products, membership in professional organizations, and tuition assistance.

147. A: This is an example of a moral hazard, which describes a situation where one person does something (employee driving fast) but another suffers the consequences for it (company and/or insurance company).

148. C: The turnover rate shows the percentage of employees who left the company within a certain time frame. It is calculated by dividing the number of terminations by the average number of employees multiplied by 100: 4/40 x 100 = 10%. It is important to distinguish between turnover rate and retention rate. The retention rate is the opposite of the turnover rate and gives the percentage of employees who remain employed.

149. B: The concierge manager displays the ethical practice competency by recognizing the behavior as unethical and taking the necessary steps to address it. The concierge should be impartial, find the best dining experience for his guests, and not send guests to restaurants because he's returning a favor. Unethical behavior can reflect negatively on the company and needs to be stopped right away. Together with the HR department, the concierge manager should conduct an investigation and then determine the right course of action to address the behavior.

150. C: The HR manager displays the business acumen competency by applying knowledge she has gained to the business operation. This shows that she is aware of the day-to-day practices of the concierges and recognizes potential legal risks. By advising managers to pay the concierges during their breaks, she takes the necessary steps to protect the company from legal exposure.

151. D: The concierge manager displays the communication competency by recognizing the employee's need for further coaching. The concierge manager should observe the concierge's interactions with customers to ensure that he understands the company's expectations and applies them to his work. Direct observation also allows the manager to correct his behavior immediately and provide feedback on improvement opportunities.

152. B: This is an example of incremental budgeting because the last year's budget is used as a baseline and then increased by a set percentage. Incremental budgeting also allows for extra fund requests for additional needs.

153. C: A company's value chain is the sum of all interrelated actions, inputs, and processes that contribute to the design, creation, and production of a product or service until it is received by a customer.

154. A: The age discrimination in employment act forbids discrimination against employees and applicants over the age of 40.

155. B: The study showed that there were significantly fewer employee safety incidents in companies with high employee engagement. The other performance outcomes were: customer ratings, profitability, productivity, turnover, thefts, absenteeism, and quality defects.

156. B: During an organizational intervention, it is the role of HR to conduct a structural diagnosis, analyze problems the organization faces, and identify the root cause of those problems.

157. A: A flatter organizational structure often results in fewer, but broader pay ranges, which is called broad banding.

158. C: The Portal-to-Portal Act regulates whether the time an employee spends traveling during the workday has to be paid. It also determines when an employee has to be paid while they are on call, waiting for an assignment, taking a meal break, commuting, or attending training.

159. D: During an M&A (merger and acquisition), HR should compare four aspects of the two companies that are being merged: 1) structural issues such as conflicts in culture between the organizations, 2) legal issues such as compliance provisions, 3) technological considerations such as which technologies are being used by the companies, and 4) financial considerations such as existing labor contracts.

160. C: The growth-share matrix considers a business line that ranks high in market share and market growth rate a "star." Scenario analysis, SWOT analysis, and PESTLE analysis are also environmental scanning tools. But they do not use the term "star."

How to Overcome Test Anxiety

Just the thought of taking a test is enough to make most people a little nervous. A test is an important event that can have a long-term impact on your future, so it's important to take it seriously and it's natural to feel anxious about performing well. But just because anxiety is normal, that doesn't mean that it's helpful in test taking, or that you should simply accept it as part of your life. Anxiety can have a variety of effects. These effects can be mild, like making you feel slightly nervous, or severe, like blocking your ability to focus or remember even a simple detail.

If you experience test anxiety—whether severe or mild—it's important to know how to beat it. To discover this, first you need to understand what causes test anxiety.

Causes of Test Anxiety

While we often think of anxiety as an uncontrollable emotional state, it can actually be caused by simple, practical things. One of the most common causes of test anxiety is that a person does not feel adequately prepared for their test. This feeling can be the result of many different issues such as poor study habits or lack of organization, but the most common culprit is time management. Starting to study too late, failing to organize your study time to cover all of the material, or being distracted while you study will mean that you're not well prepared for the test. This may lead to cramming the night before, which will cause you to be physically and mentally exhausted for the test. Poor time management also contributes to feelings of stress, fear, and hopelessness as you realize you are not well prepared but don't know what to do about it.

Other times, test anxiety is not related to your preparation for the test but comes from unresolved fear. This may be a past failure on a test, or poor performance on tests in general. It may come from comparing yourself to others who seem to be performing better or from the stress of living up to expectations. Anxiety may be driven by fears of the future—how failure on this test would affect your educational and career goals. These fears are often completely irrational, but they can still negatively impact your test performance.

Review Video: 3 Reasons You Have Test Anxiety
Visit mometrix.com/academy and enter code: 428468

Elements of Test Anxiety

As mentioned earlier, test anxiety is considered to be an emotional state, but it has physical and mental components as well. Sometimes you may not even realize that you are suffering from test anxiety until you notice the physical symptoms. These can include trembling hands, rapid heartbeat, sweating, nausea, and tense muscles. Extreme anxiety may lead to fainting or vomiting. Obviously, any of these symptoms can have a negative impact on testing. It is important to recognize them as soon as they begin to occur so that you can address the problem before it damages your performance.

Review Video: **3 Ways to Tell You Have Test Anxiety**
Visit mometrix.com/academy and enter code: 927847

The mental components of test anxiety include trouble focusing and inability to remember learned information. During a test, your mind is on high alert, which can help you recall information and stay focused for an extended period of time. However, anxiety interferes with your mind's natural processes, causing you to blank out, even on the questions you know well. The strain of testing during anxiety makes it difficult to stay focused, especially on a test that may take several hours. Extreme anxiety can take a huge mental toll, making it difficult not only to recall test information but even to understand the test questions or pull your thoughts together.

Review Video: **How Test Anxiety Affects Memory**
Visit mometrix.com/academy and enter code: 609003

Effects of Test Anxiety

Test anxiety is like a disease—if left untreated, it will get progressively worse. Anxiety leads to poor performance, and this reinforces the feelings of fear and failure, which in turn lead to poor performances on subsequent tests. It can grow from a mild nervousness to a crippling condition. If allowed to progress, test anxiety can have a big impact on your schooling, and consequently on your future.

Test anxiety can spread to other parts of your life. Anxiety on tests can become anxiety in any stressful situation, and blanking on a test can turn into panicking in a job situation. But fortunately, you don't have to let anxiety rule your testing and determine your grades. There are a number of relatively simple steps you can take to move past anxiety and function normally on a test and in the rest of life.

Review Video: **How Test Anxiety Impacts Your Grades**
Visit mometrix.com/academy and enter code: 939819

Physical Steps for Beating Test Anxiety

While test anxiety is a serious problem, the good news is that it can be overcome. It doesn't have to control your ability to think and remember information. While it may take time, you can begin taking steps today to beat anxiety.

Just as your first hint that you may be struggling with anxiety comes from the physical symptoms, the first step to treating it is also physical. Rest is crucial for having a clear, strong mind. If you are tired, it is much easier to give in to anxiety. But if you establish good sleep habits, your body and mind will be ready to perform optimally, without the strain of exhaustion. Additionally, sleeping well helps you to retain information better, so you're more likely to recall the answers when you see the test questions.

Getting good sleep means more than going to bed on time. It's important to allow your brain time to relax. Take study breaks from time to time so it doesn't get overworked, and don't study right before bed. Take time to rest your mind before trying to rest your body, or you may find it difficult to fall asleep.

Review Video: The Importance of Sleep for Your Brain
Visit mometrix.com/academy and enter code: 319338

Along with sleep, other aspects of physical health are important in preparing for a test. Good nutrition is vital for good brain function. Sugary foods and drinks may give a burst of energy but this burst is followed by a crash, both physically and emotionally. Instead, fuel your body with protein and vitamin-rich foods.

Also, drink plenty of water. Dehydration can lead to headaches and exhaustion, especially if your brain is already under stress from the rigors of the test. Particularly if your test is a long one, drink water during the breaks. And if possible, take an energy-boosting snack to eat between sections.

Review Video: How Diet Can Affect your Mood
Visit mometrix.com/academy and enter code: 624317

Along with sleep and diet, a third important part of physical health is exercise. Maintaining a steady workout schedule is helpful, but even taking 5-minute study breaks to walk can help get your blood pumping faster and clear your head. Exercise also releases endorphins, which contribute to a positive feeling and can help combat test anxiety.

When you nurture your physical health, you are also contributing to your mental health. If your body is healthy, your mind is much more likely to be healthy as well. So take time to rest, nourish your body with healthy food and water, and get moving as much as possible. Taking these physical steps will make you stronger and more able to take the mental steps necessary to overcome test anxiety.

Mental Steps for Beating Test Anxiety

Working on the mental side of test anxiety can be more challenging, but as with the physical side, there are clear steps you can take to overcome it. As mentioned earlier, test anxiety often stems from lack of preparation, so the obvious solution is to prepare for the test. Effective studying may be the most important weapon you have for beating test anxiety, but you can and should employ several other mental tools to combat fear.

First, boost your confidence by reminding yourself of past success—tests or projects that you aced. If you're putting as much effort into preparing for this test as you did for those, there's no reason you should expect to fail here. Work hard to prepare; then trust your preparation.

Second, surround yourself with encouraging people. It can be helpful to find a study group, but be sure that the people you're around will encourage a positive attitude. If you spend time with others who are anxious or cynical, this will only contribute to your own anxiety. Look for others who are motivated to study hard from a desire to succeed, not from a fear of failure.

Third, reward yourself. A test is physically and mentally tiring, even without anxiety, and it can be helpful to have something to look forward to. Plan an activity following the test, regardless of the outcome, such as going to a movie or getting ice cream.

When you are taking the test, if you find yourself beginning to feel anxious, remind yourself that you know the material. Visualize successfully completing the test. Then take a few deep, relaxing breaths and return to it. Work through the questions carefully but with confidence, knowing that you are capable of succeeding.

Developing a healthy mental approach to test taking will also aid in other areas of life. Test anxiety affects more than just the actual test—it can be damaging to your mental health and even contribute to depression. It's important to beat test anxiety before it becomes a problem for more than testing.

Review Video: <u>Test Anxiety and Depression</u>
Visit mometrix.com/academy and enter code: 904704

Study Strategy

Being prepared for the test is necessary to combat anxiety, but what does being prepared look like? You may study for hours on end and still not feel prepared. What you need is a strategy for test prep. The next few pages outline our recommended steps to help you plan out and conquer the challenge of preparation.

Step 1: Scope Out the Test

Learn everything you can about the format (multiple choice, essay, etc.) and what will be on the test. Gather any study materials, course outlines, or sample exams that may be available. Not only will this help you to prepare, but knowing what to expect can help to alleviate test anxiety.

Step 2: Map Out the Material

Look through the textbook or study guide and make note of how many chapters or sections it has. Then divide these over the time you have. For example, if a book has 15 chapters and you have five days to study, you need to cover three chapters each day. Even better, if you have the time, leave an extra day at the end for overall review after you have gone through the material in depth.

If time is limited, you may need to prioritize the material. Look through it and make note of which sections you think you already have a good grasp on, and which need review. While you are studying, skim quickly through the familiar sections and take more time on the challenging parts. Write out your plan so you don't get lost as you go. Having a written plan also helps you feel more in control of the study, so anxiety is less likely to arise from feeling overwhelmed at the amount to cover. A sample plan may look like this:

- Day 1: Skim chapters 1–4, study chapter 5 (especially pages 31–33)
- Day 2: Study chapters 6–7, skim chapters 8–9
- Day 3: Skim chapter 10, study chapters 11–12 (especially pages 87–90)
- Day 4: Study chapters 13–15
- Day 5: Overall review (focus most on chapters 5, 6, and 12), take practice test

Step 3: Gather Your Tools

Decide what study method works best for you. Do you prefer to highlight in the book as you study and then go back over the highlighted portions? Or do you type out notes of the important information? Or is it helpful to make flashcards that you can carry with you? Assemble the pens, index cards, highlighters, post-it notes, and any other materials you may need so you won't be distracted by getting up to find things while you study.

If you're having a hard time retaining the information or organizing your notes, experiment with different methods. For example, try color-coding by subject with colored pens, highlighters, or post-it notes. If you learn better by hearing, try recording yourself reading your notes so you can listen while in the car, working out, or simply sitting at your desk. Ask a friend to quiz you from your flashcards, or try teaching someone the material to solidify it in your mind.

Step 4: Create Your Environment

It's important to avoid distractions while you study. This includes both the obvious distractions like visitors and the subtle distractions like an uncomfortable chair (or a too-comfortable couch that makes you want to fall asleep). Set up the best study environment possible: good lighting and a comfortable work area. If background music helps you focus, you may want to turn it on, but otherwise keep the room quiet. If you are using a computer to take notes, be sure you don't have any other windows open, especially applications like social media, games, or anything else that could distract you. Silence your phone and turn off notifications. Be sure to keep water close by so you stay hydrated while you study (but avoid unhealthy drinks and snacks).

Also, take into account the best time of day to study. Are you freshest first thing in the morning? Try to set aside some time then to work through the material. Is your mind clearer in the afternoon or evening? Schedule your study session then. Another method is to study at the same time of day that you will take the test, so that your brain gets used to working on the material at that time and will be ready to focus at test time.

Step 5: Study!

Once you have done all the study preparation, it's time to settle into the actual studying. Sit down, take a few moments to settle your mind so you can focus, and begin to follow your study plan. Don't give in to distractions or let yourself procrastinate. This is your time to prepare so you'll be ready to fearlessly approach the test. Make the most of the time and stay focused.

Of course, you don't want to burn out. If you study too long you may find that you're not retaining the information very well. Take regular study breaks. For example, taking five minutes out of every hour to walk briskly, breathing deeply and swinging your arms, can help your mind stay fresh.

As you get to the end of each chapter or section, it's a good idea to do a quick review. Remind yourself of what you learned and work on any difficult parts. When you feel that you've mastered the material, move on to the next part. At the end of your study session, briefly skim through your notes again.

But while review is helpful, cramming last minute is NOT. If at all possible, work ahead so that you won't need to fit all your study into the last day. Cramming overloads your brain with more information than it can process and retain, and your tired mind may struggle to recall even previously learned information when it is overwhelmed with last-minute study. Also, the urgent nature of cramming and the stress placed on your brain contribute to anxiety. You'll be more likely to go to the test feeling unprepared and having trouble thinking clearly.

So don't cram, and don't stay up late before the test, even just to review your notes at a leisurely pace. Your brain needs rest more than it needs to go over the information again. In fact, plan to finish your studies by noon or early afternoon the day before the test. Give your brain the rest of the day to relax or focus on other things, and get a good night's sleep. Then you will be fresh for the test and better able to recall what you've studied.

Step 6: Take a practice test

Many courses offer sample tests, either online or in the study materials. This is an excellent resource to check whether you have mastered the material, as well as to prepare for the test format and environment.

Check the test format ahead of time: the number of questions, the type (multiple choice, free response, etc.), and the time limit. Then create a plan for working through them. For example, if you have 30 minutes to take a 60-question test, your limit is 30 seconds per question. Spend less time on the questions you know well so that you can take more time on the difficult ones.

If you have time to take several practice tests, take the first one open book, with no time limit. Work through the questions at your own pace and make sure you fully understand them. Gradually work up to taking a test under test conditions: sit at a desk with all study materials put away and set a timer. Pace yourself to make sure you finish the test with time to spare and go back to check your answers if you have time.

After each test, check your answers. On the questions you missed, be sure you understand why you missed them. Did you misread the question (tests can use tricky wording)? Did you forget the information? Or was it something you hadn't learned? Go back and study any shaky areas that the practice tests reveal.

Taking these tests not only helps with your grade, but also aids in combating test anxiety. If you're already used to the test conditions, you're less likely to worry about it, and working through tests until you're scoring well gives you a confidence boost. Go through the practice tests until you feel comfortable, and then you can go into the test knowing that you're ready for it.

Test Tips

On test day, you should be confident, knowing that you've prepared well and are ready to answer the questions. But aside from preparation, there are several test day strategies you can employ to maximize your performance.

First, as stated before, get a good night's sleep the night before the test (and for several nights before that, if possible). Go into the test with a fresh, alert mind rather than staying up late to study.

Try not to change too much about your normal routine on the day of the test. It's important to eat a nutritious breakfast, but if you normally don't eat breakfast at all, consider eating just a protein bar. If you're a coffee drinker, go ahead and have your normal coffee. Just make sure you time it so that the caffeine doesn't wear off right in the middle of your test. Avoid sugary beverages, and drink enough water to stay hydrated but not so much that you need a restroom break 10 minutes into the test. If your test isn't first thing in the morning, consider going for a walk or doing a light workout before the test to get your blood flowing.

Allow yourself enough time to get ready, and leave for the test with plenty of time to spare so you won't have the anxiety of scrambling to arrive in time. Another reason to be early is to select a good seat. It's helpful to sit away from doors and windows, which can be distracting. Find a good seat, get out your supplies, and settle your mind before the test begins.

When the test begins, start by going over the instructions carefully, even if you already know what to expect. Make sure you avoid any careless mistakes by following the directions.

Then begin working through the questions, pacing yourself as you've practiced. If you're not sure on an answer, don't spend too much time on it, and don't let it shake your confidence. Either skip it and come back later, or eliminate as many wrong answers as possible and guess among the remaining ones. Don't dwell on these questions as you continue—put them out of your mind and focus on what lies ahead.

Be sure to read all of the answer choices, even if you're sure the first one is the right answer. Sometimes you'll find a better one if you keep reading. But don't second-guess yourself if you do immediately know the answer. Your gut instinct is usually right. Don't let test anxiety rob you of the information you know.

If you have time at the end of the test (and if the test format allows), go back and review your answers. Be cautious about changing any, since your first instinct tends to be correct, but make sure you didn't misread any of the questions or accidentally mark the wrong answer choice. Look over any you skipped and make an educated guess.

At the end, leave the test feeling confident. You've done your best, so don't waste time worrying about your performance or wishing you could change anything. Instead, celebrate the successful completion of this test. And finally, use this test to learn how to deal with anxiety even better next time.

Review Video: 5 Tips to Beat Test Anxiety
Visit mometrix.com/academy and enter code: 570656

Important Qualification

Not all anxiety is created equal. If your test anxiety is causing major issues in your life beyond the classroom or testing center, or if you are experiencing troubling physical symptoms related to your anxiety, it may be a sign of a serious physiological or psychological condition. If this sounds like your situation, we strongly encourage you to seek professional help.

Tell Us Your Story

We at Mometrix would like to extend our heartfelt thanks to you for letting us be a part of your journey. It is an honor to serve people from all walks of life, people like you, who are committed to building the best future they can for themselves.

We know that each person's situation is unique. But we also know that, whether you are a young student or a mother of four, you care about working to make your own life and the lives of those around you better.

That's why we want to hear your story.

We want to know why you're taking this test. We want to know about the trials you've gone through to get here. And we want to know about the successes you've experienced after taking and passing your test.

In addition to your story, which can be an inspiration both to us and to others, we value your feedback. We want to know both what you loved about our book and what you think we can improve on.

SCAN HERE

The team at Mometrix would be absolutely thrilled to hear from you! So please, send us an email at tellusyourstory@mometrix.com or visit us at mometrix.com/tellusyourstory.php and let's stay in touch.

Additional Bonus Material

Due to our efforts to try to keep this book to a manageable length, we've created a link that will give you access to all of your additional bonus material:

mometrix.com/bonus948/shrmcp